CHRONICLING

THIRTY YEARS OF

THE WEST

ENVIRONMENTAL WRITING

To the memory of William O. Douglas

His roots in the West taught him to champion the land and the law and the humblest of people. In the preface to his autobiography, *Go East, Young Man*, he wrote that he wished his book somehow would help Americans to truly love this nation:

> *I hope it may help them to see in the perspective of the whole world the great and glorious tradition of liberty and freedom enshrined in our Constitution and Bill of Rights. I hope they will come to love this continent, the most beautiful in the whole world.*

> *I hope that before it is too late they will develop a reverence for our rich soils, pure waters, rolling grass country, high mountains, and mysterious estuaries.*

> *I hope that they will put their arms around this part of the wondrous planet, love it, care for it, and treat it as they would a precious and delicate child.*

Bill, you are with us always.

CHRONICLING
THIRTY YEARS OF
THE WEST
ENVIRONMENTAL WRITING

Michael Frome

THE
MOUNTAINEERS

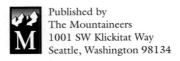 Published by
The Mountaineers
1001 SW Klickitat Way
Seattle, Washington 98134

0 9 8 7 6
5 4 3 2 1

Published simultaneously in Canada by Douglas & McIntyre, Ltd., 1615 Venables Street, Vancouver, B.C. V5L 2H1

Published simultaneously in Great Britain by Cordee, 3a DeMontfort Street, Leicester, England, LE1 7HD

Manufactured in the United States of America

Cover design by Helen Cherullo
Book design and typography by Ani Rucki
Illustrations by Fred Thomas

Cover photographs:

Library of Congress Cataloging-in-Publication Data
Frome, Michael.
    Chronicling the West : thirty years of environmental writing / Michael frome.
        p. cm.
    Includes bibliographical references (p.   ) and index.
    ISBN 0-89886-475-5
    1. Environmentalism—United States—History.   I. Title.
GE197.F77   1996
333.7'2'0978—dc20   96–6868
                                                                          CIP

♻ Printed on recycled paper

CONTENTS

CHAPTER V   175

THE PLACE, TOO, HAS ITS SOUL

CHAPTER VI   201

ON MEDIA AND EDUCATION

CHAPTER VII   225

THE WEST BEYOND TOMORROW

FOREWORD

This collection of Michael Frome's writings, arranged in a cohesive and integrated format, provides an incomparably rich history of the environmental movement from the mid-1960s to the mid-1990s.

It truly "chronicles the West" during this thirty-year period, documenting the coming of age of the environmental cause, along with landmark laws and major new programs that protect the heritage of the nation.

Michael Frome saw it as it happened. His wide travels in this country and abroad, his long experience with heads of government, Congress, and environmental agencies, and his countless consultations with citizen leaders and grassroots activists qualify him uniquely as an important observer and critic, well worth hearing and heeding.

For one who has enjoyed a long friendship with Michael (over these thirty years), during which we played the roles of counselor and critic for each other, it is exciting to read his accounts of epic environmental battles. I knew Michael first in Washington, D.C., where he worked as journalist and author and I as executive director of the Wilderness Society. In time we both moved west, he to teach, first at the University of Idaho and later at Western Washington University, and I to return to my homeland, the Bitterroot Valley in western Montana. Through it all we have remained in close communication and collaboration.

Michael has always called the shots as he's seen them. He has consistently taken the high ground, reporting as factually as one man's perceptions will allow. His writings reflect the spirit, inner strength, and tenacity that have kept him in the center ring of countless environmental fights, often at the expense of his own position and comfort.

His later years as an academician, teaching environmental writing to college students, provide insights into the failure of higher education to prepare young people to face the difficult social and political issues of our day. For young people, or people of any age, Michael Frome's life and work are sheer inspiration. His essays remain as zestful and lively as ever.

For the graying and grizzled who have suffered the pain and known the joy that Michael's "thirty years" have brought, these selections hold very special meaning. They tell exciting stories of "everyday people" who courageously have nurtured grassroots political power and felt strengthened by their experiences, regardless of outcome.

But *Chronicling the West* is more than nostalgic reminiscence. High school and college students come into the environmental movement with fervor but often burn out because they lack grounding in the long-term struggle and process gone before them. This book is for them. It transcends the decades—here now the prophetic voice of thirty years ago brings the issues to contemporary consciousness as a springboard for involvement in shaping a wholesome future. In his paradigm of good people and their practice of participatory democracy, Frome sees the restoration of Jeffersonian political process, and points the way for all who want to do better in their lives.

Chronicling the West for me is fascinating reading with a far-reaching message of empowerment. Anyone who wants to help make the world a better place should welcome the message and will benefit from it.

Stewart M. Brandborg

PREFACE

The materials in this book cover more than thirty years of writing about the West, essentially from the mid-1960s until the mid-1990s. In a sense the work at hand began a decade earlier, in 1953, when I met and listened to Bernard DeVoto at the Mid-Century Conference on Resources for the Future in Washington, D.C.

DeVoto was the kind of guy I wanted to be. He was then best known for his "Easy Chair" column in *Harper's* magazine and as a historian who had won a Pulitzer Prize for *Across the Wide Missouri*. Senator Richard Neuberger of Oregon called DeVoto the most effective conservationist of the twentieth century. Wallace Stegner, DeVoto's friend and biographer, later wrote of him:

> *His conservation writings record a continuing controversy unmarred by any scramble for personal advantage or any impulse toward self-justification, a controversy in every way dignified by concern for the public good and for the future of the West from which he had exiled himself in anger as a young man.*

It distresses me that DeVoto is now virtually forgotten and unknown, and likewise Richard Neuberger, a journalist, one of my own, who entered politics without sacrificing conscience, and pretty soon maybe Wallace Stegner, who departed this world in 1993. It isn't that any of them needs to be glorified, but times and events and people ought to be remembered. As Stegner said, every action is an idea before it is an action, and perhaps a feeling before it is an idea, and every other idea rests upon other ideas that have preceded it in time.

That is why I look back. At this stage of life I suppose I could lean back, relax, take stock, and pitch slowballs. But I don't want to live in the past, there is still too much to be done. I want to learn from the past, the environmental decades that I observed at close range, and to share the lessons for what they may be worth.

I am pleased to acknowledge the cooperation and encouragement of friends and colleagues: Lisa Friend, who helped in the initial review and selection of essays and later prepared the index; Deanna Woolston, who made additional creative input regarding selection and structure and labored and laughed with me through computer glitches; Richard Navas, Scott Brennan, Diane Rydberg, David Washburn, and Margaret Washburn, for help in content and/or with the computer; the good people at Mountaineers Books, including Donna

DeShazo, Margaret Foster, and Cindy Bohn, all constructive and considerate; Carsten Lien, Alfred Runte, and Mack Prichard for their critical reading of the manuscript; and June Eastvold, my wife, for her patience and moral support while all this happened.

Michael Frome, November 1995

INTRODUCTION

On Valentine's Day 1988, I went to speak to the Alaska Environmental Assembly in Juneau. I was in my sixty-eighth year, but I didn't feel old, I felt young. The meeting was challenging and uplifting, with hope, optimism, good feeling, and the love appropriate to Valentine's Day. I talked about love of earth, love of all creatures large and small. I said, "Hug the person next to you, right or left. Or hug both." I wanted each to feel good about himself or herself.

In Alaska I was with friends. Some had never heard of me, I'm sure, but Dave Foreman, the radical, rousing activist, made the introduction and said I was a courageous, crusading environmental journalist, so the young people, especially, perked up. I told how lucky I felt in my life, with my travels and friendships, opportunities to make input into public policy, in small or large way to influence the course of history. Because the meeting was about saving the coastal wilderness of southeast Alaska, I recalled Alaskans I had met over the years, men and women who had fought for the coastal wilderness and who should not be forgotten. Those people had been through tough times, and it likely wasn't getting any easier. In fact, when we look at the revolutionary task of reordering America's priorities, it sometimes seems absolutely impossible. Even with all the enthusiasm in the meeting hall, we were still only a small cadre struggling against a vast industrial-bureaucratic complex. Still, I could say, "Look at history, recent history, across America and in Alaska: establishing equal rights in Selma, Alabama; ending the Vietnam War; saving Misty Fjords and the Brooks Range—those challenges also seemed absolutely impossible. But those who tried and hung in there proved victorious."

I told them all this and they loved it. When they applauded I offered as an encore a little quotation from Mark Twain: "To do good works is noble. To teach others to do good works is nobler, and no trouble." And they applauded again.

But it seems like only yesterday that I was a novitiate. The years fly by and I'm taken as an expert. Maybe so, but it didn't happen in a hurry. I suspect that an activist in any cause is not born into it, except to the extent that everyone comes into the world with love and trust and an innate need to do good works.

I look back to when and where I came in. I was blessed. The late 1950s,

'60s, and '70s were the best of times for environmentalism in Washington,
D.C., where I lived and worked as an independent freelance journalist. The
environment was an up-and-coming public concern, but few in the media
knew anything about it, or cared. I developed my own beat, knocking on the
doors of senators and congressmen, federal bureaus, conservation organizations, and industry trade groups. Once I joined the staff of *Field & Stream*, a
magazine with a circulation of about 1.8 million, access came easier. I could
get an hour-long interview with a senator and be invited to lunch in the private dining room of the Secretary of the Interior without even asking. I went
to the White House on occasion and met President Lyndon Johnson. He was
the consummate politician, sprinkling national parks in congressional districts
and encouraging his wife, Lady Bird, in her natural beauty crusade. Richard
Nixon, when he was president, did not have much taste for the environment
but saw the popular political value in it and compiled a decent record, at least
until the 1973 Arab oil embargo. With those people virtually everything re-
volved around politics and power, scarcely ever real principle. I can't say that
much has changed in recent years, either through the Republican administration of George Bush or the Democratic administration of Bill Clinton. Now,
as then, politics and power prevail over principle.

In those days I never dreamed of living in the West, although I traveled
considerably, supplementing my work in covering Washington. I explored marvelous places, many, many of them in the West. I loved the places, especially the
spacious, wild out-of-doors, and the experience of meeting and interviewing
people at various levels of life. I learned about politics, people, science, mother
nature, myself—lessons about learning.

I picked my own heroes, like William O. Douglas, the Supreme Court
justice whose entire life stands as a record of courage and willingness to hold
fast against odds. By profession he was a lawyer, not a writer, but he published
more than most professional authors. For a while it seemed that whenever I
went to some hot spot of conservation controversy he had already been there,
hiking, camping, and communing with people who cared. Detractors detested
his activism, demanding he exercise "judicial restraint," but he brushed them
off. "A man or woman who becomes a justice," he said, "should try to stay
alive; a lifetime diet of the law turns most judges into dull, dry husks."

From people like Douglas, well known, lesser known, and unknown, I
learned a choice lesson. Consider that many issues on which I reported twenty
and thirty years ago—clearcutting public and private forests, subsidized

overgrazing of public rangelands, the wildlife crisis—are still pressing, are still tragically contemporary. Reviewing history that repeats itself can be damn discouraging. But I saw and learned that individuals can and do make the difference and bring positive change. They do better working together than alone, but I've seen loners cling to a dream and make reality of it. Institutions fall short. Whether private or public, profit-making or eleemosynary, academic or professional, institutions fail to provide needed ideas and ideals; instead, they breed conformity and compliance. The larger and older an institution becomes, the less vision it expresses or tolerates. Douglas once proposed that every ten years federal agencies like the Forest Service be dissolved and reconstituted. He might have suggested the same for institutionalized professions. Certainly the two in which I have worked, journalism and higher education, foster colorless impersonality at the cost of emotion, the most powerful human force. But the individual who realizes the power of his or her own life and never sells it short is free to speak and to make a difference.

Life has shown me the world is full of miracles. I never thought I would be a university professor, let alone earn a doctorate, which I achieved after the age of seventy. Now I can say that I view emotion and imagination as qualities that open the heart to feeling and open the mind to articulate expression. To write something meaningful about the natural world requires vision, caring, courage, and hope. Any writer, or an activist in any field, with those qualities will have a creative, rewarding career, maybe not wholly profitable, but productive and positive all the way.

My environmental career began in Washington, D.C., but my dream of journalism began in high school in New York City, in the mid-1930s, when I discovered the *Autobiography of Lincoln Steffens*, the fascinating story of a man who made a career of probing power without fear of the powerful. Steffens was born and bred in the West, studied in Europe, began his professional career as a police reporter in New York, then rose to prominence as one of the best of the "muckrakers," investigative reporters who uncovered political and economic corruption. He pursued his work with integrity, honesty, and fairness; he influenced the course of events rather than merely reporting them. Re-reading the *Autobiography* shows Steffens to be still relevant, as, for example, his chapter on "Timber Fraud in Oregon":

> *Senators, representatives and appointees to Federal office from these [Western] states had built up, protected, and used the Federal departments to further the frauds, so that this whole story was a clear sight of the*

interlocking of the local, State, and Federal machine as all one
system. . . . [S]o a Federal department [Interior] created to execute land,
timber, and mineral laws in the public interest was organized (by political
appointments) and bought by systematic bribery to take the part of the land
grafters, timber thieves, and big mine-jumpers.

I wanted somehow to follow Steffens's path, although the odds seemed
hopelessly against it. I was in and out of college, without finishing. When I
did get a break, I started at the bottom, as a copy boy at the *Washington Post*,
and advanced from there the hard way.

In World War II, I joined the Army Air Corps (later the Air Force), trained
as an air transport navigator, and saw the world: Africa, Asia, Australia, Europe, South America. On the long missions across watery wilderness my geography was in the heavens; I measured celestial distances, learned to respect
weather and the elements, experienced the harmonious pattern of the universe, of time beyond time and space beyond space joined in cosmic unity.
I'm certain that all who fly are moved by the depths of the skies to find new
dimensions in their thinking, though the full meaning of my experience came
to me later. When I first read the words of Charles A. Lindbergh, "In wildness
I sense the miracle of life, and beside it our scientific accomplishments fade to
trivia," I felt a shared truth.

Early in 1946, I returned to the *Washington Post*, now as a reporter. I
covered local news and wrote obituaries, but I brought in stories on my own
as well. Through good fortune and connections with old military friends, I
went to Eastern Europe, where I interviewed leaders of the government and
opposition parties in Czechoslovakia and Poland for dispatches that the *Post*
featured on the front page.

I drew better assignments but was eager to get ahead—so eager that I
jumped at an opportunity to be a larger fish on a smaller paper elsewhere. It
was a mistake and within a year I was back in Washington, looking for a job. I
found one in public relations for the American Automobile Association. On
the face of it, it seemed like just another public relations job, but every experience is a plus in the long run, even when it appears to be a minus at the
moment. It proved to be that for me.

While at AAA, I became aware of conservation groups and began com-
municating with them. During my ten years with the association I traveled
around the country and learned a lot about it. I discovered national parks and
their problems. The parks clearly were significant touring destinations, but

their postwar popularity was soaring beyond adequate staffing and protection. Bernard DeVoto wrote a classic piece on the subject, "Let's Close the National Parks," in *Harper's* (October 1953). To be concerned with this issue was a logical part of my work, considering that auto clubs in their early days had encouraged the establishment of national parks and now thousands of their members faced difficulties in obtaining campsites and lodgings.

I met many individuals, in and out of government, who played particular roles in park policy, including Alfred Knopf, the publisher, who was chairman of the National Parks Advisory Board; Horace M. Albright, who had been present when the National Park Service was established and later became the agency's second director; Laurance Rockefeller, continuing his father's philanthropic interest in conservation; writers of note like DeVoto, Wallace Stegner, and Sigurd Olson; and John Oakes, editor of the editorial page of the *New York Times*. I had become acquainted with Oakes's work before his appointment as editor, when he contributed a conservation column that was buried in the back pages of the Sunday travel section. I read the travel pages of various major newspapers as part of my work, but John Oakes showed me something special that I found in no other paper. For instance, in the edition of May 13, 1956, he introduced me to new legislation designed by Senator Hubert Humphrey to establish a national wilderness preservation system:

This isn't just a question of city folks seeking outdoor recreation, or enjoying spectacular scenery, or breathing unpoisoned air. It goes much deeper; it springs from the inextricable relationship of man with nature, a relationship that even the most insensitive and complex civilization can never dissipate.

Through these contacts and readings I felt challenged to explore new fields, to find avenues where I could write under my own name and hopefully even make a living at it. I went on my own in the late 1950s, contributing travel articles to magazines and newspapers, including the *New York Times*, *Christian Science Monitor*, *Washington Post*, and *Chicago Tribune*. A friend steered me to Doubleday, for which firm I wrote my first books. They were travel guides, but I emphasized activities in national parks and national forests and the value of conservation. Travel writing was fun, but in due course I figured there must more to life than glorifying places that had lost their glory.

The great change came when I accepted an invitation from the Forest Service to join a pack trip in the Bridger Wilderness of Wyoming. After following the trail through tall timbers and alpine meadows, alongside a thousand clear lakes and living glaciers, sleeping out at eleven thousand feet and touching the heavens, I could never be the same again. And if the Forest Service was protecting such wild places as part of a program of multiple use, I was all for it. When I came out of the wilderness, Jim Harrower, a local historian, hardware dealer, and mayor (of Pinedale, Wyoming), took me to the bluff overlooking the site where the fur trappers rendezvoused in the 1830s. It was the same place he had taken DeVoto in researching *Across the Wide Missouri*. DeVoto was a hero to me then (and still is), so I felt I was tracking not only history but the historian as well.

Beginning in the mid-1960s, when *American Forests* first made me a columnist, I wrote columns for various magazines and newspapers: *Woman's Day* (on travel); *Field & Stream* and *Western Outdoors* (on conservation), and the *Los Angeles Times* (where the column was called "Environmental Trails" and combined travel and the environment). After I was fired from *Field & Stream* in 1974, I wrote a column, "Crusade for Wildlife," for *Defenders of Wildlife*, for eighteen years.

In the beginning, I was considered "safe"—independent but certainly not extreme. That was how I thought of myself. My 1962 book, *Whose Woods These Are: The Story of the National Forests*, strongly supported the U.S. Forest Service and its programs. The editor at *American Forests*, James B. Craig, said that I would bring a needed fresh perspective, "to ward off blandness." I didn't write blandly, but I never wanted to be a dissenter in the ranks; I didn't want to be fired or labeled a mischief maker. I simply wanted to tell it "like it is."

It took a while for me to become critical, or, as TIME later wrote, "tough and tendentious." Early in my career I trusted and believed. In my very first column in *American Forests*, in May 1966, I reported on a meeting at the rim of the Grand Canyon. The subject at hand was the government's proposal to construct two new dams on the Colorado River, which would seriously change the level and flow of water through the Grand Canyon. At that meeting I watched David Brower, then executive director of the Sierra Club, in action and considered him extreme, intolerant of positions differing from his own. Three or four years later, however, when Brower and I were on a program together in Wyoming, I thought he was the moderate, while I probably sounded like the extremist. By then I understood that all David was trying to do was protect the sacredness of the Grand Canyon from Goliath.

In tackling critical issues, I stepped on the wrong toes. When I began writing about conservation I respected and admired public agencies and the professionals in charge. I thought rangers the best of men (and until recently they were all men) and the resource colleges they had attended the best of places. In due course I felt disappointed and disillusioned, let down by individuals and institutions I had trusted. I became disturbed about management practices in the national forests and the liaison between industry, the Forest Service, and forestry schools that rationalized abusive overcutting and clear-cutting. I felt compelled to express serious concerns in my column in *American Forests*—after all, I had been hired to express an independent viewpoint. The American Forestry Association presumably was a membership organization serving the public interest, but its board of directors was dominated by representatives of large timber companies and the Forest Service. In 1971 the executive director of the American Forestry Association ordered that I was "not to write critically about the U.S. Forest Service, the forestry industry, the profession or about controversial forestry issues." I couldn't accept the censorship and was fired.

Of course, I still had *Field & Stream* and its much larger audience. When I first joined the staff as conservation editor and columnist, I was really a stranger to the "hook-and-bullet" world, but I found hunters and fishermen receptive and responsive. They flooded the magazine with mail about the degradation of particular places they cared about. The tougher I wrote the better they liked it, and so did the editor, Clare Conley, who gave me strong support.

But we drew flak too. Conley got the boot first. The new editor directed that I write in generalities without naming names. Yet that to me has always been precisely the point: The naming of names, the assessment of responsibility for actions affecting the environment and quality of life, is the fulfillment of free expression through what Jefferson called "open avenues of truth." When I was dismissed in late 1974 many individuals and organizations protested. One reader wrote to me: "I feel that the true outdoor people are the key to the environmental problem because they, at least, know something about how the real Earth operates. And, up to the present, you have been one of the few, with access to this group, that have been making strenuous efforts to alert these people to the 'shadows of coming events.' I will miss your column." Tom Bell editorialized in *High Country News*:

> We tout our system as being one of freedom for the individual, and we particularly tout our freedom of speech and expression. His [Frome's] experiences give the lie to just how much freedom we really do have.

That was not my feeling, however. Truthtelling ultimately will prevail. Too many writers self-censor their own work, anticipate trouble, and sanitize their writing to the point of banality. That is their choice. I learned that when one door closes, another opens. After *Field & Stream*, I became a columnist for *Defenders of Wildlife*, writing as I wished without fear or favor until a new executive director wanted to pick my subjects for me.

In 1982 I was blessed anew. After deciding to leave Washington and change my life, I joined the University of Idaho as a visiting professor. I came for one year and stayed four, then moved to Western Washington University, where I remained until retiring from teaching in 1995. Yea, verily, there is plenty to do. If I don't get it done, maybe the students will. That I found continued uncensored outlets for my writing, and a place to lecture in another career, reinforces my faith in the system. Or perhaps it proves the world is full of miracles waiting and wanting to happen.

As the end of the twentieth century approaches, this country, including my beloved West, can use the miracles. Newt Gingrich, the congressional kingpin, in discussing his grand design "To Renew America," has talked and written about "civilizational collapses," of the family, the inner city, and our school systems, coupled with rising crime and the drug culture. I wish he had said something about the degraded environment, the impoverishment of land and of decent human beings, that results directly from unrestrained greed and pursuit of profit.

Yes, the issue of "moral values" needs to be addressed but in a more fundamental way than Gingrich and his allies in the wise-use/property rights movement have chosen. Those groups have been most active in the West, picking up where the Sagebrush Rebellion of the Reagan years left off. I can't deny they constitute a grassroots movement with considerable citizen involvement, but the power and purse behind it come from industries that see Gingrich's "Contract with America" as a contract *on* America. For all their grievances with government and their righteous clamor about the rights of ownership, profit-making—the freedom to exploit God's own earth for their small purpose—plainly is paramount in their design. The moral values are on a higher road. Finding that road, to common caring and sharing, is the challenge.

CHAPTER I

THE VIEW FROM THE RIVER

Early in September of 1991 I was called to substitute for Wallace Stegner as the keynote speaker at a conference at Utah State University on "The Future of Western Water: Defining the Public Interest." It was then two years before Stegner's death. He had come down with a bad back and suggested I be invited in his stead. Considering that we were not special friends in any way, I was surprised, but I also felt privileged and challenged.

Stegner, one of the finest writers of the twentieth century, was a powerful intellectual influence on the West. He was water-conscious; his collection of choice essays, in fact, is titled *Sounds of Mountain Water*. In 1955 he edited *This Is Dinosaur*, an important and effective weapon in the historic fight to keep dams out of Dinosaur National Monument.

I don't know what Stegner would have said as keynote speaker, but I thought it fitting to discuss broad issues of water in the West from a humanistic, or ethical, standpoint, especially before the forum at hand, which was composed mostly of technical experts. Those technicians needed to look beyond their expertise. Considering the problems of toxic wastes, poisoned air and water, erosion, desertification, and acid rain, clearly it is time to ask new questions in the search for new and better answers, and the best answers come not from engineering, but from the spirit.

I believe this idea is reflected in the essays that follow. It isn't exactly water that counts so much as a way of looking at water as more than a commodity, though this has been difficult to do in a region long focused on growth, opportunity, and wealth. In 1911 when Theodore Roosevelt dedicated the dam named for him at the confluence of Tonto Creek and the Salt River, it symbolized America on the march: the highest dam in the world, impounding as much water as the world's previous three largest reservoirs combined. It created arable land out of desert, and if it worked in arid Arizona it was expected to work anywhere.

In 1966 when the Grand Canyon was threatened by plans to build two dams, David Brower of the Sierra Club challenged the notion that such dams were valid even in Arizona, while Representative Morris K. Udall, as I wrote in *American Forests*, "set courage to one side in pursuit of the maximum political mileage." In his book *Too Funny to Be President*, published in 1988, Udall recalled the confrontation:

> *The weakness of the argument in favor of the dams was borne home to me the day I had to debate David Brower—as clever, tough, and tenacious an opponent as you could want—in front of a gaggle of national press at the worst possible venue: the rim of the Grand Canyon. This was a tough assignment—comparable to debating the merits of chastity in Hugh Hefner's hot tub in front of an audience of centerfold models, and me being on the side of abstinence.*

A good story, but it wasn't funny at the time. Mo Udall and his older brother, Stewart, Secretary of the Interior from the beginning of the Kennedy administration to the end of Lyndon Johnson's, were both highly motivated. They worked earnestly to advance the cause of conservation, but times came when they were locked in, victimized by a political system larger and tougher than personal principle. Stewart supported the proposed Hooker Dam in New

Mexico, which would have flooded the Gila Wilderness, established through the efforts of Aldo Leopold in 1924 as the country's first designated wilderness. In an interview with me years after leaving office, Stewart recalled how President Eisenhower had turned off the flow of federal funds for building dams in the West; then John F. Kennedy in his election campaign promised to turn it back on, and it was up to Udall to deliver. That's politics.

Brower has looked back with regret at his mistakes, too. In the 1950s, he was instrumental in the campaign to protect Dinosaur National Monument, but he failed to fight the dam at Glen Canyon on the Colorado River, understandably at the time, since the canyon lies outside the national parks. But history has shown that the Glen Canyon dam had serious negative impacts on the Grand Canyon itself, not to mention that a choice piece of natural beauty was lost.

Nevertheless, saving the Grand Canyon was a monumental attainment. The Bureau of Reclamation had all the power that comes from pork-barrel politics. After my column appeared in *American Forests*, Ottis Peterson, the publicity chief of the bureau, busily selling his wares, dispatched a letter to the editor chiding both Brower and me. Even if the two proposed dams were built, Peterson wrote, I could still see the same view. Moreover:

Supposing there was another sudden volcanic eruption in the vicinity of the Grand Canyon which choked up the inner gorge with lava once more. It would be a geologic oddity and wonder which would send Dave Brower and company into ecstasy. Is it so sinful for man to accomplish the same end result in a manner which will be useful to the onrushing pace of the Pacific Southwest?

Happily, the bureau's view did not prevail. There is more to the use of water than serving the onrushing pace of the Southwest or, in the case of the Snake River at Hells Canyon, the Northwest. Water is a limited resource in the West, requiring and deserving husbandry and stewardship. But it's more than that. The West needs its sacred places and its appreciation of water as a sacred gift of spirit.

Yet rivers, streams, and lakes are contaminated by chemical runoffs from factories, farms, forests, rangelands, and spreading, sprawling cities, and from train derailments. I read an account of one case in California where a ruptured tank car spilled at least 13,000 gallons of a concentrated herbicide into the Sacramento River, killing more than 100,000 fish and many other forms of life. The mighty Columbia River and its principal tributary, the Snake, which once supported more than 11 million native Pacific salmon, may soon bear witness to the tragic extinction of wild native salmon.

The awesome extent of the poisoning of Kesterson National Wildlife Refuge in the San Joaquin Valley of California has raised serious questions about irrigated agriculture and drainage. The tragedy began in 1980 when the Bureau of Reclamation diverted irrigation drainwater containing selenium, arsenic, boron, lead, and other metallic poisons from arid lands upstream into the wildlife refuge. The safe limit for selenium in drinking water is ten parts per billion; at Kesterson the concentration rose to 1,400 parts, and selenium may have made its way into the Central Valley aquifer.

On the other hand, there's an upbeat side. In 1979 I quoted the American Rivers Conservation Council on the aftermath of the collapse of Teton Dam: "A few heads will roll in the Bureau of Reclamation as scapegoats, and then Congress will continue funding bad projects." Well, it hasn't quite worked out that way. Congress may still fund bad projects but nowhere near as many. Reclamation has been significantly downsized and is no longer the powerhouse that once virtually wrote its own ticket. And part of the reason has been the activity of the American Rivers Conservation Council, now known as American Rivers, and allied groups. Citizens who care make the difference and have their day.

The same with Hells Canyon, which I wrote about in 1969 when it looked like all this would be "lost to the sight of man." In 1976 Congress responded to citizen efforts by establishing the Hells Canyon National Recreation Area—652,000 acres of national forest, embracing 100 miles of the free-flowing Snake, its gorge, and the wild rim country and its wildlife. Unfortunately, the Forest Service couldn't handle it—the agency has complained in years since that it didn't have the money for wilderness and recreation, but it did find money to build a lot of logging roads and to sanction more logging, continued grazing, and an upsurge in jet boating, most of it commercial, providing tourists a cheap, quick thrill. Thus the Hells Canyon Preservation Council has been campaigning for a national park preserve, with a focus on preservation and appropriate recreation.

In 1986, just before my four years in Idaho came to an end, I went backpacking in the Seven Devils with my friend, Bill Loftus, outdoors editor of the *Lewiston Tribune*. It was Bill's idea of bidding adieu. In my article in *Field & Stream* I had described the view from the river, of sheer solid walls rising almost vertically, yielding into stairsteps and great benches, snow-patched mountains against the sky. Here my friend had scattered the ashes of his father, so it was sacred ground for him. Earth, water, sky—the West is blessed with its sacred space.

At the Edge of the Grand Canyon

American Forests
May 1966

In the process of formulating a personal position on any public question, particularly in the field of conservation, there is no better way than seeing with one's own eyes, listening to articulate advocates of both sides, weighing the arguments and searching for the truth in one's own mind. This is my belief and always I reserve the right to be wrong.

Thus I was led recently to join a two-day tour of writers departing from Kennedy Airport in New York for the Grand Canyon, there to observe at close range proposed sites for hydroelectric power dams. The invitation had come from the *Reader's Digest*, apparently as part of a program to publicize an article on the subject. Though intuitively opposed to the Marble Canyon and Bridge Canyon dams, whether within or adjacent to the main Grand Canyon, on the grounds that dams and national parks make poor companions, the opportunity for a close-up study was too important to miss.

On the plane heading west, I sat for a time next to Congressman Morris Udall of Arizona, who expected to be one of the principal speakers on the pro-reclamation side later in the day. We talked about many aspects of conservation. Congressman Udall is at least as perceptive as his older brother, the Secretary of the Interior. He deserves points for courage, too, having fought for legislation like the Wilderness Act, which gives little political mileage in his own state. It may be that in his strong support of the Bridge Canyon and Marble Canyon dams Mr. Udall has set courage to one side in pursuit of the maximum political mileage. It may also be that he is following his principles and that he is right.

The purpose of the program at the Grand Canyon, according to a news release distributed aboard the plane, was "to give both sides of the controversy an opportunity to be heard." But this was not quite the spirit in which the day proceeded.

Members of the press were not the only ones invited to the workshop, forum, or "backgrounder," as it was variously called. Over one hundred members of the Sierra Club, a conservation organization enthusiastically opposed to the two dams, arrived by plane from various cities of the West. I never quite figured out whether it was the *Digest* or the Sierra Club that conceived of holding a press briefing and an anti-dam pep rally in the same room at the same time.

"It was apparent from club members' remarks that they thought the workshop was to be a one-sided affair," reported the *Arizona Republic*, "keyed to their interests in preventing dam construction."

I do not wish to give a blow-by-blow account of a dismal, disappointing day. Soon after the program at El Tovar Hotel began, Congressman Udall rose from the center of the audience demanding to know when his side would have a chance to be heard, if at all. When he threatened to call an impromptu press conference the magazine people agreed to let him and two other reclamationists follow five anti-dam spokesmen.

This disappointed the opening speaker, David Brower, executive director of the Sierra Club. "What was to be a presentation of one view," he lamented, "is now a continued contest." As a keynoter, Mr. Brower neither stated nor discussed the issues. He read a telegram of protest to Secretary Udall on the activities of the Bureau of Reclamation. He decried the "ominous silence from the National Park Service" on the issue of dams. He said the agency was required to be silent, and again that it was "effectively silenced." At this very time, as I learned later, the workshop sponsors had letters from two former Park Service directors, Horace M. Albright and Conrad L. Wirth, containing background material for reading to the workshop, but these too were "effectively silenced." And Merill D. Beal, the chief naturalist of Grand Canyon National Park, was standing by, ready (but never called upon) to give a naturalist's view of the canyon, which I would have welcomed as a basis for probing the issues.

But invective was more in fashion than investigation. The talks of Congressman Udall and the others of his side were punctuated by cat-calls, guffaws, and laughter from the audience. "I have never had such a difficult time in offering welcoming words from the governor," said the governor's representative. The question period, ostensibly for the press as at thousands of press briefings I have attended, was marked by speeches from the floor by Sierra Club members. However, some brave fellow from the Arizona Game and Fish Department dared to rise and suggest that his people also considered themselves to be conservationists, and even preservationists.

Next morning Barry Goldwater arrived from Phoenix. He came in response to a plea from the governor's representative to help save the day for the dam builders' cause. But Mr. Goldwater surprised the reclamationists, the Sierra Club members, the press, and perhaps even himself. He raised the tone of the whole affair to a level of reason and rationality, where it belonged, by combining an articulate statement of Arizona's critical water needs with compassion for those fighting to save the intrinsic majesty of the Grand Canyon. As a patriot of his state, he said that he was not convinced of the need to dam Marble Canyon, a region of sheer beauty which he had sought to have added to the national park while he was in the Senate. He felt there were valid points that had never been discussed, key questions still to be probed. "There should not be foregone conclusions on your part, nor on ours," said the former Senator like a man through running for office in Arizona.

This approach touched even Mr. Brower, who spoke with reason himself, or so it seemed to me. Had he done so on the previous day, I thought, this could have been a different conference. In searching for the truth in a controversy such as that over the Grand Canyon, the definition of needs and the establishment of areas of agreement enable the discussion to proceed on a much healthier basis, with a minimum of mud-slinging, misrepresentation, and anger.

When the tour departed I chose to remain behind another day, in order to review the conflicting literature I had received on the scene, to think through the arguments without benefit of passion or invective, and to look into the Grand Canyon for the answers.

At 5:30 A.M. I walked to the rim to watch the sunrise. The entire canyon was in darkness, and so was the sky except for a thin band of white at the horizon. From one second to the next the scene changed and the world brightened. This was Arizona, the arid place, wide, wild, and wonderful, which Barry Goldwater and Morris Udall extolled for its natural beauty and pledged to defend to the bitter end.

If I were an Arizonian, I would ask myself, "Why do we really need these dams?" "What effect will they have upon the values we treasure?" Everybody in the arid country wants dams, or thinks he wants dams, like a panacea, or religion, that is said to guarantee a better life, inducing prosperity, boom, bank deposits, building, freeways, congestion, and sprawl. Arizona, I fear, demands the right to make the same mistakes of planlessness that every other place has made, and to urbanize in the universal pattern.

If I were an Arizonian, I would ask myself, "How much do we really

know about the water crisis in expanding cities like Phoenix, which are packed
with wastefulness and ugliness, as well as with swimming pools?" "How much
do we really understand about water?" The truth is that we know little about
storage, evaporation, transfer, the influence of artificial impoundments on
earth stresses. Where we should have fundamental research and rational delib-
eration keyed to long-range needs of a total community living in harmony
with an arid natural environment, we are governed by political hysterics.

If I were an Arizonian, and especially an Arizona politician, I suppose that
I would rise in righteous wrath to attack the *Reader's Digest* and the Sierra
Club, but I would read their arguments through, and be glad that people in
distant places, with little to gain for themselves, are concerned over the fate of
the Grand Canyon.

If I were an Arizonian, I would go up to the Canyon at daybreak and feel
that I held its future in my hands. Harnessing natural features and improving
upon rivers represent man's splendid ingenuity, beyond a doubt. The greater
ingenuity is to show that man can survive while leaving some features of the
earth to their own devices. This is the true test of our mechanical, intellectual,
and moral skills. There is no better place to feel it than on the Grand Canyon
of the Colorado River.

When the Teton Dam Collapsed

Defenders of Wildlife
April 1979

When the Teton Dam collapsed in 1976 one might have expected, or at least hoped or dreamed, that out of such tragedy a new federal policy governing water resource development would emerge. That Idaho disaster, after all, was foreseeable and avoidable, as well as unforgivable, and clearly part of a larger frightening pattern.

The American Rivers Conservation Council knew better. "The dam collapse which killed a score of people and destroyed thousands of acres of land will quickly be swept under the bureaucratic rug, if the public works committees and appropriations committees have their way," the Rivers Council forecast with bitterness born of harsh experience. "A few heads will roll in the Bureau of Reclamation as scapegoats, and then Congress will continue funding bad projects, pretending that avoidable death and destruction had not occurred."

That prophecy has been largely fulfilled. Key members of Congress are determined to pursue the same old wasteful and wanton course: appropriating billions of dollars for water resource projects demonstrably unsound economically, utterly destructive ecologically, and suspiciously unsafe.

Congress, of course, is not alone. Last year President Carter vetoed the $3.4 billion public works bill, forcing Congress to cut $1 billion worth of pork out of the barrel. But this is another year, with another set of political considerations. It finds the President and his administration either retreating from strong positions or supporting what dam fighters call "the worst old dogs," such as the Central Arizona Project, Central Utah Project, and the Tennessee-Tombigbee Waterway.

Interior Secretary Cecil D. Andrus has declared, "Water construction projects will continue in the West. We just want to make sure they are good, safe projects." That assumes that projects may be either good or safe, which I seriously doubt. It also reminds us that Secretary Andrus served as governor of Idaho while the Teton Dam was built.

Following the Teton tragedy Mr. Andrus and Senator Frank Church, his fellow Idahoan and Democrat, wrung their hands in righteous wrath, demanding punishment for the guilty. "It appears certain," Senator Church observed, "that the federal government shares primary responsibility." Andrus and Church both conveniently overlooked their own earlier support of the project, when they should have known better. That, I suppose, reflects the political game of weaving, bobbing, throwing a punch, and ducking at the right time.

In the summer of 1971 I was in Idaho. By appointment I had met the then Secretary of the Interior, Rogers C. B. Morton, at Jackson, Wyoming, and flown with him to Boise for dedication of the Birds of Prey Natural Area at the edge of the Snake River. It was the kind of gala day that brought out the politicians for another moment in the sun.

For a little while I found myself with Senator Church, whom I knew in Washington, and Governor Andrus, just the three of us together. I couldn't think of a better representation to make to them than the widespread opposition of sportsmen and environmentalists to the Teton Dam. There was still a chance to stop it. Senator Church might use his powerful influence for a new study. Secretary Morton had directed his own review and was believed ready to scrap the project; it was likely that he would welcome encouragement to do so from the governor in order to offset other pressures.

In our discussion Senator Church was vigorous in his advocacy of the Lower Teton Project as valid, beneficial, needed. The governor said little, though generally nodding assent to Senator Church's expressions. "Direct and personal appeals to Idaho's congressional delegation and to governor Cecil Andrus for review of the project and an evaluation of alternate methods of doing what the dam would do have all been fruitless," Pete Henault, one of the conservationists leading the fight, wrote in the following summer, 1972.

Then in 1973 the citizens went to court. They exposed the Bureau of Reclamation for doctoring figures in order to understate costs and exaggerate benefits; the whole project, in fact, was intended to subsidize irrigationists already using more than their share of the state's water. The conservationists denounced the environmental impact statement as a poor rationalization, especially in its failure to recognize wildlife losses.

The Sierra Club, Trout Unlimited, and the Idaho Environmental Council in their suit showed there would be major losses in prize trout streams. Flooding canyon slopes along the Teton River would eliminate vital winter range that provides food and shelter for mule deer, elk, and moose during winter storms. Populations of bobcat, otter, ruffed grouse, and other species would likewise be driven out. The Bureau of Reclamation talked of mitigation of losses, a mythical palliative that rarely, if ever, seems to work, but the Fish and Wildlife Service declared, "There is no alternative sanctuary."

The Bureau of Reclamation in its scanty environmental impact statement made no mention of leakage and seepage. However, the environmentalists produced as a witness a former Bureau geologist, Shirley Pytlak. She had been part of a survey team that had drilled holes in the floor of the reservoir to determine how well it might hold water. She testified that tests revealed serious seepage.

"If this much water can be absorbed by drill holes," Ms. Pytlak then asked aloud, "how much would leak from a whole reservoir?" Her question went unanswered. The warnings of other geologists went unheeded (including the advice that cameras be positioned to record the devastation that was sure to come).

Three years later, in 1976, the Teton Dam collapsed. The floodtide killed at least eight or ten persons and left thousands homeless. Thousands of head of livestock were lost and farm acreage ruined; property damage was estimated at $1 billion or more. Then followed the investigations, which seem a part of the political pattern associated with tragedy. An independent panel concluded the design of the dam had been faulty to begin with, with "less than conventional precautions" accounting for the collapse. The same viewpoint was expressed by the General Accounting Office, which charged BuRec with "unnecessary safety risks."

If something like the Teton disaster had happened in private industry, I daresay that someone would be subject to imprisonment for fraudulent misrepresentation or use of phony data. It makes me think of Watergate, except that in this case people lost their lives and the dirty political linen has never really been laid out to air before the public.

Out of the Teton Dam has emerged a new appreciation of safety in dam building—at least for now. The engineers of BuRec and the Army Corps of Engineers are not geniuses after all; they are not infallible, and may not even be competent.

As long as a decade ago a group of scientists called the Glen Canyon Study Group expressed deep concern about "enormous losses of water, the uglification of the gorgeous wilderness, raw changes in the balance of nature, and portents of pollution" at the Glen Canyon Reservoir near the Utah-Arizona border in the Southwest. They found leakage into surrounding sandstone walls at the rate of one million acre-feet a year equal to 15 percent of the flow of the entire Colorado River. Evaporation off the reservoir, swept by high, dry winds, is around five feet a year—so great, in fact, that humidity of the area is substantially increased.

More recently it has been determined that one of the worst (and, at the moment, most hotly contested) boondoggles, the Central Arizona Project, would annually lose through evaporation over its four huge reservoirs and lengthy desert canals at least 100,000 acre-feet of water. And the Arizona Bureau of Mines has questioned the safety of the major unit, the Orme Dam, since the site is located over geologic faults near Phoenix. Likewise, the Auburn Dam, designed to throttle the historic American River in California as part of the massive Central Valley Project, has been seriously challenged in a variety of safety investigations. The Association of Engineering Geologists, for instance, warns that the thin concrete arch of Auburn Dam would crack "over thousands of feet horizontally and hundreds of feet vertically" as a result of a single upstream direction shock. If the dam were to fail, the geologists warn, a 100-foot wall of water would descend on Sacramento; loss of life could exceed 100,000.

To my mind it's not enough to examine each dam on its own merits, whether for safety, economics, environmental impact, political practicality or any single factor. That's not enough when the whole idea is wrong.

We should now recognize the cumulative problems caused by deviating flow of a river. Little is actually known about evaporation, storage, transfer, or the influence of artificial impoundments on earth stresses. High dams may induce earthquakes since the great weight of impounded waters triggers release of tectonic forces. In another fashion, the Aswan Dam of Egypt has become a classic of miscalculation. It took completion of the dam for the world to recognize that Aswan catches soil nutrients in its reservoir, holding them back from the Mediterranean Sea. This lack of nutrients is destroying fish populations which for thousands of years have fed residents of the eastern Mediterranean.

Virtually all dams change flow patterns, water temperatures, chemistry, and quality of waters, and biological relationships in clearwater streams below them. Fluctuating water levels periodically expose, then inundate timberlands and scenery so that beauty and quality are sacrificed. Mud settles in the reservoir, where it accumulates in the form of sediment and silt. As the reservoir fills its value diminishes, while danger of flood increases.

Dam builders and their supporters like to cite statistics of public use. The Army Engineers will say their 300 lakes (artificial reservoirs, really) receive a heavier volume of visitors than all games of baseball, football, soccer, hockey, and assorted other spectator sports combined. This may be impressive, but only in terms of numbers. It would be national folly to sacrifice the few remaining moving rivers, a part of our living heritage. These areas must be left alone, free of that unholy alliance of engineers, builders, self-serving politicians and profit-makers, so that Americans may come as individuals to develop sensitivity to inspirational and scientific values found only in undisturbed nature.

The Bureau of Reclamation backs hydropower as a clean source of energy, free of thermal pollution and other environmental problems associated with coal or nuclear power. But building hydro projects sacrifices land that produces food, trees, or wildlife, often forcing people—and always the little people—to leave their homes.

Reservoirs inundate wildlife habitat, pressing animals into adjacent habitat generally already supporting wildlife at full capacity. Often, in parts of the arid West, the habitat suitable for many species is found only in the river bottoms. Deepening and straightening streams destroys bank cover and habitat niches valuable to fish, fur animals, and other aquatic life.

Historically the nation's water policy has encouraged over-use and waste. It has fostered construction of unsound projects. Water-saving measures and alternatives to dams, though invariably less costly, are rarely considered. Water conservation was declared to be the cornerstone of this administration's water policy announced last June, though I have not observed the principle applied in fact. The President's directive that federal agencies start to remove incentives for water misuse and add incentives for conservation could bring tremendous savings, but I see no signs of action along these lines.

If the President is serious, the Bureau of Reclamation should be disassembled as a self-perpetuating bureaucracy that has outlived its time and costs more than it's worth. The same goes for the civil works program of the Army Engineers, an agency that should be redirected to concentrate on its primary military mission.

The government needs to be forthright with the people. I have at hand a news release issued by the Interior Department on August 21, 1975, on awarding another construction contract for the Central Utah Project. It says:

The Vat tunnel is an integral part of the 27-mile Strawberry Aqueduct feature of the Central Utah Project which will develop most of Utah's share of Colorado River water for municipal and industrial purposes along the heavily populated Wasatch Front area of the state, plus providing water for irrigation, recreation, hydro-electric, and fish and game habitat.

The "benefits" alleged will include complete inundation of 53 miles of stream and drastic reduction of flow in 261 miles, net loss of thirty square miles of big-game habitat, 43 square miles of upland game habitat, 43 square miles of waterfowl habitat, and nine square miles of marshland. That news release might have been issued yesterday, or tomorrow. The same people in the Department continue to produce such propaganda, loaded with misrepresentation, to cover up the hard facts, and to help shape policy on "good" and "safe" projects.

It's encouraging at least that environmentalists are no longer alone. In a full page advertisement published in the *Washington Post* last October, Howard Jarvis, chairman of the American Tax Reduction Movement, denounced the public works appropriations bill as a measure that would add bureaucrats, bloat big government, fuel inflation, benefit a select few, waste water, and waste taxes. *Forbes* magazine, a free-enterprise, business-oriented journal, after examining the Tennessee-Tombigbee Waterway, reported: "Each year its costs escalate while its relative benefits shrink rapidly. Yet its real importance, if any, to the economy goes virtually unquestioned in Washington. The U.S. taxpayer could still save a billion or two by stopping Tenn-Tom now."

These good-sense influences are being felt. The politics have changed across the country, at the grass roots. The tide is too strong for worn-out ways to control us much longer.

"These Temple Destroyers, devotees of raging commercialism, seem to have a perfect contempt for Nature, and, instead of lifting their eyes to the God of the Mountains, lift them to the Almighty Dollar," wrote John Muir in 1913 while fighting the Hetch Hetchy Dam that ultimately destroyed one of Yosemite's most beautiful valleys.

In our time we cannot be satisfied with a block-building construction economy in an environmental desert of quicksand. To insure maximum benefits over the long-term future, government must be required to guard the public interest against inroads of development for short-term monetary gain. The hour is right to end the dam-building misadventure.

My First Trip into Hells Canyon

Field & Stream
July 1969

At the confluence of the Snake and Clearwater Rivers, where Lewis and Clark pitched camp in October 1805, and where the pioneers found shelter the following year enroute home, I arrived at the gateway to glad tidings, the kind we need in this age when emasculation of the landscape is almost a national psychosis.

It was not precisely the immediate setting that gave me the feeling of promise. The community of Lewiston, Idaho, seemed far from a fitting mirror of its heritage. An old logging mill town, rundown around the edges and bursting planlessly at the seams, with sulfurous pulp fumes drifting down the narrow canyon, Lewiston recalls a thousand other places that absolutely ignore the natural and historic endowments placed in their midst, and in their trust.

But the surrounding region, embracing portions of Idaho, Washington, and Oregon, is wide open country, the Northwest that Easterners dream about—uncrowded, uncluttered. Here one can go for endless miles without running out of pride in the native land. This is due largely to protection over more than half a century by the U.S. Forest Service, which began with the homesteaders, hard-rock miners, stockmen, and loggers, and found itself growing up with hikers, hunters, and fishermen, boatmen, scientists, and scholars. Critics may feel that occasionally the Forest Service slips in its responsibility, but here it has clearly held firm. And of all the national forest land in this tri-state area, Hells Canyon of the Snake River sums up our yesterdays, todays, and tomorrows with the special challenge, hope, and second chance for this generation of Americans.

The United States Supreme Court afforded the second chance for Hells Canyon in 1967 when it questioned the need of damming the last free-flowing stretch of the Snake River, thus reopening a case that seemed already signed and sealed. Aren't there other criteria than economics, the High Court asked, for determining the fate of wild land not specifically protected?

To put it another way, Hells Canyon may not be as renowned a phenomenon as the Grand Canyon of the Colorado, simply because it is more remote, but this doesn't mean that it is any less of a national treasure, or less worth saving in its natural state.

I had come to observe the river in question for *Field & Stream* and my own conscience, in company with Ernie Day, of Boise, Idaho, noted out-doorsman and photographer, and director of the National Wildlife Federation. We were joined by three men of the Forest Service. From the Idaho side was Everett Sanderson, supervisor of the Nez Perce National Forest, which embraces some of the finest wilderness and backcountry recreation in America: the Selway-Bitterroot, Salmon River Breaks, Seven Devils Range, and a large portion of Hells Canyon. From Oregon we had Wade Hall, who has been on the staff of the Wallowa-Whitman National Forest, which borders the Snake, since 1926. He is almost part of the heritage of the river country because, as he explained, his mother had come to eastern Oregon in 1880 in a covered wagon at the age of 4. Then there was Alex Smith, a good friend of Ernie's and mine from the regional office in Ogden, Utah, and also a veteran of the Oregon forests.

It was a bright morning in October when we started from the hotel (of course named Lewis and Clark) for Hells Canyon. At the river front we boarded the *Idaho Queen II*, whose owner and captain, Dick Rivers, holds the mail contract for delivery to isolated ranches over the 92-mile stretch of river from Lewiston to the head of navigation. Daring and dramatic riverboat trips started over this route a century ago, when sternwheelers clawed, rammed, and winched as far as they could to unload supplies for gold seekers and home-steaders, who had no other link with the outside world. The 48-foot *Queen*, powered by twin 260-horsepower diesel engines, was clearly a work boat, but not unattractive, nor unpleasant to be aboard. Nor were we alone. A snug cabin had accommodations for about forty passengers and every seat seemed filled. Many were older people, derived from the group of travelers sometimes called "the tennis-shoe set." And around us along the wharf were jet-powered boats of various sizes, which also carry sightseeing passengers and fishermen. . . .

This was my first trip into Hells Canyon, though I had become acquainted over the years with the Snake River in other portions of its thousand-mile journey from the Rocky Mountains to its merger with the Columbia. The second longest river in the Northwest, the Snake rises in western Wyoming, motherland of glorious rivers, including the Green, which becomes the main stem of the Colorado; the Madison and Gallatin Forks of the Missouri; and the Yellowstone. After joining the waters of littler streams from high lakes and forests in the Teton and Yellowstone country, the Snake flows through a beautiful forested canyon south of Jackson, then winds across the sagebrush plains of southern Idaho before turning sharply north along the Oregon border for its final journey. Captain William Clark named it the Lewis River, after his intrepid partner, and the tributary now known as the Salmon River, a great stream in its own right, he called the South Fork. But others insisted on using the Indian name of Shoshoneah, which translated into English as Snake, and Snake it is.

In recent years, the Snake has been plugged by twelve major dams and reservoirs of varying sizes, shapes, and purposes. In the lurid dam-building orgy of the past decade that destroyed beautiful stretches of river and canyon all over America in the name of profit, politics, and progress, the Corps of Engineers imposed four impoundments downstream from Lewiston. And upstream, in the deep series of gorges along the Idaho-Oregon border, carved by the river in the last twenty-five million years, the Idaho Power Company added three more, named Brownlee, Oxbox, and Hells Canyon. Today, only a little more than one hundred miles remain of native river, untamed, unspoiled, approaching the natural conditions in which man found it. This area is in the very middle and embraces the wildest stretches of white water, flowing through the deepest canyons. And even this is threatened, for still another dam, Asotin, has been authorized at the upstream edge of Lewiston, and that will reduce the free-flowing segment of the river to 75 miles.

Such is the tragedy of the Northwest. The mighty Columbia, once the proudest river on the continent, is only a shadow of itself, almost entirely bottled by eleven main dams. Proposals have been actively advanced to construct dam No. 12. Named generously for Ben Franklin, No. 12 would eliminate the last natural steelhead fishery, as well as wipe out a trout and whitefish fishery, plus spawning areas of summer-run steelhead. Turbulence, temperature changes, and oxygen-deficient releases from reservoirs are a constant threat. Fishermen may be promised tailrace fishing below such projects, but with pumped-storage peaking operations a fact of the future, these fishing areas will vanish also under violent water fluctuations. In the name of power production for industrial development, the Ben Franklin dam would also flood wildlife and waterfowl habitat, mule deer fawning areas, and nesting areas which produce 15 percent of Washington's Canada geese. No wonder the Washington Department of Game, sportsmen, and other conservationists are up in arms against this project of the Corps of Engineers.

The issues are parallel on the Snake River, which leads one to ask: Must the entire face of America be reshaped to look alike—overindustrialized, overpolluted, overpopulated?

The stubby *Idaho Queen II* headed upstream, for the first thirty miles between low hills on the flanking Idaho and Washington shores. A road paralleled our course on the Washington side to the Grande Ronde River, and then it stopped; I learned that other roads furnish access to points on both banks below the deepest part of the gorge, while hiking trails run forty or fifty miles along the river and numerous connecting trails feed in from side canyons.

At the mouth of the Grande Ronde, we saw fishermen casting from a gravel bar. Wade Hall mentioned that in summer water skiers come out in numbers. The hills grew higher as we continued upstream, with 3,000-foot cliffs rising from the water and white beaches.

It's the annual flooding action of the river that builds and refreshes these sand beaches and gravel bars, and that flushes the algae which accumulate during warm summer months. And it's the erosive power of the river in flood stage that sculptures and colors the striking canyon walls and midstream boulders. Such is life in a natural environment. Light-green broadleaf foliage growing on the beaches, bars, and at the mouths of tributary creeks contrasted softly with the walls of basalt and granite. On the warm canyon floor were white alder, wild cherry, and elderberry, while on the slopes were bitterbrush, serviceberry, blue bunch wheatgrass, western hackberry, mountain mahogany, and maple, the lower brushy draws furnishing ideal cover. . . .

At Garden Creek Ranch on the Idaho side, facing the Washington-Oregon border, the *Queen* made her first stop, the first of about a dozen. The ports along the way are bits of beach into which a boat can ram its bow and back off again after letters, magazines, and parcel post are put ashore. The schedule being purely flexible, we stopped to fish a while. A few fish were caught at our several stops. I noted that periodically the canyon would relent and fall back, allowing a bench on which some pioneer once staked his future. The various ranches that now survive actually began as either mining claims or homesteads operated by hardy souls struggling to survive.

The voyage through the turbulent stream was an adventure. The boat crashed headlong through rapids and ripples, the skipper heading straight for one bank, cutting close to a jagged boulder, then whirling the wheel. Rivermen once had to learn and memorize the rapids and channels, but now they have target boards on shore, which they line up like gun sights, enabling them to work their way upriver in switchbacks.

In due course all of us were impressed by the depth of Hells Canyon. The maximum measurable depth is 6,550 feet. It is deeper than Yosemite, and more than a thousand feet deeper than the Grand Canyon. Kings Canyon in California is rated first and deepest of those formed by any major river in America.

Presently the boat came abreast of the most celebrated stretch in the river, the battleground, which engineers, lawyers, planners, profiteers, and politicians seem about to destroy.

In quick succession we passed the site of the proposed Nez Perce Dam, the confluence with the Salmon River on the Idaho side, marked by spectacular facing of metamorphic basalt; and, a half-mile above the confluence, the site of the proposed High Mountain Sheep Dam; followed by the Imnaha River, flowing in from the Oregon side down a steep narrow valley with rocky grandeur, and then Dug Bar, the point where Chief Joseph and his Nez Perce followers crossed the Snake on their historic flight for freedom.

A veritable concentration of treasures, indeed. The Salmon River flows from its source in the Sawtooth Mountains and Whiteclouds north across the heart of Idaho, then west through rocky canyons between North Fork and Riggins before turning north again, without a single dam to mar its way. The Salmon is noted for its recreational value, as well as for being a spawning ground of steelhead and salmon, important to fisheries in the Northwest, Canada, and Alaska. Little wonder the Sport Fishing Institute proposed recently that the Salmon be designated as the first National Anadromous Fish Spawning Sanctuary, with restrictions on any diversions and downstream development that might adversely affect its natural function. The Imnaha is also a major migratory fish stream. In fact, half the steelhead still caught in the Columbia are produced in the Snake River system. Chief Joseph was of this country, born near the mouth of the Imnaha. He and his people wintered here. The Nez Perce came down the breaks and smooth benches of the Imnaha in 1877, then retreated over the river before the cavalry, without loss of a single human or animal. Archaeologists have reported that Native Americans have lived along the Snake for 8,000 years. Rock shelters, caves, carvings, paintings in nearly 200 villages and campsites are available for investigation— one of the last opportunities for such studies in the entire Columbia Basin.

This section and the whole river have a magic fascination for scientists, boatmen, fishermen, hikers, hunters, photographers, botanists, archaeologists, and all who love the outdoors. The Middle Snake presents an array of free-flowing pure water, rivershore trail, campsites, and canyon scenery. The word "unique" is often overdone, but there is no doubt that in fisheries alone this river is superb, not only for its anadromous fish, but for the resident species of smallmouth bass, channel catfish, and the immense white sturgeon, the largest fresh-water fish in North America.

The trouble with such values is that you can't measure them in terms of economic profitability, or market them for the glory of the Gross National Product. Accordingly, for many years assorted boomers of federal, private, and public power have been competing for the privilege of desecrating the scene on the theory that nature must be controlled, harnessed, distorted, but never left to God's own simple ways.

In 1964, a syndicate of four private utilities called Pacific Northwest Power Company (PNP) was awarded a license by the Federal Power Commission to construct the 670-foot High Mountain Sheep Dam. However, it was opposed in a legal dispute by a combine of eighteen public power utilities, the Washington Public Power Supply System (WPPSS), which placed its bets on the Nez Perce site for best hydropower development, although blocking access to the Salmon River fishery. The issue ultimately went to the Supreme Court, which in June 1967 handed down one of the most important resource-related decisions in its history. The Court directed the FPC to reconsider its license to PNP on the grounds that it had not adequately considered the feasibility of the federal role, as provided by the Federal Power Act. Then the Court raised the question of whether any dam should be built on the Middle Snake. In a decision written by Justice William O. Douglas, a veteran Northwesterner, champion of law, human rights, and of the outdoors, the Court declared: "The test is whether the project will be in the public interest and that determination can be made only after an exploration of all issues relevant to the public interest. These include future power demand and supply in the area, alternate sources of power, and preserving reaches of wild river in wilderness areas, and the preservation of anadromous fish for commercial and recreational purposes, and the protection of wildlife."

The Court decision gave heart to conservation groups, both local and national—the Idaho Wildlife Federation, Idaho Alpine Club, Federation of Western Outdoor Clubs, Sierra Club, and Wilderness Society. The Hells Canyon Preservation Council was organized to fight any dams. It was the second chance come alive, after all had seemed lost.

The other side was not inactive. The old rivals, PNP and WPPS, patched up their differences. Deciding there would be enough to divide between them, they applied for a joint license to build the High Mountain Sheep Dam. Then in May 1968, the federals jumped in. The Secretary of the Interior Stewart L. Udall generously proposed instead that his outfit build and operate a dam at the Appaloosa site, about eight miles above the mouth of the Salmon, on grounds that it would afford better protection to the fishery resource and make more use of the Snake for recreation. And besides (as he might have mentioned), Interior's dam builders, having been frustrated at the Grand Canyon, were in need of work. Anybody who thinks of the Interior as a "Department of Conservation" has another think coming. While a few of its bureaus truly endeavor to safeguard natural resources, other bureaus and many political appointees are devoted to the cause of everlasting construction, development, exploitation of oil, gas, metals, water, and land.

In building dams for power these days, the principal structure is often accompanied by a secondary, or re-regulating, dam placed downstream in order to recycle water. Thus the Appaloosa dam would require a re-regulating dam at the Low Mountain Sheep site, just above the mouth of the Imnaha. Another dam under consideration upstream at a site called Pleasant Valley also would need a re-regulating dam. High Mountain Sheep Dam would not only block the Imnaha itself, but require another dam at China Gardens, twenty miles below the mouth of the Salmon River, which would possibly have as much adverse effect as Nez Perce itself. And all kinds of complicated devices were offered with the competing designs in order to prove compliance with the Supreme Court order.

Hearings were held by the Federal Power Commission at Portland, Oregon, and Lewiston during 1968, but the dam proponents failed, and rather dismally, I think. They produced the usual assortment of economists, power technicians, and planners to warn gloomily that the Northwest must have every potential kilowatt of hydropower or face peril. Yet Northwest utilities and Bonneville Power have launched a multi-billion dollar nuclear power program for the next twenty years. As the vice president of Portland General Electric admitted, "If High Mountain Sheep does not become available in any particular assumed year, it does not follow that the lights in the Northwest will be turned out, but merely that in the planning process we will advance an alternate nuclear plant by seven months to a year to fill the gap." The assistant administrator of the Bonneville Power Authority conceded further when he said, "Viewed as merely an additional 3 million kilowatts in the regional power growth, Appaloosa is hardly distinguishable from the approximately 25 million kilowatts of hydro and 16 million kilowatts of thermal that will be added by 1987." But the developers must have Appaloosa for other reasons, he insisted; like all dams, it is guaranteed to control floods, boost payrolls and taxes, expand recreation, and bring a flood of tourists. The Bureau of Outdoor Recreation obligingly produced a plan full of everything a chamber of commerce would dream of: picnicking, swimming, boating, water skiing, sightseeing, fishing, hunting, horse-back riding, hiking, nature study—precisely what people can do at a thousand other places. The BOR failed to mention that water fluctuations of as much as 170 feet would leave Hells Canyon biologically barren and unsightly, with stained canyon walls and mudflats degrading to recreational concepts, and equally degrading to a quality environment in which the natural river serves as an eco-logical lifeline. It neglected to mention the superabundance of reservoir-type recreation already in the Northwest, including nearby Brownlee, in sharp con-trast with the critical shortage of recreation forms which only wilderness and wild rivers can fulfill.

The Supreme Court made such considerations important. It forced rec-ognition of the natural environment, of the values of fish and wildlife. The Interior Department obliged by proposing expensive, complicated multi-level devices for the Appaloosa design in order to reintroduce oxygen and remove nitrogen, which it claimed would actually increase productivity. But a reading of the testimony indicates the Department's biologists did not have their hearts in it. They admitted that any dam would have harmful effects on fish produc-tion, that the whole project was an immense game of guesswork, without precedent, and certain to cost many millions of dollars. There might be an outside chance of saving part of the production for commercial fishing, but to maintain the sport fishery in a "pooled-up" river would be virtually impos-sible. The river would be changed to an impoundment and, quite apart from steelhead and salmon, the native sturgeon, smallmouth, and catfish would be essentially lost—even though nowhere does a fishery of such excellent quan-tity and quality exist for all three species in the same water. . . .

Professional experts of Oregon, Idaho, and Washington fish and game departments were unanimous in their testimony that no dam could possibly benefit the sports resources. After all, with the construction of each new project, additional habitat and spawning areas of Oregon, Idaho, and Washington have been wiped out. Despite the application of all known measures, and the expenditure of $250 million for anadromous fish passages in the Columbia Basin, the fishery resource has gone steadily downhill. Clearly, the perpetua-tion of salmon and steelhead doesn't rest in mechanics and machinations but in honoring the life-cycle of the fish as they travel thousands of miles from the mountains to the ocean and home again, and in respecting the natural laws. With more than 50 percent of the Snake no longer accessible to anadromous fish, the remaining areas are more important and more critical.

"If all the dam construction projects now under construction, authorized, or seriously considered are completed," John R. Woodworth, Idaho's Director of Fish and Game, declared at the Lewiston hearing last September, "it will not be very long until the entire Columbia River within the United States upstream from Bonneville Dam, the entire Snake River from its mouth upstream to Weiser, Idaho, and major portions of the Clearwater and Grande Ronde River drainages will be impounded. It is our opinion that under the theory of true multiple-use development of water resources, maintenance of a stretch of the mid-Snake River in a free-flowing condition, coupled with its unique fishery and scenic attractions, would be in the best interest of the public and future generations hereafter."

Officials and the dam promoters were not alone at these hearings. The spokesmen for the people came, too, citing the interests and values of natural science, history, outdoor sports, the therapy of nature to man. It's tough to battle big industry and big government, with their resources and paid staffs, but at the Hells Canyon hearings the people were represented by their own technical experts, many with national reputations, who came to testify without pay.

Dr. William L. Blackadar, of Salmon, Idaho, was a star performer. He turned up after riding thirty-five miles in his kayak through huge waves and rapids from Hells Canyon to Pittsburgh Landing. "We do not realize the potential of this area," he testified. "Eight years ago the first fiber-glass slalom kayak was designed. At that time less than 500 people were rafting the Middle Fork of the Salmon River annually. Now over ten times that number run the river and for the first time sizable numbers of kayaks have appeared. This area will soon be alive with these 'banana' boats. Isn't it great that these challenges await us? Wouldn't it be sad to think that these bigger waves might be hidden under hundreds of feet of water? There are few areas left and these will become priceless."

I said earlier the dam builders had failed in their presentation. They made this plain last November, when the old enemies, PNP, WPPS, and the Interior Department, joined in a three-way bid to finance, build, and operate the Appaloosa Dam—rather ironic considering the troubles with "intervening non-federal ownerships" in Northwest power projects. Almost at once the new partners requested a delay in FPC proceedings, preferring to seek Congressional approval and avoiding the whole license question. Fortunately, the only conflict they resolved was the one among themselves, and not the issue of principle before the people. . . .

In later afternoon we pulled in at Copper Creek, our home for the night, where Rivers operates a camp for use on the midweek scheduled run. It was a pleasant setting with several furnished cabins clustered in the meadow. After we were settled, we all fished a while and watched an osprey upstream diving for his dinner. The number and variety of birds along the river is amazing. Eagles and falcons use the high canyons for their necessary isolation in breeding. Herons soar high overhead and gather food along the riverbanks. Canada geese nest in the cliffs. Hungarian partridge, quail, and grouse are common. But if any one game bird stands out as numerous, it's the chukar. Apparently foodstuffs little utilized by other species make this an ideal habitat, for coveys of these rugged birds seemed to pop out everywhere, although the species was introduced only fifteen years ago.

The next morning we continued a little while with Rivers and the party on the boat, then were put ashore on the Oregon side where arrangements had been made for saddle horses. The horses were waiting. So was Jack Hooker, a well-known outfitter of northeast Oregon, and a wrangler. Continuing our journey in this way we'd be able to get another perspective of Hells Canyon and also to travel beyond the end of navigation.

We rode past the Circle C Ranch at Pittsburgh Landing (the Pleasant Valley dam site) on the Idaho side which is an oasis of green alfalfa fields surrounded by dry hillsides. This is one of the main access points, reached by road from Riggins and Whitebird. A jet boat zipped upstream. It was named fittingly Hell's Angel, which Everett explained is between Lewiston and his fishing camp at Willow Creek, which we would reach soon. Then the dramatic topography yielded into stairsteps, great benches, and terraced cliffs. Snow-patched mountains towered against the sky. They were part of the Seven Devils, comprising a famous recreation area. "You can see the trails," said Everett, "that any citizen can use to hike or ride into the bottom of Hells Canyon within a day."

The river flowed swift and deep, winding through bend after bend of great gorges, with rapids seeming like boiling water. We passed a ranch on Kirkwood Creek, where Senator Len Jordan once lived, and then rested opposite the location of Harvey's tent camp. It was an ideal wilderness setting, sheltered beneath a cliffside. Our interest was in the stream, for here the sturgeon find running-water habitat of deep holes, swift flowing rapids and shallow riffles they need for spawning and survival. We watched closely and spotted two sturgeon near the surface. They looked about 9 feet long. One came floating to the top, then both vanished.

The great white sturgeon once was common in the United States. Fish were caught commercially weighing a thousand pounds and more. Records indicate that fish 10 to 15 feet long were not uncommon before the dams were built on the Snake and Columbia. Now the sturgeon is reduced to its last stronghold in places like the Middle Snake, a fishery that technology cannot match.

Beyond Johnson Bar, the end of navigation, the river became much rougher, apparently too dangerous except for extraordinary boatmen. Our trail seemed to take full advantage of every possible break in topography, one moment at water level, almost within feel of the spray, then climbing hundreds of feet to skirt huge rims. We crossed a dramatic stretch aptly called Eagle's Nest, then another, Devil's Slide, where the trail was carved out of solid rock.

We rode through semi-desert and foothills covered with cactus, hackberry, grasses, juniper, and pinyon pine. A rattlesnake crossed our trail. I became more conscious of wildlife. A whitetail deer bounded through the timber, then a larger mule deer skirted over a dry open hillside. A coyote "topped out" over the crest. Because it is remote, Hells Canyon is blessed with a variety and abundance of wildlife. That night, while camping at a site where a person could enjoy the same atmosphere as the first white man to see the place, we talked about this point. . . .

While we talked, an eagle rode the evening breeze, broad-winged, silent, patient.

It takes patience to shape the land, to balance the life forms, and to absorb the true meaning of life, and perhaps the appreciation of patience is God's gift to man at Hells Canyon. Such were my thoughts when we adjourned and I crawled under canvas flaps that night.

We rode out next morning into big country. The elevation changed rapidly—5,000 feet in five hours—as we rode through ponderosa pine and Douglas-fir cloaking steep, narrow-sided valleys, high plateaus of spruce and fir, and finally topped out in a breezy world of alpine sedge and grass, before meeting our ride to the town of Imnaha and another world.

As for the future of Hells Canyon, the Department of Agriculture recently gave support to the Forest Service position against any dam on the Middle Snake. This is heartening. Both Idaho Senators, Frank Church and Len Jordan, have proposed the so-called Moratorium Bill, providing for a 10-year study period. Their reasons differ, Church hoping to save the anadromous fish runs and the recreational resource, Jordan apparently wanting time to decide whether Idaho should claim the water for downstate irrigation.

There is still another way. Conservationists now are pressing for establishment of a Hells Canyon-Snake National River. This would embrace 721,000 acres, including a quarter-mile shoreline along the Snake and Salmon, a Seven Devils Unit of 256,000 acres in Idaho, and an Imnaha Unit of 335,000 acres in Oregon. Existing activities, such as ranching and grazing, would be protected as part of the historic pioneer tableau, but no contrary developments would be allowed to compromise the scenic values of the rivers. Virtually all the land involved lies within national forest boundaries and the Forest Service has for years recognized that the Snake merits special management consideration. In 1963, it designated the 130,000-acre Hells Canyon-Seven Devils Scenic Area, and judiciously administered it primarily for recreation, scenery, and scientific values. Under the National River plan, an enlarged system of trails, campsites, and boat ramps would make the area more usable, and would disperse use in order to eliminate concentrations and conserve the atmosphere. Some of the steep slopes, canyon breaks, and rugged terrain appear suitable to reintroduction of mountain sheep, which once ranged here and were observed as recently as fifteen years ago.

The price of all these would be minimal. Indeed, it costs virtually nothing but disciplined restraint to protect the vital, rich records of geology, archaeology, and ecology, as compared with half a billion dollars or more for a scrubby dam and rancid reservoir that would submerge irreplaceable treasures under 500 feet of water. The boomers of power and concrete speak in almost lustful terms of Hells Canyon as "the last major hydroelectric site in the United States," as though it's indecent and sinful to leave alone the works that God hath wrought. But Americans with ethics, morality, and good sense may build the monument of this age by preserving the wonders of nature—so that all this will not be lost to the sight of man.

CHAPTER II

PUBLIC LANDS,
LAST OF THE WIDE-OPEN SPACES

Public lands are heart and body of the West, and maybe soul, too. I learned through the years to identify public lands as the source of Western art, literature, history, and mystery, the mystery of people trying to relate to the earth around them, failing, falling, picking up to try again. Take away the public lands from Albuquerque, Denver, Salt Lake City, Seattle, and they, and all the other cities, would be the most ordinary of places. Take away the public lands and there wouldn't be much to the economy either. Public lands are the last open spaces, last wilderness, last wildlife haven. Without public lands the West would be an impoverished province.

My first awareness of public lands came with the national parks. I can't imagine the West without Yellowstone, Yosemite, the Grand Canyon, Mesa Verde, Mount Rainier—those and other superlative landmarks set aside, safeguarded forever, as we like to think. Then my trail led to national forests, where I learned to appreciate trees as trees, as well as timber, and about the concept of wilderness, which Forest Service personnel initiated. At *Field & Stream* and again at *Defenders,* I focused on wildlife, finding endless connections with the public lands.

"Home on the Range, Where Livestock Roam," originally called, "The Wide Open Spaces in a Year of Decision," was an early piece I wrote for *Field & Stream*, about public lands administered by the Bureau of Land Management (BLM). Possibly because BLM functions are virtually wholly western, I found that the agency got very little public attention in the East but not much in the urban West either. In fact over the years conservationists, except for Charlie Watson, a heroic lone figure in Nevada, have paid little consistent heed to the BLM.

In that early report I made my mistakes, overrating rest-rotation grazing, the Vale Project, and the willingness of stockmen to cooperate in conserving, but I tried and kept trying. Good professionals wanted to make something of the bureau as a land steward, to reverse course from its old role of giving land away, and were desperate for help. BLM people shared inside information, including stories about questionable land dealings by their superiors.

I think the essays here show how difficult it was, and still is, to administer lands professionally, in the public interest. History shows that the idea of designating and protecting public lands has forever been attacked and, where attacks failed, subverted. As chairman of the House Interior Committee through the 1960s, Wayne Aspinall, a Democrat of Colorado, dominated congressional policy on natural resources, principally on behalf of commercial users. After his defeat in 1972, he returned to the House floor, lobbying his old colleagues as a paid hand of the mining industry. In the Nixon days, Harrison Loesch, a Colorado lawyer, came on board as Assistant Secretary of the Interior in charge of public lands, and when he left sold his skills to Peabody Coal.

For public lands, the Reagan-Bush years were lean and mean. The anti-government was in charge of governing, yet nothing in the past, certainly not in my experience, compares with the anti-federal frenzy of the mid-1990s, generated by the wise-use/property-rights movement and reflected by the majority in Congress. Field personnel of the BLM and Forest Service in Nevada and New Mexico, and likely other places as well, have been threatened with violence. So have everyday citizens, at open meetings, where they came to listen and dialogue. The anti-government clamor over public lands has lost "civility" and reason.

"The Western frontier, to the lasting sorrow of old hunters like yourself, has now practically disappeared," wrote Gifford Pinchot in the introduction to Hamlin Garland's 1910 novel, *Cavanagh, Forest Ranger.* "Its people faced life with a manly dependence on their own courage and capacity which did them, and still does them, high honor." I don't see significant courage or honor in tearing apart public lands. The frontier has long disappeared, and frontier myths and machismo should disappear with it.

It's not that public agencies are above criticism. In the best of years I found them wanting. The Bitterroot Valley and national forests of western Montana are still overcut and mismanaged by "The Boys Who Brought Back DDT," and, as Dale Burk said then: "The agency remains glued to the same old cut, cut, and cut-some-more philosophy that led it into disgrace in the first place." Political pressures and bureaucracy mix a wicked brew.

When Bill Clinton was elected president in 1992 he appointed Bruce Babbitt, the former governor of Arizona, as the Secretary of the Interior. Babbitt came with excellent credentials and good intentions. He appointed Jim Baca, who had achieved an impressive record as the elected commissioner of natural resources in New Mexico, as director of the Bureau of Land Management. Baca took his new job seriously, determined to revive the spirit of his agency by enforcing regulations and reducing grazing damage on the range. Within two years politics forced him out. Babbitt himself fizzled for the most part. For a time he went around the West holding meetings with ranchers, trying to cajole, mollify, and appease them into accepting increasing fees and decreasing stock numbers, but they could go to their congressional delegations at any time and continue to do things their way.

As of 1995 national parks, the "crown jewels," are administered no better than any other public lands. Every three or four years a new director comes on board. An important early mission for him is to inspect the parks, especially the glamour spots (Everglades and maybe Virgin Islands in winter; Alaska, Yosemite, Yellowstone, and Grand Teton in summer), many of which he's never seen before. He will also appoint a new study team, which reviews the studies of previous teams, invariably with considerable travel, circulation of draft reports, and revisions that keep everybody busy. Under Babbitt's appointed director, Roger Kennedy (who came from the Smithsonian), the National Park Service undertook a reorganization designed to improve efficiency and reduce the number of personnel. It seemed mostly to move things around without meaningful change, but it continued keeping everybody too busy to face the chronic issues of overuse, misuse, and degradation of park resources.

Not the best of times, but over the long haul, in the span I have covered, many good things have happened. The Classification and Multiple Use Act of 1964 meant that public domain was no longer to be disassembled and given away. The Wilderness Act and its implementation have led to nearly 100 million acres being included in the National Wilderness Preservation System, plus a healthy public wilderness awareness. New national parks have been established in the Great Basin, the North Cascades, the desert and redwood forests of California, and in Alaska from Glacier Bay north to the Gates of the Arctic in the Brooks Range.

Things may indeed be difficult today, but tough times have come before. James G. Watt's tenure as Secretary of the Interior was one of those times. His mischief-making stirred the public conscience so much that President Reagan had to get rid of him. The 1990s are not the end of public lands but only the prelude to the mystery and opportunity of the twenty-first century.

Home on the Range, Where Livestock Roam

Field & Stream
April 1968

As recently as fifteen years ago if a Western politician of one party mildly criticized a federal land management agency, the chances were that a politician of the opposite party would immediately allege that his opponent hadn't gone far enough, and then thoroughly denounce the outfit in question. It was good politics, the thing to do, and it served the powerful special interests that have run the West for a century.

The late Senator Pat McCarran, a tub-thumper for Nevada mining and livestock industries, delighted in shooting down what he called "swivel chair cowboys and Eastern bureaucrats." He kept the Bureau of Land Management weak and off balance with a six-year-long Senate investigation and forestalled efforts to raise grazing fees. Frank Barrett, Congressman and later Senator from Wyoming, singled out the Forest Service as his special target and conducted a series of vituperative public hearings. The Forest Service, said he, while trying to promote a stockmen's monopoly over national forest grazing lands, was "arrogant, bigoted, tyrannical—void of respect of law or the rights of other people."

Times have changed since the McCarran-Barrett era. The special interests still exercise immense political influence, but the stranglehold is loosening. This was clearly shown last fall in Wyoming when Governor Stanley Hathaway, speaking for the cattlemen who form the power structure of his state, attacked proposed new BLM regulations to manage scattered tracts of grazing land as "another step by the federal government to bring the livestock industry under complete bureaucratic control." If the new regulations were put into effect, the governor predicted darkly, "a one billion dollar annual industry in the state will be under the heels of the federal government." This was to be expected, but the reaction of Senator Gale McGee was not. Instead of playing a me-too game, the senator countered by telling the stockmen to their faces that the new regulations were not all that serious, and furthermore that the government obligation is "to administer the public lands as a public trust, not in behalf of a few individuals." He probably could not have gotten away with that fifteen years ago.

The key to the difference in this short span of time perhaps is most readily found in California. The population there is growing by 1,500 persons every day of the year. For each new ten persons one acre of open space must be eliminated from the California landscape. The roving room that remains becomes that much more precious—too valuable to waste, or to furnish to one commercial use only, or to surrender to landgrabbers. The smart, honest Western politicians are learning that they can stand up and meet higher responsibilities than those called for by the special economic interests.

They recognize that the people of the West and all the country are now awakening to the "public lands," the domain administered by the Bureau of Land Management in the Department of the Interior, as they have been awake for years to national parks, national forests, and wildlife refuges. Public lands cover 175 million acres (an area greater in size than California and Nevada combined) in the eleven Western states, plus 282 million acres in Alaska, but they have been a vague concept for too long. Though they belong to all the people, they have been run by the Western bloc in Congress in behalf of a handful of their "pioneer" constituents, the miners, loggers, stockmen, oil and gas interests, and land speculators, and generously ignored by the Eastern bloc.

As a consequence, millions upon millions of acres are in poor condition, an eroded and unproductive wasteland. Congress has kept the BLM laboring under a cloud of uncertainty, though it administers 60 percent of all federal land. The agency has been forced to suffer shifts and changes through the years, a sequence of traumatic experiences from which the Fish and Wildlife, Forest, and National Park services have been gently spared.

Now, however, the public has a better chance. Representative Wayne Aspinall of Colorado, an imperious, provincial old liner, runs the House Interior Committee, of which he is chairman, with a firm hand. But in his own oblique way he responds to the strength and challenge of a new young Western leadership, and of the Eastern conscience, expressed by Representative John Saylor of Pennsylvania. For years the Interior Department, like a closed corporation, was dominated by Western vested interests and politicians, riddled with patronage appointees in key posts. Secretary Stewart L. Udall has had a small measure of success in reshaping it into a national agency more responsive to public interest. There is still too much lip service where courage and performance are called for, but the several layers of Interior officials, from the Secretary on down, are out in the open with no place to hide.

The public lands are worthy of all the attention they may now receive, after being ignored for so long. They are the "leftover lands" of the old public domain, which nobody wanted in the development of the West. They were given minimum protection, no mandate of management. Their principal mission was grazing. Today we recognize in them the largest undeveloped potential for wildlife and recreation in America. Given proper management, they are capable of producing more game and fish than any other federal lands.

Sportsmen have an immense stake in the future of the public lands, a tremendously diverse country. They are the home grounds of caribou and mountain goat in Alaska; antelope in Wyoming; elk in Idaho; barbary sheep in New Mexico; bighorn in Nevada; javelina, wild turkey, and mountain lion in Arizona; one of the country's heaviest concentrations of deer in Colorado—plus millions of small game, upland birds, and waterfowl. One of the finest stretches of the rugged Rogue River, famous for steelhead and salmon, runs through steep-walled canyons of the public lands in Oregon.

In addition, the deserts are a dramatic geological phenomenon unmatched by any other region. They are sparsely vegetated, water is scarce, summers are hot, and lands are fragile. But portions deserve to be set aside as wilderness, for primitive hiking, camping, and scientific research. During spring other portions can be enjoyed by rockhounds, picnickers, photographers, and all kinds of people who want to get out and sample America's last frontier.

Indeed, public lands comprise the last untapped, smog-free frontier. They embrace everything from cactus and creosote desert to grassland, Douglas-fir forests, and the tundra and barren icecaps of the north. Given wise development and management, they could provide beach recreation, winter sports, bird and wildlife watching, and a whole host of activities. . . .

The biggest difficulty is that Congress has deliberately perpetuated ancient land laws, passed before the turn of the century. These laws, designed for other purposes in other periods, serve today to prevent sound management, to keep the agency weak, and to favor the special interests. To understand them in the context of our times, consider this background of history:

The public domain, the landed estate of the American people, originally included practically all the land within the boundaries of the first forty-eight states, except the original thirteen and Texas. From the earliest days land was sold to provide revenue for State and Federal Government. Land was given to

Revolutionary soldiers in lieu of wages. And land passed into the hands of profiteers and speculators in the beginning even as now.

In 1812, the General Land Office, a direct predecessor of the BLM, was established. Its mission was to give land away. The expression "doing a land office business" came into the lexicon when government land offices were established and everything possible was done to help a citizen get his legal, rightful quota of the public domain. But with the opening of the West, land laws were short-cut and subverted, leading to fraud, intense speculation, and concentration of wealth. Millions of acres changed hands under laws designed to aid the settler.

For example, the Homestead Act of 1862 required construction of a dwelling, but since proofs of compliance were by affidavit, the tiniest possible house could be erected, about fourteen by sixteen inches, not feet. Under terms of the Swamp and Overflow Act, claimants testified to the "overflowed" character of the land by swearing they had crossed it in a boat, neatly forgetting to mention that the boat was being hauled behind a wagon. On the other hand, irrigation ditches built under the Desert Land Act often failed to carry any water and that law is still on the books, long obsolete but used deviously today by large land companies.

Railroads were given 130 million acres, directly or through the states, in alternate, checkerboard sections along their routes, "in aid," to finance construction. Their holdings were intended for sale to settlers, but through "indemnity acts" they were able to trade for some of the finest timber stands of the West. Then there were the lumber companies, which transported hired "entrymen" to file claims for $2.50 an acre under the Timber and Stone Act and thus obtained through sheer fraud millions of acres of priceless redwood and Douglas-fir forest.

The marvel of the era was that in 1872, in the face of dissolution of the nation's treasures, Yellowstone should be set aside as a public trust, or "withdrawn" from any possible private claim. This was a new course that ultimately led to establishment of national parks, forests, and wildlife refuges.

Nevertheless, in the same year, the nation's basic mining law was passed. It authorized anyone to roam the public lands in order to stake mining claims and attempt to discover valuable minerals; and, if he made a discovery, to purchase land for $2.50 or $5 an acre. The law is horribly outdated—everybody knows it and has known it for years. In 1920 the law was modified to provide for leasing, instead of purchase, of oil and gas, oil shale, potash, phosphate, and coal deposits. It was modified again in 1955 to eliminate claims on some common varieties of minerals. But the basic law is still in effect and applies to a great many varieties, common and uncommon. The legitimate miners and pseudo-miners receive the same "incentive and reward" as the "hardy pioneer opening new frontiers" of almost one century ago, irrespective of all the new values in the lands.

Thus, claims are filed to obtain title to land for speculation in areas of booming real estate, for summer cabins, filling stations, and timber. In 1966 alone, thousands of claims were filed for a mineral called dawsonite and other little-known metals in the Green River Basin of Colorado, Utah, and Wyoming, an area containing what could prove a treasure in oil shale resources. Oil shale is covered by the leasing act, which provides rentals and royalties in favor of the United States, but dawsonite, the claimants hope, is not. And no matter who files a claim, much of the property has ended up with the nation's major petroleum firms. Once a tract is disposed of, it is gone forever as far as use by the public is concerned.

The development of minerals might easily be placed entirely on a leasing basis, with supervision and control of the surface remaining in government hands. But mining interests exercise an almost primeval freedom and power, and enjoy privileges unmatched by other users of our natural resources. The mineral and petroleum interests speak softly, but their voices are heard clearly in the halls of Congress. And so the ancient mining laws are sacrosanct.

Livestock men once exercised more power over the public lands than they do today, although the range is still badly overgrazed almost everywhere. Some parts of the arid desert should never have been grazed at all, considering they provide scant forage and contribute virtually nothing to stability of the grazing industry. But grazing began and grew as sheer anarchy. The stockman, as Major John Wesley Powell once wrote, was "a trespasser on the public domain, an obstacle to settlement, and at best a crude forerunner of civilization."

In one sense, public land policies or the lack of them forced overgrazing. Stockmen discovered that, in the absence of order, he who was first was best. They were forced to any extent to control water, and they knew that whatever grass they left others would get; so they concentrated on leaving no grass at all. Range wars were a way of life between the cattlemen and the sheepmen, the latter roving with flocks of thousands. The cattlemen and sheepmen both fought the homesteaders, many of whom wasted their lives and their savings trying to farm, at government invitation, desert lands which were too dry, rough or rocky, and grasslands which were too fragile for agriculture.

After half a century of anarchy and deteriorating range over millions of acres, the Taylor Grazing Act of 1934 marked the first step to introduce some semblance of protection, if not management, into the public lands. It established grazing districts and a permit system. A priority of use in granting permits was based on the number of stock on the public range during the five preceding years. Preference was accorded to owners of land and water who could support their stock during the off months as a ranching unit.

The grazing districts, initially covering 80 million acres, were administered by a new agency, the Grazing Division, while the old General Land Office continued to issue leases for using the rest of the public domain (these two later merged to become the Bureau of Land Management), but the real power was vested in local stockmen's associations, which chose members of governing advisory boards. They determined rules, regulations, allotments, and carrying capacity, and gave more orders than advice to government agents.

The Taylor Grazing Act was fraught with shortcomings. It failed to furnish authority really needed to manage the resources. It enabled some ranchers to overrate the numbers of stock they had run during the priority period, and it discriminated unfairly against others, driving honest men to bankruptcy. But it stopped range wars and unregulated, competitive grazing, and marked a breakthrough to bringing order out of chaos.

The favored ranchers supported the Taylor Grazing Act. But they insisted on exercising political influence to keep administration weak. For years personnel was insufficient to conduct range surveys; the saying went that one or two men were responsible for supervising grazing on a district of two to eight million acres. Few people knew or cared anything about their affairs. They were alone, except for the stockmen, who were with them always. There was no organized program, no way of determining the actual carrying capacity of the land, and very little range improvement. One committee of Congress was unwilling to accept the principle of management or to increase grazing fees, while another committee declined to increase BLM's appropriation until it showed more revenue from increased fees. . . .

The outlook until recent years could scarcely have been more dismal. The changing times, however, have demanded that politicians depart from their traditional inaction, indecision, and vacillation. In 1957, BLM received appropriations for an intensive ten-year grazing review, called adjudication, an inventory of forage production and demand, and determination of the adjustment necessary to bring them in balance.

Adjudication has been a tremendous project, involving surveys of the federal range and 17,000 ranch properties, covering almost 200 million acres. It showed, clearly and simply, that the range was in poor condition and therefore unfit for wildlife and watershed protection, and not much good for grazing.

But adjudication represents the beginning. Last summer in Eastern Oregon I saw in action the next step in range management.

"Adjudication was a nasty word around here," Max Lieurance, manager of the Vale District of BLM, said to me. "It meant reduction to the stockmen and nobody knew what he would come out with. In some units legitimate priority existed for more than twice the carrying capacity. But reduction alone wouldn't do the job—it still meant congregating stock in the accessible areas with water. We needed a cooperative program, of working together, to manage the land and stock in the best interest of all."

Max, a husky native Northwesterner schooled on the range, and I drove over part of the Vale District, which covers as much land as the State of Maryland. ("It's a long way to anywhere, from here to there," he said.) It is a high, dry country, with short growing season and a thin skin of soil. A century ago it supported healthy stands of native perennial grasses, but sagebrush is now the dominant vegetation, surrounded by clusters of cheatgrass, an annual which provides little forage and burns like flash fuel. The Vale District is the scene of about 330 ranching operations, with licenses to graze about 90,000 head of cattle and 45,000 head of sheep on public lands.

"Until 1962 we couldn't move," Max continued. "We had little money, few personnel. We were jumping from unit to unit, making surveys, talking about adjudication, while the resource was going downhill and looking more like desert pavement every day. We had no fire towers, firebreaks or guard stations, and no maintenance. Finally the Oregon delegation in Congress accepted our program and said, 'We'll get the money. Let's see what you can do.'"

That was when "Vale Project" began—the largest rangeland renewal program ever attempted, a model area of national and international importance.

The uphill struggle of the Vale Project constitutes a story in itself. Brush has been controlled by aerial spray on 300,000 acres, releasing moisture for grasses. Drought-resistant grass has been seeded on 200,000 acres. More than a thousand miles of fences have been built, and nearly 600 water troughs and storage tanks installed. The point that impresses me most, however, is not the role of the government but of the ranchers. When they finally realized their backs were to the wall and the range was doomed, they accepted voluntary reductions in the number of stock and in the number of months on the public range. They accepted the practice of resting some pastures, of rotating use on others, of moving their cattle from one range unit to another. In short, they accepted the principle of management. . . .

Vale is the showplace of the BLM range, but hardly typical. Thus far, on all the public lands, a total of 700 management plans have been completed, covering less than eighteen million acres. Approximately 12,800 such plans are needed in order to rehabilitate depleted range, to correct erosion, to improve all the natural resources, for water, wildlife, wilderness and recreation, as well as forage for livestock.

Three years ago the BLM initiated a more intensive program of range management. Bureau range managers believe that it is possible to double forage production by proper management alone without costly investments in seeding, land treatments, and brush sprayings. As a part of this effort a system of "rest-rotation" grazing management was started, first in a series of demonstration areas, and now each district has planned or initiated at least one "rest-rotation" system. Developed by Gus Hormay, a longtime employee of the Forest Service who now works for the BLM, the results have been spectacular. Even in areas plagued by drought, vegetation conditions have improved significantly.

The stockman is often pictured by conservationists as the bad guy, but I insist this view is sorely outmoded for the bulk of them. BLM management is based on the interdependence of public and private property; therefore, it serves to stimulate a healthy land resource on both and enlarges the vistas and potentials of Western open space. It should not be forgotten that when snows come game herds filter to lower valleys and private lands. If these lands are lost, the game is lost. . . .

As for wildlife, the greatest need is to assure that the range is grazed within carrying capacity. Wildlife and livestock do not have to be serious competitors, if both are kept in bounds. What is good for one can often be good for the other. On the Vale Project, new roads to move livestock are also used by hunters and other outdoor recreationists. Reseedings for cattle receive substantial use by antelope. Other seedings of nomad alfalfa and bitterbrush are designed for wildlife; and portions of sagebrush are spared from chemical treatment for the benefit of sage grouse, antelope, and deer. In developing the multiple-use plan, the Oregon Game Department furnishes the wildlife requirements, which help strengthen public support for the whole program.

The Vale Project is part of the new look, the upturn of recent years. In

1962, the old state and national advisory board were expanded from single-use grazing membership to a broader base of community representation. A livewire, creative director of BLM, Charles Stoddard, who served from 1963 to 1966, brought in good new talents, including Bob Smith, Arizona Game and Fish Director, to head up the wildlife program; Glen Fulcher, professor of agricultural economics at the University of Nevada, a BLM critic, to direct the range staff, and Albert M. Day, former director of the Fish and Wildlife Service, to serve as a consultant. Stoddard sparked interest in modern multiple-use land planning that transcends spending soil and water conservation money for livestock only, surveying strictly for applicants for federal lands, or running a forestry program just for timber sales. He gave the agency a legacy of lofty goals to fulfill in years to come.

Before 1964, the whole concept of public lands was directed toward disposal. The Taylor Grazing Act was only a part-way measure that authorized administration "pending final disposal" and established grazing as the primary use. BLM and the Interior Department asked Congress for a permanent multiple-use law, patterned after the National Forest Multiple Use Act of 1960. Congress demurred, in its own fashion; it countered by establishing the Public Land Law Review Commission to study laws and procedures of all federal land agencies. BLM came off with another temporary measure, the Classification and Multiple Use Act, but this time there was meat on the bone.

The Act gave authority to classify lands for disposition or for retention in multiple-use management in manners that "best meet the present and future needs of the American people." Until the Commission's report is submitted, according to the Act, BLM can manage retained lands for grazing, occupancy, industrial development, fish and wildlife, timber, outdoor recreation, mineral development, watershed, wilderness preservation, or preservation of public values "that would be lost if the land passed from federal ownership." It also adopted the streamlined Public Land Sales Act, which provides for the sale of suitable large tracts for community growth and development with requisites of zoning. . . .

So far, more than sixty-six million acres have been classified, almost entirely for multiple-use management. The first classification involved 600,000 acres in Valley County, Montana, where the Valley County Advisory Group, appointed by the county commissioners, held twenty-five open meetings to inform the public and seek local views. Those early hearings set a pattern of healthy public expression and interest in continuing federal ownership. In

North Dakota, where BLM thought of disposing of all its remaining hold-ings, wildlife groups pointed out that pothole country contained excellent habitat for migrating birds. In area after area, the public surprisingly has in-sisted on retaining isolated tracts for picnicking, fishing, rock-hounding, and camping. These isolated tracts include the roughest, toughest parts of the Deschutes River in Oregon, with some of the finest potential for steelhead and salmon fishing in the Northwest, and thirty miles of the Salmon River, near the confluence of the Snake River in Idaho, with fishing for catfish, bass, and sturgeon. Another area classified for retention covers one hundred miles along the Gila River near Phoenix, Arizona, a green belt in the arid desert regarded as the finest whitewing nesting habitat in the United States, and heavily populated with mourning dove, quail, songbirds, and mule deer.

It is roughly estimated that 150 million of the 175 million acres in the Western States may ultimately be classified for retention. BLM has begun a monumental program of posting signs, so that sportsmen and other recre-ation users will know when they are on public land and when they are not. Maps of public lands in each state are now available for the first time. In Wyoming, the agency has negotiated some agreements with the state and land owners to permit access across private property, a critical need through-out the West considering the pattern of intermingled ownership.

The BLM maps illustrate the horrible pattern of "checkerboard" owner-ship. The railroads, as I mentioned earlier, received alternating sections along their routes. The states received grants specified as "school sections." Settlers claimed the arable bottom lands and miners patented other tracts scattered over the public domain. The checkerboard system is nobody's fault; the origi-nal intention was to give all the land away. But today it stands in the way of efficient, economic land management. Land exchange with private owners in order to fill in the blocks is a must, but BLM does not have the same authority to conduct workable exchanges as do the park and forest services.

This is just one of a thousand public land problems which now confront the Public Land Law Review Commission and, more importantly, the public itself. An opportunity is before the people to create a whole new system of managed lands bearing some such title as Resource Conservation Areas, with names comparable to national parks and national forests, with boundaries, and with signs at entrances and exits—a real identity for the public lands. . . .

Many of the big decisions are hanging fire, pending the report of the Public Land Law Review Commission. Some decisions and actions cannot wait.

To continue to dispose of land under antiquated laws deprives the Commission and Congress of their options; therefore, actions under creaky statutes like the Desert Land Law and the Mining Law should be contained. Several thousand cases of illegal occupancy on government lands—some involving squatters with affluence and influence—should be cleared up with dispatch. This can be done without any new Congressional sanction. And other BLM state offices can follow the pattern in Arizona of clearing billboards and other forms of blight from the public lands.

Just as management plans are being prepared for grazing allotments, so should detailed management plans be prepared for wildlife and recreation. BLM has the authority now to identify and safeguard scenic, scientific, and natural values. Yet when I traveled the Rogue River last year I found that timber cutting practices leave a lot to be desired in protecting the wild character of the river and its fisheries resource. . . .

Our best interest will be served by looking at the public land as the property of all the people, with benefits measured in higher terms than revenues to the government or profits to the powerful few. To be specific, why do we need so urgently to develop the oil shale resource of the Green River Basin? "Known and anticipated reserves are considered wholly adequate to carry us into the next century on the basis of our best judgment on demand," Secretary Udall wrote recently. In the next breath he added that, "We cannot be entirely sure that some discovery or event may [not] require a sharp increase in petroleum energy demand," but he might also have noted that some other discovery could very easily enable a sharp decrease in demand.

In the heart of the Green River Basin, the Piceance Creek drainage of northwestern Colorado is one of the most famous and productive hunting areas in North America, a wintering ground for 30,000 to 60,000 mule deer. Industrial development certainly could endanger the wildlife habitat. Strip mining for oil shale could ruin the land surface for other uses. It could create enormous spoil piles and problems in stream and air pollution. More valuable are the intangibles which have no price tag.

The public lands, as I wrote earlier, constitute the nation's last smog-free frontier. And so they can remain, for the benefit of this generation and generations hence. It won't be easy to protect them as such, but the effort is worth it. After all these lands are ours.

The Bitterroot Valley: Destruction beyond Imagination

American Forests
February 1970

It is obvious from reports on the scene that all is not well these days in the woods of western Montana.

"The Forest Service, it appears, has gone completely mad and is destroying our once beautiful mountains with a vengeance," according to one correspondent. "The country is being torn apart by logging roads and clearcutting of the forest. Sadly, there seems to be no end in sight. If the Forest Service has its way, the process will be speeded up."

This letter came to me out of the blue. I do not know the author. He could be looking for mischief. But I doubt it, for he writes with clear style and impressive feeling. People are that way; they love the land.

Besides, his communique is only one of a dozen to reach me within the past two months from Missoula, the metropolis of western Montana, and from the Bitterroot Valley, which lies south of it. The letters are from members of the faculty and student body at the forestry school of the University of Montana, from foresters and retired foresters of the Forest Service, and from everyday citizens. All sound the same alarm. . . .

"The issue is bigger than clearcutting," to quote the words of a young fellow looking forward to fulfilling his constructive role in a world of beauty. "The real issue is the complete lack of application of any semblance of scientific forestry or a land ethic. The Forest Service headquarters here apparently has burned all the books containing that information. The destruction is simply beyond imagination. The soil disturbance has most serious implications for recreation, fishery, wildlife, and water yield."

People write me about such land issues because they think I am a good listener, which I try to be. I believe the land belongs to we the people; that land management must be for the people; that administrators of public land, whether of the national forests or any other areas, are servants of the people, fulfilling policies which we alone have the power to determine, above the bureaucrats, politicians, and special economic interests. In short, Carl Sandburg reckoned, The People, Yes.

Ten years ago I visited the Bitterroot Valley, a lovely country, and found its slopes carpeted with ponderosa and lodgepole pine and a thousand kinds of wildflowers. The high mountain lakes and streams are loaded with fish (or were then) and bordered by snowy peaks and ridges thrusting skyward. The upper reaches are a wilderness sportsman's delight, with rough going and plenty of cover for game. It was in the Bitterroot that Lewis and Clark held their historic encounter with the Flathead Indians in 1805 and that Father Pierre-Jean DeSmet, the Jesuit missionary of the Rocky Mountains, established St. Mary's Mission in 1840.

I discovered the lofty cliffs and canyons surrounding the valley were composed almost solidly of national forests—the Bitterroot, Lolo, Nez Perce, Clearwater, Deerlodge, and Beaverhead. In my book on the national forests, *Whose Woods These Are*, I wrote that Easterners on viewing the magnificent distances would understand why many Idahoans and Montanans are not anxious to attract industrial wealth or new population; they figure they have ample wealth already.

The Forest Service grew up with the country, and maybe that's part of the problem. As early as 1899 Hank Tuttle and Than Wilkinson built one of the earliest ranger stations anywhere. They had to buy hinges, nails, and the one glass window from their own funds, since the government had made no appropriation for such things. In recent years their cabin has been restored by the Lions Club, as an expression of pride in times past.

Times present are another matter. The current dispute is not the first challenge in the Bitterroot of the competence of the Forest Service and of its over-emphasis on timber as a way of life.

Students of conservation issues may recall that in 1966 the agency prepared to build a logging road into the Magruder Corridor, a rugged, steep mountain area, embracing the headwaters of the Selway River, and to conduct an extensive logging program to be followed and justified by the development of mass recreation facilities. Forest officials, for all practical purposes, ignored citizen protests; they insisted upon the infallibility of their professional judgment, a habit to which too many land managers are hopelessly addicted.

When the Idaho and Montana people found discussion with the regional headquarters to be futile, they took the issue into the political arena, in which citizen conservationists properly belong. Through their United States senators, they persuaded the Secretary of Agriculture to appoint an impartial investigating committee, composed of citizen experts in various natural resource fields, including forestry. The committee report, which the Secretary made public with his acceptance, did not sustain the Forest Service.

The report questioned the wisdom of a logging road and the economic feasibility of logging stands of marginal value. It stressed the alternative need of protecting from erosion the watershed and fisheries values in the Upper Selway drainage. The agency's professional studies were perhaps not so well thought through, after all; for, as the committee commented, "The Forest Service was preparing to initiate timber road building and timber cutting in this area without clearly stated limitations or restrictions relating to this use or to other values." It noted also that wildlife resources had not received "commensurate consideration."

From current reports, one may wonder whether there has been any change. The story of the Forest Service in the Bitterroot Valley today has been recounted fully in a series of nine articles in the daily *Missoulian*. The author, Dale Burk, writes with sensitivity about natural resources, and clearly with much digging and research. He interviewed scores of people, including loggers, ranchers, old Bitterrooters, and G. M. Brandborg, who served as supervisor of the Bitterroot National Forest for twenty years before his retirement. Mr. Burk gave officials of the Forest Service fair and ample opportunity to state their case, too; they have no complaints coming.

Mr. Burk recorded the testimony of a local logger to the effect that, "Most people working in the woods feel the Forest Service is setting the forest back 150 years." The supervisor of the Bitterroot National Forest explained the benedictions of clearcutting in lengthy replies to written questions. By eliminating trees from the mountain slopes, he advised, the valley would get more water. "However, we get it all at the wrong time," countered two ranchers, complaining they must now suffer with siltation and debris in their water supplies and irrigation ditches.

Clearcutting on a large scale represents a signal victory of technology over nature. Thanks to new types of machinery, it is now possible to up-end as many as 1,500 to 1,800 trees in the course of a day, thus leveling a timber stand over hundreds of acres in short order. It flattens various sized areas, destroying the accumulated growth in one swoop, with the promise of planting something better and faster growing. This could be so in some circumstances, though hardly likely in an area of steep slopes and shallow soils that normally cannot support healthy vegetation without long passage of time. At best, it epitomizes single-use management.

The pictures appearing with Mr. Burk's articles suggest the mechanical terracing, with shadeless bulldozer trenches, that comes in the wake of strip mining. The *Missoulian* is not the only paper to carry such photographs. Miles Romney, publisher of the *Western News*, a man who lives in and loves the Bitterroot, sent a copy of his Christmas holiday edition. It featured pictures of before—the beauty of a carefully managed open ponderosa forest—and after—"a terraced wasteland," as he calls it.

People are concerned over how such practices affect the livability, economic, and social stability of their communities, not only in the Bitterroot but elsewhere. The Forest Service is being put to the test. I suppose that forestry is being tested, too. Perhaps it is professional zeal that presses for manipulation of slow growing, uneconomic sites, whose ultimate value is not in timber, but rather in recreation.

In Wyoming, as William E. Towell noted in the November issue of *American Forests*, concerned citizens objected to timber sales adjacent to the Bridger Wilderness. They argued that past cutting had been poorly planned, that future cutting would destroy the esthetics of the area, that the narrow buffer to the wilderness should be set aside for natural beauty and recreation.

The Forest Service gave them scant encouragement. In the search for help, they turned to national conservation organizations, which sent a team to investigate. Members of this group (which included Mr. Towell) corroborated the substance of the complaints. They criticized the agency for laying out roads badly, for conducting large cuttings that led to erosion, for endeavoring to log spruce in high elevations with poor prospects of regeneration; they found good reason for a Wind River National Recovery Area. As a result, the regional forester of the Intermountain Region agreed to defer further timbering activity pending a detailed study, with more public input.

He was wise to do so. There is no reason for the public to subsidize environmental deterioration on its own land.

In Oregon, a substantial body of citizens has been objecting to proposed logging of the scenic French Pete Creek drainage of the Willamette National Forest. To express their viewpoint they conducted summer marches before the regional headquarters in Portland; in November, a thousand persons demonstrated before the national forest office in Eugene, known in other days as "logging capital of the world." Conservation organizations paid for newspaper advertisements, complete with coupons for mailing to members of the Oregon Congressional delegation.

As a result, the two senators and the congressman of the district elicited a pledge from the Secretary of Agriculture to delay timber sales in the French Pete Creek drainage in order to allow more time for public discussion.

Never have people been so aroused—it is part of the revolution in thought sweeping the world. Alert industry leaders are aware of it. Robert V. Hansberger, president of the Boise Cascade Corporation, for example, in a statement last year foresaw the need to intensify pollution abatement. "I don't think the Nixon administration will soften any demands," he declared. "The pressure of society is too great."

The Forest Service also has the feeling that something big is going on around it. Last spring the information and education men of the Forest Service held their annual meeting in the Washington area. A copy of the summary has come to me. "As the meeting unfolded," it discloses, "several things became undeniably apparent. First of all, the Forest Service has not consistently been hitting its mark in the field of responding to and serving the needs of the public."

The keynoter at the meeting of the public relations men, the chief of the Forest Service himself, said the agency must "foster confidence through good performance." The deputy chief added, "We must obtain more involvement of people and groups outside the Forest Service. We have to learn what the public wants. We have to provide more goods and services to meet their needs."

Manifestly, no major land use plan or program today will succeed or long survive unless it is consistent with public interest or welfare, and has public support. The difficulty is that Forest Service people, or any other group of land management officials, deal largely with men experienced in their own fields. Competence is judged to a great extent within the bounds of their professions. They are not at home in the thought world of our environment. People with a sense of mission and social conscience must guide those who are drifting, who want to do something significant, but know not how.

As for the Bitterroot Valley, Chief Charlot of the Flatheads, in protesting the forced movement of his people to the Jocko Canyon reservation, remained with a handful of followers through years of desultory harassment and destitution. Today, one might perceive the shaping manifestations of retribution. Or he could look hopefully for redemption through protection of beauty and respect for the earth.

The Boys Who Brought Back DDT

Written for *Field & Stream*

November 1974

Unpublished, my last column

My old friends of the Forest Service, the boys who brought back DDT, have devised a new approach to involve the public in the process of decision-making. Certainly something new and different is needed. Public forests have been run for the private benefit of timber and livestock industries long enough. The fishermen and hunters and other outdoor sportsmen come in last. So do the fish and wildlife and forest environment, despite a basic mandate from Congress directing the Forest Service to consider all aspects of multiple use. It is a mandate generously ignored.

On the face of it, the new thrust sounds for once like a determined effort to deal the little people in on the action. We have been offered the draft of something called the "Environmental Program for the Future," and been told it reflects the spirit of the National Environmental Policy Act. We have been invited to furnish input, to indicate a choice of several alternatives, to really influence the development of a broad, long-term forestry plan for the nation.

That's how it sounds. When you live intimately with these issues, however, as I have over the years, you learn from bitter disappointment the difference between propaganda and performance. While eternally hoping for change, you learn to read the fine print and to keep your guard up.

Through one form of public involvement exercise after another, grassroots conservationists have been trained to keep their guard up in dealing with the Forest Service. In past years there were the "show-me trips" and the "listening sessions." The "listening," alas, was accompanied by a stream of color brochures and other promotions extolling clearcutting, a thoroughly "efficient and economic system" of placing timber production above all other values. Cutting soared, tripling in volume over a period of twenty years; the resource, in turn, suffered and wildlife habitat deteriorated.

"Public comments are invited but the consultant atmosphere appears to be lacking," complained Senator Jennings Randolph, of West Virginia, in early 1972, after an investigation at the behest of his constituents. "The prevailing feeling expressed by those after attending the hearings is that decisions have already been made and their expressed concerns have only been accepted as an empty polite gesture."

In the same year, Charles Prigmore, president of the Alabama Conservancy, charged much the same: "The Forest Service indeed holds hearings at infrequent intervals, particularly when public pressure becomes irresistible. But this is an attitude of patient tolerance of public concern and thinking, rather than any real encouragement of joint decision-making. Forest Service personnel consider themselves to be the experts, and the public to be ignorant at best and obstructionists at worst."

Then there was the editorial in the September 1973 issue of *Montana Outdoors*, published by Montana's Fish and Game Department. The headline told the story: "Yes, We believe in Public Involvement, But We Gotta Cut Those Trees." The editorial dealt with the four public involvement meetings at which 90 percent of those present opposed the Cedar-Bassett Creek timber sale, in an area highly coveted by sportsmen. Despite written objections of the State Fish and Game Department and the public, the Forest Service decided to log anyway.

I could cite scores of such cases, current as well as past, throughout the National Forest System. Montana, the outdoorsman's paradise, seems a prime target; it will never be the same when the foresters are through with it.

Are we now, however, facing the dawn of a bright new day through the Environmental Program for the Future? The plan, according to the prospectus, "will enable the public to become more systematically informed on important issues facing the managers of the National Forest System and the other programs of the Forest Service and to participate in those issues along with the Congress and specific forest users." Who could ask for anything more promising?

The document, I fear, does not fulfill the promise. The emphasis in the text is not on sustaining land health over the long run, but on gaining maximum production of commodities over the short run, without fundamental concern for the future. Three levels of operation are offered to the public: low, moderate, and high. However, the low level of timber cutting, 16.4 billion board feet, is just a shade below the moderate level and not much below the high (of 20 billion board feet). There is no choice of indicating that today's cutting level is already too high, that foresters should revert to a sensible dimension in order to insure perpetual yield.

In his statement presenting the Environmental Program before a briefing conference which I attended, John R. McGuire, Chief of the Forest Service, declared: "We have tried to tie every action to its effects on every related action or use of the forest resource. For example, we spell out that meeting demands for more recreation opportunity wilderness, recreation areas, and campgrounds will necessarily mean less area devoted to timber growing for houses and other products."

Such is the tenor throughout: You must choose between two conflicting objectives: (1) assuring appropriate esthetic and amenity values of the forest environment, and (2) assuring adequate flows of goods and services at reasonable prices. By implication, the trout fisherman who desires clean cold water in a setting of solitude is depriving the urban and rural poor adequate low-cost housing. The objective of land health, completely compatible with that fisherman's search for "amenities," is ignored. So too are the impacts of timber export, shortened rotations producing pulp instead of housing materials, and the damage caused by clearcutting and conversion to monoculture.

Page after page of the draft program yields misleading data. Three examples follow:

"The controversy over clearcutting stems primarily from its visual impact; a newly clear-cut area looks bad. No other system of producing a forest leaves such a conspicuous mark on the landscape." Visual impact is the very least of the controversy, as compared with the impact on wildlife habitat, soil stability, soil nutrients, and water quality; whether this system produces or destroys a forest is an open question in itself—the answer cannot be assumed on the forester's say-so.

"The technique (clearcutting) is used primarily for those species that cannot tolerate shade, are subject to windthrow, or for other reasons grow best in even-aged stands." But clearcutting actually is applied to virtually all species, not for silvicultural but rather for economic reasons.

"The Environmental Program for the Future statement is aimed at the broadest possible review of the environmental, economic, and social effects of Forest Service programs, but it in no way obviates the need for specific environmental impact studies and statements prior to all major actions proposed. The Forest Service is also firmly committed to comply with all federal air-and water-quality standards as part of all programs." This sounds too good to be true; but as Dale Burk, one of the country's ablest writers on the outdoors environment, reports in the daily *Missoulian,* published in western Montana, it simply doesn't work this way in practice.

Dale was born into a logging family and knows trees from timber. He has won assorted prizes for his courage and perception, particularly for coverage of the eco-disaster on the Bitterroot National Forest. His most recent series focuses on the projected Moose Creek timber sale, on the headwaters of the East Fork of the Bitterroot River. According to a recent article by him, three local citizen organizations (Montana Wilderness Association, Montana Wildlife Federation, and Western Montana Fish and Game Association), backed by four national organizations, have protested the sale. They charge the sale violates the National Environmental Policy Act, Multiple Use Act, Wilderness Act, and the Forest Service's own directives on roadless area inventory; that the impact statement is filled with factual errors, with insufficient consideration for wildlife and watershed values. We also learn from this account that the Environmental Protection Agency believes the Forest Service made its decision to road and log the area with insufficient scientific information.

There is little for sportsmen to cheer about. Wildlife in the Environmental Program is treated as merely another "output." Under the "low supply alternative," habitat would be improved on national forests and national grasslands through coordination with other management activities on 15.8 million acres out of a total of 187 million acres; endangered species would be protected through special practices on 110,000 acres; fish and wildlife habitat would be improved on 900,000 acres, and wildlife technical assistance would be furnished to private woodland owners on 1.4 million acres. The moderate and high alternatives provide little more. There is no implicit recognition that wildlife is a user of all forest lands, nor a stated objective of achieving at long last a semblance of balance as between wildlife versus timber cutting and grazing of domestic stock.

Endangered species are especially subject to short shrift. According to the far-reaching Endangered Species Act, which became law on December 28, 1973, all federal agencies are directed to insure that actions authorized, funded or carried out by them do not jeopardize the continued existence of any species or result in the destruction of its habitat. Thus, priority must be assigned throughout the National Forest System, but the environmental program offers "special practices" for only a very small portion.

Reading this document carefully convinces me that my friends of the Forest Service have found a new package for the old sales pitch. What they really want to generate is not public involvement in decision making but public support for increased appropriations to cut more trees, build more roads, spread more chemical poisons, graze more livestock. The draft Environmental

Program supposedly represents the basis of furnishing public input, but page after page is filled with the most suggestive comments on why the low level alternative will not do, and why the high level alternative will best meet "national production goals for 1984." Almost as an afterthought, hunters and fishermen are promised greater access, but in many cases there is too much access already for the game and the true sportsman.

Forests should never be conceived simply as factories for pulp and timber. In any long-term forestry plan the capacity of ecosystems should be the basic concern, rather than self-fulfilling prophecies of unrestrained growth in a wasteful society. Aldo Leopold once noted that foresters could be divided into two groups, as follows:

Group A, quite content to grow trees like cabbages, with cellulose as the basic forest commodity. It feels no inhibition against violence; its ideology is agronomic.

Group B, sees forestry as fundamentally different from agronomy because it employs natural species and manages a natural environment rather than creating an artificial one. It worries on biotic as well as economic grounds. It worries about a whole series of secondary forest functions: wildlife, recreation, watershed, and wilderness.

Group A is plainly and firmly in charge, and there lies the trouble. The first step in developing an environmental program should probably be an intensive educational effort within the Forest Service and forestry profession. . . .

Other disciplines need to be involved in forest policy and administration. The Fish and Wildlife Service, state fish and game departments, and the Environmental Protection Agency should all play active roles, more active than at present.

Then, at last, there is the public at the grass roots. A series of regional town meetings out where the rubber meets the road should discuss the future of our public and private forests. Sportsmen don't need to wait for someone else to ring the bell. Get out to see the woodlands, then call in your friends and local media for an open forum. You'll find the way to make your influence felt. Remember, it's your world—don't leave it to the experts.

Clearcutting: A Frightening Pattern

Defenders of Wildlife
December 1974

The recent reintroduction of DDT into the forests of the Pacific Northwest was a shocker in itself. It also reveals basic and scary lessons about the long-range prospects for forests everywhere in America, and especially for the native wildlife—mammals, fish, birds, insects, and plants which they embrace. The worst, I fear, is yet to come.

Consider first the issue in the Northwest. A condition of political hysteria was created through publicized warnings of the timber industry, Forest Service, and the forestry profession that grave damage would befall the region if the Douglas-fir forests were not sprayed to prevent a possible tussock moth infestation. The governors and congressional delegations of Oregon, Washington, and Idaho all endorsed the Forest Service plea for an exemption from the pesticide law banning the use of DDT. Russell E. Train, administrator of the Environmental Protection Agency, granted this exemption because he would have felt the wrath of Congress and placed his own outfit in jeopardy had he chosen otherwise.

The Forest Service, an agency addicted to tree cutting and the use of chemical poisons, provided the basic advance data on potential losses if there were no control applied. These were measured only in timber values. The contingency noted that livestock and other domestic animals would have to be removed, but at whose expense was not considered. Hunters would be warned as to the possibility of DDT residues in game animals, but there was absolutely no evaluation of resultant economic loss. After all, who wants to eat the meat of DDT-infested animals? The weight of judgment was all on the side of short-term commercial values—the extraction of a single resource without implicit regard for the other components in the total forest environment.

Such is the frightening pattern that I find on public and private forests everywhere. The most dangerous poisons are implicit forestry tools, as though it were essential, or even possible, to impose synthetic control over a natural system. Millions of acres are being sprayed by the Forest Service, other federal agencies, and the timber industry, all with the inevitable result. The more poisons are used, the more they are needed.

A healthy forest can never be protected for its timber alone, nor even for game animals. All that is green and trees is not a forest. Forests are not collections of animal and plant species chosen by a manager because they are useful and understood by men. To worry about board feet of timber, or deer, or even endangered carnivores like wolves is not enough. All elements of the ecosystem must be present: The more complex and diverse the forest community the greater its interaction and stability, and its productivity in the long run.

But forestry in our time denies this law of earth science. Forestry is not synonymous with conservation. Intensive forest management, according to Dr. W. Leslie Pengelly, a well-known wildlife biology professor at the University of Montana and member of the Montana Fish and Game Commission, is seldom compatible with wildlife issues. Professor Pengelly may be optimistic. Having viewed so-called intensive, or high-yield, management in every forest ecosystem in the United States, I doubt that contemporary forestry is ever compatible with conservation or wildlife. . . .

Widespread advertising and promotion are employed to justify clearcutting, in which hundreds, or even thousands, of acres of forest are knocked over virtually in a fell swoop; use of toxic herbicides and pesticides; drainage of wetlands; and conversion of native mixed stands to plantations of pine standing in rows like corn or cabbages. And always, because the condition of our forests cannot be separated from the condition of fish and game, foresters and timbermen bombard the nation's sportsmen with endless materials on the benefactions to be derived from their particular brand of exploitation.

They never let up nor allow logic or science to stand in their way. For example, in 1972 the Southern Region of the Forest Service published a color brochure, "New Forests for Wildlife—How Even-Aged Management Benefits the Sportsmen," paid for with pubic funds. This booklet is filled with misleading and inaccurate statements suggesting that clearcutting provides the best technique for wildlife management such as: "Even-aged management means a greater variety of game species—more deer, grouse, quail, doves, and rabbits."

This kind of irrational propaganda disturbed me deeply, and I was not alone. "It is axiomatic in wildlife management," wrote Dr. John Grandy, a biologist with the National Parks and Conservation Association, to the

Regional Forester in November 1972, "that wildlife is maximized by maximizing edge and diversity. Clearcuts as used in even-aged management do not normally maximize either edge or diversity. It seems to me the species mentioned above would be favored by group selection or small patch cutting. For example, what is more valuable for wildlife generally: a 40-acre clearcut or 40 separated one-acre clearcuts? An understanding of wildlife management indicates only one answer to that question."

I also wrote to the Southern Region, citing Dr. Grandy's cogent observation, and received this response from an assistant regional forester, Stanford M. Adams: "Dr. Grandy's comments are from the standpoint of pure wildlife management. If you look at only the wildlife resource, which he is doing, he makes some good points. There are better ways to maximize wildlife production. For that matter, if you look at only the timber resource, there are more effective and economical ways to produce timber than Forest Service coordination guides will permit."

Whatever "pure wildlife management" may be I cannot imagine. There is only sound land management, from which all resource values benefit. The alternative is mismanagement, from which none benefit. On national forests, as I have witnessed management in action, timber is not produced but merely extracted, the so-called coordination guides notwithstanding. Or as Dr. Edward Crafts, a former deputy chief of the Forest Service, conceded in 1973: "The clearcutting excesses which have led to controversy have been timber oriented and not conducted to improve wildlife habitat. Moreover, clearcutting is often cheaper, easier, and more profitable to apply than other options. It is a simplistic approach."

Sportsmen's groups and state fish and game agencies have demonstrated rising alarm and resentment at habitat destruction on public and private forests. "Already thousands of acres in blocks, ranging from 160 to well over 1,000 acres," records the *Louisiana Conservationist,* "have been stripped of existing timber, bulldozed, chopped, or burned clean, and then seeded or planted with pine. The small stream bottoms which have historically supported hardwoods are now the main targets. They provide a last and most critical retreat for game within the great sea of pine."

Another serious criticism was made early in 1974 by the Southeast Wild Turkey Subcommittee of the Wildlife Society through a resolution charging that "acts devastating to wild turkeys and other wildlife species have been and are presently being perpetrated in the guise of progressive forest management."

These acts were defined as "the conversion of large areas to even-aged short-rotation pine monoculture characterized by intensive site preparation accomplished by bulldozing, roll-chopping, and/or burning." The subcommittee condemned the prevalent forestry practices that have "permanently defaced the natural beauty of our landscapes and harmfully affected the esthetic qualities of the forested lands of the Southeastern United States . . . [and] caused and continue to cause disastrous and unnecessary damage to fishes and aquatic wildlife through siltation of springs, streams, estuaries, and harbors . . . (and proven) destructive to wild turkey habitat and detrimental to many other wildlife species."

The timber-forestry axis has promoted clearcutting among sportsmen on the basis of opening access and making it easier to kill game. According to Wayne Bailey, very likely the country's foremost wild turkey specialist who serves as chairman of the wild turkey subcommittee, however, "Turkeys often suffer from an excess of access. One study recommended that no more than six miles of roads per 10,000 acres should be open to public vehicular traffic in an area where wild turkey are to be encouraged. . . . Walking is, or should be, an intrinsic part of turkey hunting. The myriad sounds of a spring dawn, the deep-throated gobbling that lets you know the quarry is there, and use of the various tactics designed to outsmart him are the true rewards. The kill is secondary."

I heard much the same type of comments from Charles D. Kelley, Alabama's state fish and game director, speaking at the annual meeting of the Alabama Conservancy in 1972. The heart of Mr. Kelley's remarks consisted of reports from field biologists on his staff. They talked of erosion, siltation, and flooding as a direct result of clearcutting; of immediate damage to all species of wildlife, permanent loss of squirrel and turkey habitat in areas planted to pine, and long-range damage affecting all species of wildlife.

"I am convinced that clearcutting is the most serious threat to wildlife that we face today," reported one of the Alabama biologists. "Wildlife losses are greater than benefits received."

I am likewise convinced. Unhappily, distortion and suppression of the truth in such matters is practiced to an awesome, frightening degree. Cover-ups were not invented with the Watergate affair, nor are they restricted to politics. I have learned this repeatedly from personal experience in the forestry domain. For example, in the July 1969 issue of *Field & Stream* I reported receiving word from concerned citizens in Tennessee that a large paper corporation, Bowaters Southern, had spread poison grain over a wide area as part of its conversion program to a pulp-producing monoculture. I noted in my column that members of three hunting clubs had taken separate inspection tours of Signal Mountain, outside Chattanooga, and all had declared it a terrible tragedy for wildlife.

My report evoked a letter of protest from Bowaters public relations manager, Clarence Streetman, accusing me of "misleading statements and fabrications." His viewpoint was supported by the Tennessee Fish and Game Department, U.S. Bureau of Sport Fisheries and Wildlife (here I learned that predator and rodent controllers are as active in the South as in the West, equally for the benefit of the special interests), and a consulting wildlife biology professor at the Forestry Department of the University of Tennessee, Dr. Ralph Dimmick by name, who had prescribed the poison, zinc phosphide. They all assured me in correspondence that environmental risks were slight and of a temporary nature, that all complaints had been carefully investigated and had proven groundless or insignificant. They insisted the only targets—a species of rodent called voles—were affected and that there was no hazard to birds or game. But I was deeply concerned that expressions from all of them transcended by far any concern for the biological and ecological resource.

I interviewed people in the mountains. They were upset. One man told me poison corn had been sprayed all over his property, which adjoins the Bowaters land. Another said, "I found poison in the water and was afraid to drink. People fear to hunt and eat game with poison in the system." I learned the report of Marzine Hudson, of the state office of the Bureau of Sport Fisheries and Wildlife, confirming the damage, was being suppressed: despite pleas to all levels of the Department of the Interior, I was never able to obtain a copy. I made the trip into the hills accompanied by a television camera crew from Chattanooga at the request of the TV station. The program has never been shown.

Although Bowaters and its supporters insisted that zinc phosphide "kills only voles," I found that every piece of current literature stresses this to be an intense, extremely dangerous and long lasting poison. Warnings such as the following are plain and plentiful: "Zinc phosphide must be used with care, as it is toxic to all forms of animal life. It has poisoned humans as well as domestic and wild animals. . . . Be certain to remove and destroy all uneaten baits at the end of the poisoning period."

Even more important, total annihilation programs for rodents are rarely, if ever, successful: declines are followed by greater reproductive success.

Instead of looking for panaceas in the bag of trick poisons, Bowaters (and other companies conducting similar pursuits) would be well advised to undertake careful ecological research and serious self-study concerning forest management practices that may account for high vole populations. For example, I saw huge bulldozed piles of dead hardwood—an utterly wasted natural resource serving as a clear source of protection for rodents.

During this episode I was subjected to assorted pressures, directly and indirectly. The president of the American Forestry Institute, a public relations front for the industry, dispatched a warning letter to the advertising director at *Field & Stream*. Years ago this kind of high-handed maneuvering was standard procedure in the relations between industry and media: apparently it has not been given up.

Pressures notwithstanding, sportsmen and other conservationists increasingly are challenging the system. In 1973, a group of hunting organizations brought legal action to block the Department of Natural Resources of Washington State from intensive timber cutting on the Olympic Peninsula. Their complaint declared: "These four elk herds all exist in the herds and the natural state that they do because of stands of virgin timber which have no access roads into them. These stands of timber provide safety and sanctuary for these elk in times when such are needed. Once these stands of virgin timber, relatively small in size though they are, are logged and have had access roads put into them, these elk herds will be reduced considerably in numbers and, speaking in terms of their natural states, will almost cease to exist on lands owned by the State of Washington."

The concentrated effort to harvest all remaining old-growth forests not protected by wilderness (which at best is not large enough or low enough in elevation) in the Pacific Northwest and to convert these forests into young, thinned, even-aged stands will have a devastating effect on elk and a long list of flora and fauna. The coniferous forests of Oregon alone support more than 20 hole-nesting bird species, as well as several species of hole-nesting mammals.

Even though logging may improve deer habitat under some circumstances, serious disturbance eliminates such species as spotted owls, pine martens, and goshawks. After five years of ecological research on numerous avian predators, Richard T. Reynolds of Oregon State University warns: "Several of these predators and their prey are totally dependent on a specific forest type, namely old-growth or mature forests. At the present rate of harvest of mature forests both predators and prey will be extirpated as viable populations within our lifetime."

Birds actually furnish the most efficient, least costly form of insect control in the forest. A single woodpecker, for example, has been estimated to consume the larvae of 13,675 highly destructive wood-boring beetles per year. It is fair to generalize that the more numerous and varied the bird population, the broader the spectrum of natural insect control. John Smail, executive director of the Point Reyes Bird Observatory, a California research organization focusing on the ecology of nongame species, has reported on an analysis of nine breeding-bird censuses in coniferous forests in California, Colorado, and South Dakota. The analysis showed that 25 percent of the total number of birds using these forests are species that nest in holes. These hole-nesters require older trees with some decayed portions in order to breed successfully (and feed large broods of young on destructive insects), although they forage on trees of various ages. "Any forestry practice producing solid stands of trees of the same age reduces the diversity of bird species able to breed, and this in turn reduces possible insect control," according to Mr. Smail. "Clearcutting is the most drastic example."

Clearcutting and "high-yield" forestry are promoted to sportsmen on grounds they produce more game. It is true that clearcuts result in quail habitat, often where none existed before, and that an abundance of browse is produced on many clearcut areas. Biologists note these benefits are temporary: before many years quail habitat and deer browse decline. Squirrel and raccoon are adversely affected by the absence of mast foods such as berries and nuts and den trees. The clearcut provides the deer only browse, while the selective cut provides both browse and mast.

Tree monoculture leads to animal monoculture. On moist sites, following cutting and burning of debris, or slash, a rapid invasion of grasses and herbaceous plants often makes ideal habitat for white-footed deer mice, meadow voles, ground squirrels, and mountain beaver. By consuming seeds and seedlings, they create damage problems; so costly control programs utilizing poisons, repellents, traps, and fencing are instituted.

Then deer, elk, and black bear emerge in numbers. Wildlife is no longer an asset but a forest pest, and hunters are called on to "bring the population into balance." The valuable evergreen forest of western Washington suffers particular damage from the black bear. Because they live on "tree farms," bears are forced into unusual or exaggerated feeding habits when they come out of hibernation in spring and early summer, stripping outer bark and sapwood of the Douglas-fir. The typical "managed" forest represents a controlled environment, protected artificially from fire and insects. It lacks variety of open spaces, variety of plants and animals, variety of bear food. To offset bear damage, corporate owners hire professional trappers and encourage sport hunting. In 1972, more than 3,000 bears were killed in western Washington. An antibear cult, supported by a yearly festival, brings visitors to the town of McCleary. Thousands gather to chant the glory of dead bears and to eat several hundred gallons of bear stew. It makes little sense.

Logging that exposes game to harassment and is subject to animal control programs can hardly be called beneficial to wildlife. There may be forage produced through clearcutting, but in the process game animals lose their essential cover and freedom from harassment. As roads are constructed through the forest, and then logging spurs are punched in various directions, wildlife is exposed and disturbed. Then it retreats. The retreat of a species like the elk transmits the initial disturbance to new surroundings, like an ecological reverberation. The retreat into higher areas is apt to concentrate the elk in a wilderness area where the range is slim to begin with. Where relatively few jeep roads existed before in the lower elevations, many now exist, making the terrain vehicle-dominated rather than wildlife-dominated. And when timbering ends, the disturbance will continue in some other form.

The rare animals of wild places perhaps are the most seriously affected. Logging and road building in the remote valleys, the untouched upper drainages of the northern Rockies of Idaho, Montana, and Wyoming have destroyed the isolation of the few remaining grizzly bears, disrupted their food sources, and driven them out though there is really nowhere for them to go. The hunted mountain goat climbs unsuspiciously to a steeper cliff face where it considers itself safe only to be just as exposed as on the logging site it left behind.

In forests all across America wildlife is hard pressed to survive. This need not be. Unfortunately, government policies and practices are designed to aid the corporate interests rather than the small landowner or the wildlife which is compatible with his objectives.

I have at hand a recent report titled "Silviculture of Loblolly Pine in the Georgia Piedmont," written by Ernest V. Brender of the Southeastern Forest Experiment Station. It declares that the old selection method of logging, in which only the mature trees are cut out of continually standing forest, provides a structure where growth tends to be concentrated primarily on merchantable stock. Stumpage value is high on sawtimber and veneer, the principle products of uneven-aged management. The method permits the nurturing of high quality trees and those earning the highest interest rate. The landowner can expect a regular income at relatively short intervals: thus the management is adapted to small holdings. Uneven aged stands are not as vulnerable to complete destruction by fire as are young even-aged stands. Measures to control undesired species need application only to openings created by periodic harvest cuts. The stands at all times satisfy esthetic demands and are compatible with wildlife. Use of heavy machinery in logging is not possible, and professional skill is required in tree selection.

Now you would expect that this idea would be endorsed and advanced by the Fish and Wildlife Service, considering the nature of its mission. So would I, though I have never, in all my studies, crossed any serious critique of clearcutting by this agency. To the contrary, consider the following from Verlon E. Carter, regional forester of the Fish and Wildlife Service, in Atlanta:

> Based on extended research and many years of experience, foresters recommend and rely on even-aged type silviculture for growing the nation's future timber needs. Therefore, it is only reasonable to assume that the future welfare of forest wildlife will be dependent on the versions of this system that are designed to favor wildlife. These are some of the primary reasons for utilizing even-aged silviculture to create preferred seasonal habitat conditions for the broad range of wildlife on the Piedmont National Wildlife Refuge.

> The pine and hardwood composition on the 36,000-acre Piedmont Refuge is similar to that which occurs on millions of acres of the Piedmont province. Successfully coordinated management of refuge wildlife and timber will be of considerable demonstration value on these adjacent lands.

With this kind of endorsement of a program designed to aid the corporate interest instead of the small landholder, one may be sure the worst lies ahead. Pulpwood companies already are huge landowners. They complain about taxes, but these firms are acquiring, not disposing of, property in the South; they are devouring diverse woodlands all across the South, converting them into one-crop plantations for the benefit of stockholders far from the scene. They get tax breaks and write-offs not available to the small woodlot farmer. The latter has kept his land open to the sportsmen, while the former, the large corporation, is shutting land to local people, or presuming to charge large fees which only the well-to-do can pay, or poisoning the soils and streams so they aren't fit for use.

Now the timber-forestry axis has set sights on the four million nonindustrial land private owners, whose forests average 70 acres in size. The Forest

Service has declared its intention of bringing the blessings of reforestation to 45 million acres of private land which it considers to be "unstocked or poorly stocked." What is "reforestation"? By Forest Service definition (and by practice on the national forests which it administers), it consists "largely of introducing commercially valuable trees on land already occupied by other kinds of vegetation"—in other words, elimination of trees and other plants growing naturally and replacement with species which foresters consider desirable, based on their limited values.

Reforestation begins with poisoning, on hardwood sites, through the injection of 2,4,5-T or 2,4-D into standing timber. It involves "removing or killing cull trees so the growing space they occupy is available for better trees." According to the new Environmental Program for the Future, the agency's frightening plan of action for the next ten years, "Cleaning, weeding, precommericial thinning and releasing of promising young crop trees by removing overstory vegetation are other examples of cultural work that can be done under this program."

"Cull trees" are the dead and dying, but not exclusively so: they're also the unmarketable hardwoods which take space needed for "better" trees. In the South alone, modern forestry prescribes the removal and replacement of 24 billion cubic feet of cull trees: The removal of cull trees constitutes the bulk of timber stand "improvement" projected for no less than 90 million acres.

Wildlife views cull trees in rather different terms. Cull trees usually mean mast for food and denning and nesting places for housing: the dead, dying, and natural are the hope of the ivory-billed woodpecker, wherever it may be, of the red-cockaded woodpecker, and of many other birds and mammals.

Do we really need to sacrifice these intrinsic values of the original America in order to meet "the wood needs of the nation"? I don't believe so. Neither does the minority of foresters who still espouse the cause of conservative management. The best quality timber, most vital to future wood supplies, in the judgment of L. Keville Larson, a practicing consulting forester of Mobile, Alabama, will be grown in natural stands. Figures of the Southeastern Forest Experiment Station cited by Mr. Larson show that miscellaneous private ownerships, consisting primarily of natural stands, are building their growing stock by 40 percent per year; industry ownership, with a much higher percentage of plantation, however, has less volume per acre and is building growing stock by only nine percent per year.

"Although with an understanding of silviculture, natural stands can be managed for wildlife, recreation, watershed, or any other single or multiple use objective," declares Mr. Larson, "natural stands will continue to be of great importance primarily because the most common objective will be return to the owner.

"Selective management is much more intensive [than even-aged]. It is practical forestry based on the judgment of men in the woods following the basic guidelines of partial cutting, insuring full stocking, increasing the growth rate, improving the stand, considering each acre, and selecting the treatment that fits the forest condition and ownership objective."

There is still hope that Mr. Larson's sensible system may yet prevail, that the harsh assaults upon the forests may be contained and reversed. Such hope is furnished not simply by reason but by law. The epochal Endangered Species Act of 1973 (enhancing earlier laws of 1966 and 1969) now guarantees protection to any member of the plant or animal family endangered or threatened, or that is likely to become endangered on a significant portion of its range. This law recognizes at last that a species must be saved in many places if it is to be saved at all. In other words, the fact that there are still grizzlies in Alaska does not permit the Forest Service any longer to mismanage the bear habitat in the Northern Rockies.

The Endangered Species Act promises to enforce a responsibility for the earth among land management agencies which the National Environmental Policy Act has failed to achieve. Section 7 declares that all bureaus (including the Forest Service) shall insure that actions authorized, funded, or carried out do not jeopardize the continued existence of any species or result in destruction of its habitat. Terms of the act encourage action by the states in the same direction and authorize acquisition of land for the protection of endangered species.

Concern for endangered species no longer can be left in the hands of federal officials alone. Thus the act allows individuals to petition to place new species on the list and even provides for finder's fees. The regulations are still to be fully written and implemented, but the strength of law is abundant, and so is the challenge. Little doubt exists in my mind that the timber industry will try to undermine it forthwith.

Time is at hand for the people to save the forests. When the forests go downhill, the nation goes with them. So history is written over the last thousand years. Wild creatures, vegetable and animal in kind, make the forest whole. To save the least is to save the largest, and to save the whole as well.

We *Are* Loving Our National Parks to Death

Sohioan
Spring 1972

In the western wilds of Wyoming in the fall of 1870 a group of explorers, accompanied by a small military escort, spent a month amid the high mountains, majestic waterfalls, plunging canyons, and amazing geysers of the Yellowstone country. They gave names to many of the features, including Old Faithful. Then came the question of what to do with the area. Around the campfire one night they pondered claiming it for themselves, as they had a legal right to do, but the longer they talked the more they realized they must share these treasures for the benefit of all people.

Out of that expedition came the establishment of Yellowstone National Park, through action by Congress, and signature of President Ulysses S. Grant on March 1, 1872. There had never been a national park before, not in the United States, nor in any other nation. It was a new idea that has since flowered the world over.

Yellowstone is still a magic word. I think of it as the symbolic representation of all places kept free as God made them, unfettered by machines and marketplaces, where young and old can exercise their minds and bodies, and by so doing appreciate the integrity of the land.

This to me is the focal issue in the National Parks Centennial—a time for celebration and serious thought as to what Yellowstone and Yosemite and Grand Canyon mean in the context of our time and of times still to come.

Certainly as we look at them today, these national parks represent an endowment of riches that makes the United States the envy of the world. The national park system has grown to embrace more than 280 units in all parts of the country, from Alaska and Hawaii to the Virgin Islands. With their hundreds of museums, trailside exhibits, and guided walks, the parks constitute the single most important influence in cultivating the art of intelligent travel. But times are changing rapidly, and all is not well. Popularity is not enough to insure survival of the parks for the next 50 years, let alone another century. When the National Park Service was organized in 1916, the handful of regions it administered was scattered across remote areas of the West. Few

Americans could afford to visit the parks, and then only by long train trips. Now, the tempo of transportation has quickened. Population has soared. Millions of people have an abundance of leisure and seek relief from urban blight and noise. Consider these statistics. In 1946 the number of visitors throughout the national park system totaled 92,160,000. In 1972 this is expected to be 183,900,000—probably a greater volume of visitors in this single year than in the entire history of the parks up to and including World War II. Little wonder that Superintendent Jack Anderson of Yellowstone is forced to plead, "We don't want more people to come for the centennial year. We can't handle the ones we get in an ordinary year of trying to save the wilderness."

The parks are overvisited and critically understaffed. There have been heavy expenditures for roads to make it easier for millions to enter, but not corresponding increases in expenditures for park personnel to supervise the crowds or to protect the natural values. As a result, both the resources and the public have suffered.

"Crime is running rampant," a feature article in the *Billings* (Montana) *Gazette*, reported, using Yellowstone as a prime example. "The drug problem is as serious as in any city. And there are simply too many people using the park. Campers are quickly destroying the land, and automobiles are gravely polluting the air.

"Also, there are a number of people entering the park who think this wilderness is another Disneyland. They have provoked bears into violent attacks. They are destroying the natural wonders in various ways, such as by sliding on algae found around geysers. They are tossing coins and assorted junk into thermal pools, especially the once-beautiful Morning Glory pool. They have no idea about how to perform in a wilderness."

So it goes in virtually all the national parks. Air pollution, water pollution—people pollution—are prevalent. Only degree and form vary, ranging from overuse and overcrowding to litter, defacement, vandalism, crime, traffic jams, lack of sanitation, pollution of streams, erosion of soil. In one park alone, Shenandoah, in Virginia, over 700,000 pounds of garbage including styrene plastic cups, paper plates, throwaway beverage cans, and sewage from the storage tanks of camping vehicles are disposed of at five landfill dumps inharmoniously placed in wilderness. As for crime, the old helpful park ranger has been changed into a tough policemen coping with a rising tide of murder, manslaughter, rape, assault, drunkenness, disorderly conduct, drug law violations. The most widespread crime is "car-clouting"—stripping automobiles of valuable parts and contents.

Why does it happen and what can we do about it?

Adventures in the outdoors are essential to appreciation of the mechanism of the land. There is no higher or more exciting sport than that of ecological observation. But when people come into the national parks they find scant emphasis on self-reliance or on the need to respect the environment of nature.

In one sense, Congress is responsible by granting appropriations virtually in direct ratio to the rising volume of visitors, and so spurring the Park Service into devising crowd-pleasing and crowd-attracting devices.

Certainly the time is at hand to stop handling national parks as common playgrounds with space unlimited. There are too many people in the parks at a given time.

There is too much space given over to trailers and large luxury vehicles, and to profit-making concession operations, consuming valuable real estate which should be protected for more appropriate purposes.

The National Wildlife Federation and the National Parks and Conservation Association have proposed that any new tourist facilities be placed outside the national parks, where they would bring revenue to local communities and preserve the wilderness atmosphere of the parks.

We can no longer allow parks to be used as outdoor amusement centers. The primary role should be to preserve choice and representative specimens of land forms in America. Through such preservation, the parks can serve as laboratories for learning and as reservoirs of animal and plant life which may be threatened elsewhere; they can be used to interpret how these systems operate to the benefit of man as a part of nature.

"Yellowstone should be closed to all vehicular traffic for at least five years. Only persons willing and able to walk into the park should be allowed entry during this time," urges Kimbert Larsen, of the *Billings Gazette.* "It is sorrowful that such a suggestion has to be made, but Yellowstone has to be closed for several years."

He may well be right; his comment recalls the position taken by John Muir many years ago in the debate over opening Yosemite to auto traffic. "Good walkers," he said, "can go anywhere in these hospitable mountains without artificial ways."

This approach does not mean the exclusion of people, but rather insures the protection of trail and campfire country—the true park wilderness experience—for optimum use and enjoyment by people over a longer period of time. It also means the planned enlargement of regional vacation areas, with more surrounding state parks, private campgrounds, and private resorts absorbing and serving the rising tide of recreational travelers. It should also lead to a new emphasis on close-in parks and clean streams, run by cities and counties filling the needs of people as part of a wholesome environment of life, and freeing the national areas for other uses.

"As a country of sightseers, it is without parallel. As a field for scientific research it promises great results," reported Lt. Gustavus Doane, military leader of the 1870 Yellowstone expedition. "In the branches of geology, minerology, botany, zoology, and ornithology it is probably the greatest laboratory that nature furnishes on the surface of the globe."

Here may be the most significant role of the national parks in America's tomorrow: as classrooms for scientific and environmental education. When the parks were new, there were fewer Americans and lots more elbowroom. National parks are ideally suited for use as ecological centers for the urban young, who have no exposure to the natural systems.

That many youngsters are shut off from healthful outdoor experiences undoubtedly contributes to the rising tide of crime, violence, frustration, and discontent. Fortunately, the national parks already have a network of "environmental study areas" for the continuing use of school groups. And in 1971 Congress established a Youth Conservation Corps, on a limited pilot-program basis, as a means of providing summer work and outdoor education. Youth Corps work is not a goal in itself—but, rather, a means of generating understanding of the individual's role in the greater world around him.

Exactly what form the National Park Service of tomorrow will take one cannot foresee. Sometimes I feel there should be a new agency, a United States Wilderness Service, to insure saving the few remaining fragments of primeval places as our legacy to the future. In any event, our forebears included men of rare insight, who could look forward to our needs. This generation has a duty to sustain them by looking still further ahead.

When Congress set Yellowstone aside, it asserted that while utilization may be necessary, there must also be sanctuaries where kinship with all nature can be constantly renewed. Such is the everlasting value to recognize and perpetuate in celebration of the National Parks Centennial.

The Parks Cry for Support and Advocacy

Different Drummer
April 1995

For many years national parks have been an important part of my life. I've learned to view the parks as sanctuaries that open the heart to inner feeling and emotion; they enable me to appreciate the sanctity of life, of all life, and the history of the nation. Now, however, I feel deep concern for their present and fear for their future. National parks, monuments and historic sites are not well protected. They are at risk. They cry for public understanding, help, support and advocacy.

It takes commitment, conviction, deep-felt concern and courage at all levels, top to bottom, to run the national parks and to relate to caring citizens. Stephen T. Mather, the first director of the National Park Service, built a field force as a model of honorable and ethical federal employment. He inspired the "mystique," a spirit of mission, a willingness to stand tough against what he called "desecration of the people's playground for the benefit of a few individuals or corporations."

But over the past thirty years, through Democratic and Republican administrations, politics has replaced principle. Today, National Park Service personnel hunger for leadership, a leadership committed to ethical and ecological principles, and to open communication. They are tired of watching helplessly while parks are sold out politically and degraded. Many park people I know have labored long and hard and care deeply, only to feel frustrated and unfulfilled by institutional bumbling, and by weak and waffling decisions made by office-bound officials hiding behind endless paper-shuffling of plans and promises to do better.

The Park Service endeavors to please everyone, but it does not stand in the way of crowds and commercial exploitation. For example, in June 1992, a ranger, off-duty, called me from Mesa Verde National Park in Colorado to tell about two bears that wandered into a campground looking for food only to be shot dead on official orders. That didn't sound right. If it's a question of clearing an area of campers or bears, safeguarding the bears, or any native species, ought to come first. However, Robert M. Baker, regional director of the National Park Service, later wrote to me that dispatching the two bears to bear heaven was justified to prevent "an unacceptable risk to human safety and property."

I can't agree. Anyone going to a national park or wilderness ought to prepare for risk and be properly advised to do so. The preservation of wild, unmanipulated nature is a use in its own right—a "wise use," the essence of wisdom, of human intellectuality, compassion and ethics, as well as of science. Yet many of these places are run like zoos, or popcorn playgrounds, where visitors go around in padded comfort. . . .

These examples reflect politics as a powerful influence, more deadly to wildlife than the most high-powered rifle in the hands of a poacher. It's the politics of profit, weakening laws and regulations, silencing public employees, corrupting democracy.

Consequently, administrators find it convenient to support, or propose, construction projects designed to draw visitors and to sanction crowd-pleasing activities reduced to a low common denominator, rather than to hew to regulations focused on the values of the resource itself and its protection. More than 75,000 snowmobiles descend on Yellowstone during the winter. Presumably they are limited to the unplowed roads, but there is little ranger supervision or control. As the numbers continue to rise, so does the pressure to open more of the park to them. At Voyageurs National Park, in Minnesota, the park administration actually endorses snowmobile races and advocates a plan to build snowmobile trails across the Kabetogama Peninsula, an area sheltering wolf, bear and other wildlife, clearly identified for its wilderness values and potential for inclusion in the wilderness system.

The agency talks of "partnerships" to cope with its shrinking budgets, but I see and fear the liaison with money-makers to help them make more money. The leaders talk in rhetoric and jargon, of structure, rather than of substance, or challenge or hard issues, without any system of genuinely informing and involving the public as partners in protecting the public estate.

In light of the deficiencies of public administration a critic could suggest, with best intentions, that national parks ought to be dealt off to land trusts, the Nature Conservancy, or Trust for Public Lands. That is like saying that schools don't work, so let's privatize education. I don't agree: I'm for public education and making it work—and I'm for national parks and public lands and making them function in the public interest. Franklin D. Roosevelt had the right idea when he said:

I see an America whose rivers and valleys and lakes—hills and streams and plains—the mountains over our land and nature's wealth deep under the earth—are protected as the rightful heritage of the people.

"These parks did not just happen," declared J. Horace McFarland in 1916. "They came about because earnest men and women became violently excited at the possibility of these great assets passing from public control. Each one of these national parks in America is the result of some great man's thought of service to his fellow citizens."

That public enthusiasm and energy is needed desperately to restore and guard the integrity of national parks. It doesn't mean keeping people out; it means dealing them in. Theodore Roosevelt called the Grand Canyon "one of the great sights which every American if he can travel at all should see," but he didn't ask everyone to come at the same time. To the contrary, he pleaded with Americans to do nothing to mar the Canyon's grandeur. In return for what they give, national parks and other public lands deserve and need the respect of visitors who come to enjoy them. When the problems derived from overuse and abuse are explained properly, I believe that Americans will understand and respond appropriately, and, hopefully, influence the body politic that serves us.

National parks when they were new yielded discovery, adventure, and challenge. They should always do that. And they can, if we set our minds and hearts to it. As the rest of the country becomes developed, and supercivilized, national parks should be held apart, safeguarded to represent another side of America, free of technology, free of automobiles, snowmobiles and flightseeing, free of commerce and crowds, free of instant gratification, a pioneer, self-reliant side of America.

In the unending struggle to obtain and sustain a quality environment of life, national parks contribute by their existence as model ecosystems. In a world where nothing remains static, the challenge is to raise and then sustain the quality of the parks themselves. Turning over the National Park System in better condition than we found it may be the most important bequest of this generation to the future.

Wilderness *Does* Work

Spring 1995

Thirty-plus years after passage certainly marks a fitting point in history to consider whether the Wilderness Act of 1964 still works. Has wilderness preservation, as a principle and as a mechanism, failed—so that time is ripe for an alternative, as J. Baird Callicott proposes? Or do we need wilderness "now more than ever," as both Reed Noss and Dave Foreman insist? Whatever the answers, I view the discussion in *Wild Earth* by these thoughtful, able witnesses as positive and challenging. I'm glad the questions have been raised and to have the opportunity to contribute to the dialogue.

Even at its best, I see the Wilderness Act as a beginning rather than an end in itself. True enough, the National Wilderness Preservation System, which came into being with the act, has grown to embrace nearly 100 million acres of public land, but perhaps that's only a number—that doesn't necessarily mean it works, or that it works as it should, or as it was intended. I see an unfinished agenda, a time to identify weak spots, opportunities and challenges. The truth is that we have a long way to go to realize the promise of the victory one generation ago.

But more important, at least for me, is to recognize and appreciate wilderness preservation as something deep-rooted in American history and national conscience, and even beyond our own country as a universal calling, a global need. The rest of the world has taken heart from our lead, as in Great Britain, where Lady Sayer, prime mover of the Dartmoor Preservation Association, pleads for a halt to the tragic disintegration of upland moors. Her words are poignant and powerful: "The rocks and heather, the gorse and the bogs. That is wild country, and in Britain it is all we have left of truly virgin land; and it is slowly vanishing, not only in Britain, but in every part of our man-polluted planet."

Here at home it is sometimes assumed that wilderness preservation as a land use was conceived with the movement for the Wilderness Act, and that it was based largely on goals of "aesthetics" and "recreation." History, however, shows otherwise, that the Wilderness Act emerged as the culmination of ideas and efforts of diverse people, often unsung, over a considerable period of time. For example, I recently came across the August 1936 issue of *Nature Magazine*, in which Arthur Newton Pack editorialized in support of a proposal by Dr. E. Lucy Braun for a network of national primeval monuments, extending from tropical hammocks in Florida to rain forests of the Northwest, from desert flora of southern California to spruce and fir forests of Maine, "sufficiently substantial and representative areas that would preserve intact examples of every type of native vegetation." Pack applauded Dr. Braun's stated goal to safeguard historic, scientific, and aesthetic values, urging that: "A national survey should quickly be made of remaining typical areas and a complete program of acquisition adopted."

Dr. Braun, for her part, may have developed her thinking through contacts with Aldo Leopold and Robert Marshall.

In his 1933 book, *The People's Forests*, a conservation gem unfortunately lost to time, Robert Marshall proposed a national network of numerous primeval reservations in all sections of the country, saving specimens of each timber type. He in turn may have been influenced by his close friend and ally in forestry, Gifford Pinchot, who in 1920 as commissioner of forestry in Pennsylvania (ten years after leaving his federal position as chief of the Forest Service), successfully advocated establishment of forest parks, forest monuments, and special scenic areas, the basis of Pennsylvania's roadless wild areas and natural areas. Looking back into the nineteenth century, George Perkins Marsh, in pioneering the unified concept of soil, water and forest, recommended keeping a large portion of America in its primitive condition. So did Thoreau, who foresaw national preserves protected as a democratic birthright, "in which the bear and the panther may still exist, and not be 'civilized off the face of the earth.'" Thoreau, in fact, wanted each community to sustain a primitive forest of 500 or 1,000 acres around it to "keep the New World *new*."

Now, one may question whether Thoreau and others were motivated ecologically and scientifically or "merely" aesthetically. Dave Foreman, in organizing the North American Wilderness Recovery Project, has argued that true wilderness—ecological wilderness—is the only path home, that without it we are likely to be strangers and aliens in our own land. I share Dave's view, but see the rationale in other terms, perhaps best explained by treating ecology or biological diversity as a feeling rather than exclusively as factual or substantive. As Emerson revealed more than a century ago, literature, poetry and science all are homage to the unfathomed secrets of nature. John Muir

felt uplifted and exalted in the wild sanctuary. Wilderness to him was an expression of God on earth—the mountains, God's temples; the forests, sacred
groves. "In wildness I sense the miracle of life," wrote Charles A. Lindbergh,
"and beside it our scientific accomplishments fade to trivia." Ansel Adams
more recently explained it this way:

> *Here are worlds of experience beyond the world of aggressive man, be-*
> *yond history, beyond science. The moods and qualities of nature and the*
> *relations of great art are difficult to define; we can grasp them only in the*
> *depths of our perceptive spirit.*

The trouble in modern intellectual society is that the perceptive spirit is
repressed and imagination is denied. Scientists and educators require evidence, documentation, statistics, quantification. Education for the most part is
about careers, jobs, making it in a structured materialist society, rather than
about individualism, the ability to question society and to constructively change
it. Education emphasizes the cognitive—a focus on facts, with abilities to analyze, calculate and memorize. It provides a practical means of acquiring information, but the intuitive, ethical and spiritual are largely omitted or denied.

Nevertheless, wilderness, if you ask me, above all its definitions, purposes
and uses, is sacred space, with sacred power, the heart of a moral world governed by peace and love. Wilderness preservation is not so much a system or a
tactic, but a way of experiencing the world within oneself, of understanding the
sacred connection with all of life, with people, plants, animals, water, sunlight,
clouds. It's an attitude and way of life with a spiritual ecological dimension.

That is not exactly a new idea, nor uniquely American. All religions emphasize God's gifts of earth, sky, water and life, the unity and wholeness of
creation, the immorality of abusing and exploiting nature for immediate gain,
and the benefits of intimate, personal communion with nature. For centuries
Buddhists and yogis have gone to caves, mountain tops and other remote
places to find revelation. On one occasion Jesus Christ spent forty days in the
wilderness, where he had been led by the Holy Spirit. On another he and
three disciples undertook to visit a high mountain, probably Mount Hermon,
on the northern boundary of Palestine; it was a deliberately planned experience in the expectation of finding unlimited good.

All across the world the so-called primitive peoples have placed a person-
alized value on sacred qualities of land, particularly when untouched. Their
sacred places serve as common history uniting generations. In Hawaii, the
concept of *wahi pana* merges the importance of visible place with invisible

spirit. The inventory of sacred places in Hawaii includes the dwelling places of the gods and of venerable disciples, temples and shrines, cliffs, mounds, mountains, weather phenomena, forests and volcanoes. Sacred places are located widely across North America, retreats where native peoples in many different ways have sought to cleanse body, mind, and spirit, to experience visions, revelations, mystic journeys, sometimes praying and fasting on high mountain ridges, or "going to water," which means ritually washing in a sacred stream, possibly for purification when the stream is cold and icy.

Some sacred places are prominent landmarks, like Denali in Alaska and Katahdin in Maine; others are mere rocks, but not mere at all to one with faith in the sacred quality of the rock—or of the wind, for that matter. The past lives on in the present: Land, water, trees, animals, birds, rocks, human remains, and human-made objects are believed instilled with vital and sacred qualities. "Preservation" means perpetuation of living cultural conditions—beliefs, lifeways, languages, ceremonies—as well as places and properties associated with them. Native Americans are very concerned about cultural preservation, through living connection and dynamics of continuing culture. They want to be part of a modern world, while kindling and rekindling Earth-based tradition. They live in the belief better days will come, if they can mend the sacred hoop broken many times over in the past five centuries.

Wilderness does something like that for me. Over the years I've learned to love wilderness in a personal way. It enriches my body; it elevates my mind and spirit to look above and beyond my own wants and needs. It makes me a better person. Thus, I think of the Wilderness Act as an expression through law of national ethics and idealism, a symbol of hope, lighting the path to an age of reason and nonviolence, an age of respect for the earth as a source of respect for each other.

Of course, there's plenty of room for pessimism. For every step forward, society seems to take two (or more) steps backward. I can't deny Thomas Merton's gloomy critique in *Raids on the Unspeakable:*

> *We live in the time of no room, which is the time of the end. . . . The time when everyone is obsessed with lack of time, lack of space, with saving time, conquering space, projecting into time and space the anguish produced within them by the technological furies of size, volume, quantity, speed, number, price, power and acceleration.*

On the other hand, Oscar Wilde delivered a great line: "We are all in the gutter, but some of us are looking at the stars." Wilderness is a special place for looking at stars—for touching stars and being empowered by them, for daring impossible dreams. That was what Howard Zahniser did when he wrote the Wilderness Act (drafted on his dining room table), then proclaiming, "We are not fighting progress. We are making it. We are not dealing with a vanishing wilderness. We are working for a wilderness forever." In his own studious, articulate and compassionate manner, Zahniser, despite all odds and opposition, never let go of the dream—that is his greatest gift.

Nor do I see why those who care should let go of it now. Zahniser and the other citizen leaders of thirty-plus years ago left a monumental legacy, and a challenge to fulfill the dream. I was privileged to know many of those pioneers, whom I remember for their courage, honesty, and sense of purpose. They were patriots, of the best kind, demonstrating that wilderness preservation is Americanism, just as wilderness is America, the vestigial symbol of the original America as God made it. The vestiges may be in no way be perfect, nor even adequate, but they are the best we have and thus more the treasure. Leopold defended the value of places less than pristine, urging that they be left alone to evolve over the long term. In *A Sand County Almanac* he showed the earth's ability to heal itself under caring stewardship. On a larger scale, the history of national parks such as Great Smoky Mountains, in southern Appalachia, and Big Bend, in west Texas, proves that restoration is a realizable goal.

It takes serious commitment to make such things happen. But the effort in itself is rewarding, even more than whatever success the effort may bring. Involvement evokes the best in people: Albert Schweitzer taught that a person is ethical when life becomes sacred, not simply his or her own life, but that of all humans, and of plants and animals, and when he or she devotes himself or herself to other living things. Rachel Carson espoused the same idea: "The beauty of the living world I was trying to save has always been uppermost in my mind—that, and anger at the senseless brutish things that were being done. I have felt bound by a solemn obligation to do what I could—if I didn't at least try I could never again be happy in nature."

To say it another way, democracy is what we make of it, a system under which we the people get what we deserve, and what we demand. I love the work that individuals do, rising above themselves, and above institutions, challenging an entrenched system in which a small minority controls wealth and power. In this age of distrust and disillusionment, answers come when thought, hope and dream rise above the average, when intangible values of human heart take precedence. Human touch, not money, is required. There must be risk-taking, personal self-sacrifice. Those willing to sacrifice most never do it for salaries; yet crusades for social issues, whether for peace, racial equality, gender rights, or the environment, show how people—at times a very few—can and do bring needed change.

Professionalism in itself has little to do with caring for humanity or saving wilderness. Individuals work miracles, in contrast with institutions and professions that breed conformity and compliance. The technological, professorial "objective" mindset has not worked; the "subjective" embodies power, the wisdom of knowing the essence of life and caring enough to fight, no longer allowing technical experts to define terms and methods for treating issues under question. Or as Saul Alinsky wrote in *Rules for Radicals*, "All of life is partisan. There is no dispassionate objectivity."

The Wilderness Act opened the way to a new level of citizen involvement and activism, a grassroots conservation movement in which local people could be heard in behalf of wilderness areas they know best. The late 1960s and early 1970s were exciting times, a marvelous moment in conservation history, when Stewart M. Brandborg, who succeeded Howard Zahniser as executive director of the Wilderness Society (on Zahniser's death in 1964), and associates systematized grassroots wilderness activism. They grasped a provision of the act stipulating that, prior to consideration by Congress, public hearings must be held with advance notice on each proposed new wilderness unit in the vicinity of the lands in question. Harry Crandell, who worked for the Wilderness Society from 1970 to 1975, recently wrote to me about that period:

> *The Society was in the forefront and led major wilderness and public land issues. We all worked together as a team, each helping the other, but often we had to work alone for long stretches simply because there were so many balls in the air at once. Successful conclusion of issues would have been highly unlikely absent citizen involvement and telephone "trees" manned by volunteers and staff and "alerts" prepared by staff.*

This kind of thing doesn't happen much any more, at least not to my knowledge. From my observation, national organizations like the Wilderness Society and Sierra Club are led and staffed by well educated professional personnel, who have learned lots of things from course work but not enough from life or from self-sacrifice; they have their field offices, yet local citizen groups that I know in the Northwest, notably the Northwest Ecosystem Alliance and Alliance for the Wild Rockies, function on their own and do most of their own politicking in Washington.

I recall going to California (at Brandborg's suggestion) to visit the San Rafael Wilderness, the first national forest area reviewed under the 1964 act. My partner on the trail was Dick Smith, an energetic Santa Barbara newsman who knew the area intimately. Smith worked closely with the Wilderness Society to develop a wilderness concept far bolder than the official proposal from the Forest Service. Like Arthur Carhart in the northern Minnesota canoe country and Aldo Leopold in the brushy Southwest, Smith saw something special in the chaparral slopes, Indian cave paintings and sandstone cliffs others had missed. Efforts by Smith and his local allies, coordinated with the Wilderness Society, led to establishment of the San Rafael Wilderness, as the first area reviewed by Congress under the Wilderness Act, and then later of the adjacent Dick Smith Wilderness, named in his honor following his death in 1977.

Working to make a difference, to influence public policy through avenues provided by the Wilderness Act and other laws, helps individuals to understand that efforts and energies are rewarded, even in lost causes, or causes that appear lost. In Memphis, the Citizens to Preserve Overton Park during the 1960s and 1970s were determined to save one of the finest urban forests in the world from proposed construction of a highway through the middle of it. They were forced to contest not only merchants, developers and public officials, but the two powerful Memphis daily newspapers, which ridiculed park defenders and belittled any politician who dared to speak in defense of the park. The parks department and park professionals were easy pushovers, acquiescing to the planned highway, but the citizens group insisted that an established park represents an integral and sacred part of the American city, that it makes the city habitable, and that it would make more sense to locate the highway elsewhere or not build it at all. The Overton Park case, because it involved federal highway funds, was debated in Congress and before the Supreme Court. It was tough going. The citizens felt that even though the park might be lost, their lives were enriched for each day they saved it. Ultimately, Overton was spared, and it still enhances the landscape and quality of life of Memphis.

Such grassroots struggles go on everywhere, and perhaps they will continue unto eternity. Should that be the case, may those who care eternally be guided by the words of Ernie Dickerman, the wilderness warrior's warrior. Dickerman in the 1960s was a leader in the battle to save the Great Smoky Mountains from a destructive pseudo-wilderness proposal of the National Park

Service. Thirty years later, though well past eighty, he is still going strong, campaigning for wilderness in Virginia and inspiring friends and fans everywhere. In 1992 he concluded a letter as follows:

It is amazing how political democracy in the United States, despite its deficiencies and innumerable errors, permits so many of us to lead satisfying, rewarding lives.

Private citizens, Dickermans across America, need to defend and advance the wilderness cause because public officials and public agencies do so little in its behalf. Congressional policy in our time dictates that the very parks, forests and wildlife refuges John Muir helped save must be used, demonstrably, as commodities, by and for people, not in some future time, but now. Game must be produced and harvested, trees cut and transformed into cash crops, and visitors served; otherwise the areas are considered to be locked up and going to waste. Congressmen possibly may be forgiven, considering that politics is their game; they don't know anything about the ecological nature of wilderness. Perhaps those outside who do know need to try harder to enlighten Congress. But it's another story with the four federal agencies directly responsible for implementing the Wilderness Act and for protecting the separate units of the National Wilderness Preservation System. The Forest Service, Fish and Wildlife Service, National Park Service and Bureau of Land Management all ought to know better and do more.

While part of the problem certainly derives from the directives to public servants from Congress and their political superiors, agency leaders and professionals in the ranks are too willing to comply and concur. They know how the system works and adapt to it: The status and pay levels of personnel are determined not by acres of wilderness protected, nor by species of wildlife or plantlife rescued from endangerment, but by the volume of timber cut or numbers of people served. The administrator of a national forest or national park with two million visitors is higher up the ladder than the man or woman at another facility with two million acres of wilderness and half as many visitors.

Many of these personnel lack philosophy or feeling for wilderness, having been trained in forestry and range schools, rooted in traditions of agronomy, to manage and manipulate, to control the earth and to convert "resources" into commodities. They acquire the analytical type of thinking that gives power over nature but smothers the powerful in ignorance of themselves as part of nature. Wilderness to them is merely another commodity, okay in its place as long as it doesn't interfere with those that really count.

They want to impose management on wilderness, too, screening out insects, lightning fires, and natural erosive forces, rather than to identify and defend them as valid parts of a dynamic primitive landscape. They approach wild animals as if they were domestic livestock. A good scientist needs a control where manipulation is minimal, where wildlife and plant communities are allowed to regulate themselves. That is what wilderness is meant to do. Considering that domestic stock and game animals are heavily manipulated almost everywhere else, a few places ought to be reserved for systems to work without human intervention.

I've seen wilderness areas all over this country, maybe more than anybody, and found them in poor condition, mostly getting worse rather than better. In many cases degradation and dissipation of wilderness are scarcely recognized or acknowledged by those in charge. A few years ago I was invited to a National Park Service mid-level training program on "remote areas management"—the trainers in charge didn't even want to call it wilderness or face the real problems. Another time I joined a field workshop of wilderness managers of the Southwest Region of the Forest Service, conducted in the Pecos Wilderness of New Mexico. The group of twenty-five or thirty was too large for the fragile terrain. Some hadn't camped out in years, as evident in their mistreatment of the resources at hand. They busily occupied themselves with such techniques as building water bars across trails, strictly superficial to wilderness protection and enhancement, without any reference to ecosystem responsibilities. The Forest Service likes to claim it invented wilderness, citing Carhart, Leopold and Marshall, the wilderness pioneers who worked in its ranks. But Carhart's pleas for preservation were unheeded and he left the agency in despair in 1923; Leopold was dispatched from the Southwest to an office position at the Forest Products Laboratory in Madison—then he quit too; Marshall died in 1938, after which much of his wilderness work was undone. Now, the Forest Service points to its corps of wilderness rangers, which does indeed include competent and committed people, mostly at the lower levels; when it comes to predator control in wilderness or clearcut logging to the wilderness boundary, the decisions are made by district rangers and forest supervisors, the "line officers," often with different frame of reference and different sympathy.

Yes, there are people in the agencies who individually care deeply about wilderness and have labored long and hard in its behalf, but many are frustrated and unfulfilled by institutional lethargy and bureaucratic unwillingness to meet the mandate of the law. Their bosses and coworkers talk about wilderness protection only when they have to, and certainly better than they practice it. Decisions about wilderness are made in offices by people alienated from the outdoors, who hide behind paperwork and endless promises to do better.

The National Park Service in my thinking is the most culpable, precisely because it is mandated to protect and preserve and has done precious little to implement the Wilderness Act. Its leaders claim the agency's own basic legislation is adequate and effective, but all the evidence shows a continuing willingness to back away from preservation, to sacrifice wilderness to mass recreation—including snowmobiling, the least appropriate kind—and accompanying commercial development. The Park Service deliberately has kept classified wilderness small and unprotected. . . .

Citizens everywhere are way ahead of the paid professionals. In 1990 I went to attend a conference on preservation of public lands in the state of Maryland. My first reaction was that there are no public lands in Maryland, for the moment confusing the term "public lands" with the public domain of the West. Yet at the conference I learned of the Maryland Wildlands Committee's campaign to work within state parks and forests for a Maryland Wildlands Preservation System, detailed as follows:

> *Our primary goal is to protect the natural diversity of Maryland ecosystems, including biological community, species, and genetic diversity. We still lack desirable representation of Maryland ecosystem diversity, e.g., boreal bog, limestone forest, tidal marsh are missing. We still urgently need to add a few large unfragmented areas of forest wherever they are least disturbed and most valuable ecologically.*
>
> *These last big blocks of forest are hard to find within State lands. Complicating the problem is the competition among different interests: timber industry (which wants to cut), wildlife management (which wants to open up forest for edges advantageous for certain species); Wildlands people (who want to keep the forest ecosystem flourishing for all species), and the [State] Forest Service (which would like to keep everybody happy, but manage primarily for traditional forest goals).*

It's the same elsewhere in the world as well. In December 1994 I visited the Galapagos Islands, Darwin's laboratory of evolution, as part of an international group of scientists and conservationists. In briefings to the group, the executive director of the natural resources department of Ecuador, INEFAN, and the superintendent of Galapagos National Park both stressed the need to recognize and satisfy demands for commercial development by the islands's growing population—that was *their* priority. Imagine my surprise, therefore, when we were met at Puerto Ayoro, the main settlement, by a delegation of thirty-plus, children included, with an altogether different message. Their mimeographed appeal includes the following passages:

The Galapagos Islands have come of age. By this we mean that they have, like every other place on earth, including Antarctica, come, in the due course of time, under the hammer of man's restlessness and greed. The observation of Chief Seattle that by destroying nature we will die of a great loneliness of spirit, haunts us, for we sense that by the destruction of nature we wound and disfigure our own minds.

We ask for the victory of moral responsibility in the case of the Galapagos, a moral responsibility not compromised by motivation for personal gain and power. We ask that this unique archipelago, with its complexities of natural communities almost complete, be left in peace for all time, that we don't demand so much from the islands that we destroy their charm, magic and deep breathing of their inner souls.

We ask you to join forces with us to save our islands, as a last chance for mankind to show an ability to live in peace with nature. The islands require the concerned involvement of people everywhere to find solutions that will never harm the natural function of the Galapagos ecosystems.

The Galapagos already is a biosphere reserve. That helps, but clearly doesn't protect it. Ten years ago I tried to get Virgin Islands National Park in our own country *removed* from the list of biosphere reserves because it was poorly administered. The National Park Service was doing terrible things, expanding a highway, tearing down hills and uprooting palm trees to make way for parking lots, sacrificing park resources for the tourist industry. In response to my proposal, I received a stern letter of admonition from William P. Gregg, Jr., director of the biosphere program for the National Park Service, insisting that the park "is making major strides in developing the scientific basis for addressing important problems." To me, that only enables research personnel to seek more funding to conduct more studies and park managers to defer action, instead of acting on the strong, irrefutable evidence already at hand.

The biosphere reserve is a good idea. So are biodiversity, deep ecology, and conservation biology, but sometimes they come off as buzzwords, trendy new approaches to avoid facing a chronic old problem. I like to believe that wilderness represents the ultimate in land preservation, and yet today, thirty years after Zahniser, fifty years after Leopold, wilderness designation by law, without more, cannot save the wilderness or the beauty of Rachel Carson's living world. I visit the wildest and remotest areas and find them degraded by misuse and overuse, with vanishing species of wildlife driven to their last refuge and in desperate straits. The balance of the public estate, bordering wilderness, largely surrendered to private exploitation, cannot provide the buffering wilderness needs. And beyond the public lands, the state of things steadily worsens, with inevitable negative influence on wilderness.

Protecting wilderness by law no longer suffices to protect wilderness. A wholesome natural environment reflects a wholesome human environment— it's impossible to have one without the other. Aldo Leopold talked of the need of a land ethic, a code of behavior governing interactions with the environment. Now must come ethical rules governing the behavior of people toward people and political institutions that represent ideals rather than material goals catering to privilege and power.

The world as we live in it is divided between those who do not have enough and those who have more than enough. It grieves me that the United States in a presumably enlightened age should lead in widening the gap between the underprivileged—the homeless, hungry and hopeless—and the overprivileged who want still more. Clearly it is time to ask new questions in the search for new and better answers, better than established institutions have been able to provide.

Society needs transformation, a viewpoint of human concern, distress and love, and attention to the relationship of causes. Martin Luther King, Jr. saw three major evils—racism, poverty, and militarism—and found them integrally linked. I see the degraded environment as a fourth major evil, joined with the others, all symptoms of a sick society. Violence, killing, brutality, injustice are common fare; yet the poor and uneducated, society's disenfranchised, feel the fury of the justice system, assigned to the longest prison terms in the worst conditions.

Beyond the measurable, when a living species perishes anywhere on earth the whole world dies a little bit with it; we lose a little of the global soul that binds us together. When mothers in Iraq mourn the death of their sons, mothers everywhere surely mourn with them. That is sisterhood, a powerful influence for brotherhood, for realization that we are all brothers and sisters, children of the same gods. We have allowed ourselves, alas, to be separated and compartmentalized—into rich and poor; young and old; men and women; physically and mentally able and differently able; black, white, red, yellow; Christian, Jew, Muslim, Buddhist, Hindu—finding in caste, class and color the illusion of protection from others who are different. In higher education, professionals learn languages distinct to their callings, whether in law, health care, history, science, engineering, economics, forestry, wildlife, all very specialized and restrictive.

But I like to speak of the common language that calls us home, of spiritual dimensions of the natural world that bring people together to recognize difference of appearance but unity of source, and that help to heal and enrich human heart and soul. I find support in the world's great religious traditions, all appealing to children of the universe to live in harmony with the earth. Despite their differences, religions acknowledge similar mysteries of origin, similar mysteries of destiny, and the search for a world society where peace prevails. Wholeness, respect for all life, and the integrity of creation link the most profound values of all philosophies.

When the Wilderness Act was passed, the idea of ecology was new to many people. The testimony of scientists in behalf of the legislation showed wilderness as virtually the only place where life functions in conditions approaching wholeness. Since then a cadre of scientists has improved understanding of how ecosystems function, and how the size, shape, and degree of fragmentation affects its biological health and productivity. Some go further, relating scientific work to worldly issues. "What we need is a reorganization of society, a fundamental change in its direction," writes George Wald, a Nobel Prize winner for his work in physiology at Harvard, "so as to better meet human needs, to humanize what is now increasingly alienating, to serve life rather than death."

Gifford Pinchot early in this century had much the same idea. He was a social crusader for industrial democracy who did not disassociate wilderness from wise use, but felt that conservation most of all "stands for an equal opportunity for every American citizen to get his fair share of benefit from these [natural] resources, both now and hereafter." Zahniser, leader in the movement for the 1964 Wilderness Act, agreed:

To the broad vision of Pinchot we owe much in the development of attitudes that now make possible the preservation of natural areas, at a time when the need is so deeply realized.

The blessings of nature are meant to be shared, but not with blindness that sanctions destruction out of greed. Society needs to develop universal respect for nature, to learn to draw from nature with restraint, to reshape the concept of power, from domination and conquest into the power of peace and service. Wilderness helps do that. It breaks down artificial barriers between people bred to believe they are different from each other by reason of class, color, race, or gender; wilderness is teaching, real teaching. When a designated wilderness area is beyond reach, a natural area, no matter how small or imperfect, or by whatever name it may be called, is a classroom filled with learning in all kinds of fascinating subjects. Marshes offer scenes three hundred million years old, the same environment that produced the first vertebrates to walk on land. Salt marshes demonstrate a link in the ecology of the entire ocean, acting as nursery or feeding grounds for fin fish and shellfish. The desert shows the frugality of water, abundant with plants and animals that have adapted themselves to endure where water is scarce and undependable. Wilderness, large or small, reveals how living creatures struggle for water, sunlight, soil nourishment, and space; how some grow because others die, decay, and decompose, and how others benefit through cooperation or partnership. I can't think anything more captivating than deriving knowledge from experience close to the source of life, the fragile earth we hold in trust.

One lesson leads to another. Eugene Odum, the renowned ecologist of the University of Georgia, has long stressed the need to preserve a substantial portion of the biosphere in a natural state to sustain the quality of human life and carrying capacity of the earth. In a paper titled "Natural Areas as Necessary Components of Man's Total Environment," presented by Odum and his brother, Howard T. Odum, before the thirty-seventh North American Wildlife and Natural Resources Conference in 1972, "natural environment" is defined in terms of function as that part of humankind's life-support system operating "without energetic or economic input from the power flows directly controlled by man."

Because cities and other developed environments are so valuable to man they must be protected from exploitation just as is necessary for any valuable resource. Specifically, cities need the protection of an adequate life support system, many elements of which natural environment provides free of charge. Without natural recycling and other work of nature, the cost of maintaining quality life in cities would be prohibitive . . . true value of a man's total environment is determined by the diversity interaction between the "developed" and the "natural" environment and not only by the worth of each as a separate component.

Consistent with his life's work, Eugene Odum has devoted much of his later career to agricultural ecology and to links between rural and urban areas in Georgia. In *Georgia: Images of Wilderness*, published in 1992, he wrote:

> *A major reason for preserving lots of natural areas as well as prime farmlands lies in their value in providing vital and mostly non-market life-support goods and services such as clean air, clean water, good soil and so on. Without healthy watersheds, airsheds, wetlands, river corridors, farmlands and the diversity of organisms that contribute to natural recycling and regeneration of these non-market goods and services of nature, cities, industries and other producers of economic wealth cannot prosper.*
>
> *As land prices rise and shortages develop, people often complain that natural area preservation is an unaffordable luxury because "we can't eat scenery." We can reply by saying, "But we can breathe and drink it, and it can reduce your healthcare costs, maybe even save your life." We can also profit from the enhanced value of property that lies next to a protected area.*

Thanks to the influence of Odum and others, ecology is now readily accepted in the lexicon, but in 1964, the year of the Wilderness Act, the idea was new. Science itself has come a long way, often over a rough road. Still, more questions wait to be answered than have yet been asked, much more still to learn not only in science but in understanding how wilderness connects with education, ethics and religion. We need to learn more about the physical and psychic therapeutic qualities of wilderness; the contributions of individuals who have helped to save it; and the connection between the ongoing destruction of wilderness and the social issues of chauvinism, poverty, and militarism. In looking back, as part of the process of looking ahead, history proves to me the inestimable value of designating wilderness through law, of strengthening protection of public lands from the pressures of intrusive development. This protection is paramount where politics and economics are concerned. With agencies buffeted and weakened by winds of patronage and high level interference, wilderness designation is critical.

Wilderness inspires the search for undisturbed beauty and the serenity of wild places. It documents earth history and change, with baseline landmarks, against which to measure human alteration to the rest of the earth. It documents human history, too, and democratic government.

Perhaps the best of all messages is that to heal the earth is to heal the soul. Such recognition empowers individuals with responsibility and self-fulfillment to face the world with hope and heart to make it whole again.

CHAPTER III

WILDLIFE HANGS ON, AT THE BRINK

In the late 1960s I wrote a book for children, *The Varmints: Our Unwanted Wildlife*. I began page one by noting that before Europeans arrived wildlife was everywhere in America, in rich variety of species. Then I explained how settlers labeled animals as either good (the useful and understandable) or bad (the bear that invaded the pasture, the fox that stole into the hen house, and the horned owl that destroyed game birds). These became known in frontier dialect as "varmints," a term derived from the word "vermin," which usually refers to flies, lice, bedbugs, rats, and mice. And when the tide of the nation moved west, new and different varmints stood in the way. The varmints became our unwanted wildlife and were exterminated by the millions.

Perhaps I would have seen things differently had I been raised with a gun in the agrarian West. But I grew up on the sidewalks of New York, where acquaintance with wild animals began in a habitat called the Bronx Zoo. Thus, when much later I started writing seriously about wildlife and wildlife issues, it was more from the perspective of the reporter asking "What is the story here?" than of the outdoors person.

The story I found and reported, in different forms many times over, is that wildlife policy and programs are based primarily on politics, the politics of power and profit, far more than on science. Regardless of any illusions to the contrary, science and resource management for the most part serve politics, not the other way around.

For example, predator control, which I first wrote about in *Field & Stream* in 1967, has never quit serving the special interests of the Western sheep industry. Thirty years ago wildlife professionals defended this onerous system, saying, "Without regulated control, ranchers will do much worse on their own. Leave it to us, for we are the professionals." The damage might have been worse but was bad enough; officials of the Fish and Wildlife Service even warned against national parks as dangerous "reservoirs of predation" and poison indeed has been applied in our national parks. President Nixon issued an executive order banning the use of poisons against predators on federal land, but President Reagan, the self-proclaimed "sagebrush rebel," repealed it. Over time the name of the agency in charge of toxins has been changed from Branch of Predator and Rodent Control to Division of Wildlife Services and then, when citizen pressure grew too strong at Interior, it was moved to Agriculture and renamed Animal Damage Control. It was renamed Wildlife Services once again, in 1995, with new promises to be more scientific and more selective. The killing goes on with the benign acquiescence of the Forest Service and its scientists in national forest settings where the sheep industry prevails.

Science by its nature should be free of politics. Yet many state agencies are notoriously vulnerable to old politics, intimidating personnel who try to introduce new ecological thinking. The U.S. Fish and Wildlife Service is no better off. In the historic spotted owl case in the Northwest, when Fish and Wildlife personnel were silenced by politically appointed superiors concerned more with timber, the owl gained protection under the Endangered Species Act only as a result of litigation. Science, biology, and economics were examined on the record, under oath, and in public for the first time.

The national wildlife refuges are set aside primarily to preserve and enhance wildlife, but a 1989 report of the General Accounting Office reported secondary uses on more than 90 percent of all refuges. On some, oil and gas production appears to be the main business. On others, hunters line up behind dikes to shoot at ducks and geese. Military jets strafe refuges for practice. Refuge boundaries keep very little out. Refuge animals are run over by vehicles, shot, trapped, and exposed to toxins and water shortages. Kesterson in California is a spectacular, highly publicized case of a refuge poisoned by water flowing through ditches into it.

Scientists face a difficult challenge, particularly the wildlifers. They must be rational, analytical, focused on particular parts of nature. Because their standing in the community of their peers is important and valued, they must not overstate facts, nor exceed the narrow bounds of their disciplines; if they go astray they are apt to lose credibility and funding. The emerging science of conservation biology has pressed the consideration of parts fitting together in ecosystems and landscapes. Some conservation biologists have declared themselves willing to take risks, to row upstream against convention, but not so many wildlifers. In a 1985 letter, Rainer Brocke, wildlife professor at Syracuse University, New York, wrote:

We wildlifers go to our conferences, often dominated by narrow-minded state game divisions, covering the same old ground and dishing out the same old hash. We talk to ourselves and piously ask why the public has not been enlightened.

It has been my experience that the public includes many intelligent people in all walks of life who can put two and two together. All these vacillations, lack of leadership, lack of solid science are not lost on them.

I can understand when scientists struggle with political involvement, for it goes counter to their sense of mathematical order. But I've been privileged to know a few who successfully combined scientific integrity with deeply felt ethics. Freeing themselves of old shibboleths, they have communicated with feeling from the heart, as well as from laboratory and computer. Such people can make a difference, and they do.

I once wrote about the epochal work of Olaus Murie in gaining protection of what is now the Arctic National Wildlife Refuge. I remember meeting Olaus soon after he left government service in the 1950s. He wanted to live close to nature and yet to play an active role as citizen-scientist, which he did as director of the Wilderness Society. "It seems to me we should get away from the strictly scientific methods of today, so much like the laboratory technique," he wrote in the foreword to *A Naturalist in Alaska*, by his brother Adolph. "We can speak the truth, but we can use human language in doing so." Adolph, committed to the truth, was in hot water through most of his career with the National Park Service, but the national parks, Denali and Grand Teton, in particular, benefitted from his efforts.

The logging reported in "Safeguarding the Greatest Concentration of Eagles on Earth" was terminated consequent to the campaign sparked by David Cline, a biologist who heads the National Audubon Society office in Alaska. He never gave up even when the local politics in Haines favored logs over eagles, and now the state eagle preserve is the main tourist attraction and is promoted by former critics.

John and Frank Craighead have never given up either. No two people have done more to save the grizzly bear from extinction, nor taken more abuse from officialdom. As well as conducting his own research, John has been closely allied with the Montana-based Alliance for the Wild Rockies, which seeks to preserve, through legislation proposed as the Northern Rockies Ecosystem Protection Act, large biospheres and the connecting links between them. The Alliance has worked to enlist support of local citizens, Indian tribes, national environmental organizations, and appropriate business interests.

As Rainer Brocke wrote to me, the public includes many intelligent people who can put two and two together. The wildlife professional who truly wants to get something done on behalf of a species or an ecosystem will do best to work with citizens. Maurice Hornocker learned that when his pioneering studies of predation in the River of No Return Wilderness led the Idaho legislature in 1972 to reclassify the mountain lion and give it the protection of a game species. Hornocker, now the world-renowned authority on large wild cats, without hesitation came to the aid of Sharon Negri, of the California Mountain Lion Foundation in the mid-1980s. Sharon in three years had built the foundation from a membership of 300 to 32,000, a reflection of the campaign to acquire habitat for the mountain lion. The battle was fought uphill, but voters in a 1990 referendum chose decisively to support the mountain lion's cause.

Americans feel kinship with wild animals, not simply in the zoo or on television, but in the wilds that still endow the West. Most Americans, and doubtless most westerners, except for hard-core stockmen, cheered when wolves were reintroduced into Yellowstone in 1995. And next, hopefully, the grizzly, no longer "the most *horribilis* of them all."

Predators, Prejudice, and Politics

Field & Stream
December 1967

The tragic fiasco of Federal predator control as we know it today began half a century ago, during World War I. At first it was a means of eradicating wolves in order to save beef for our troops and allies. Then the sheepmen enlisted the government in a program to kill coyotes in their behalf. Wars have come and gone, but we have been stuck with predator control programs ever since.

Now the government has admitted that the principles in predator control are wrong, a needless annihilation of millions of animals, a waste of money, a political boondoggle. The Secretary of the Interior has acknowledged a fifty-year blunder by an agency of his department. This he did by accepting with praise a report of his Advisory Board on Wildlife Management, a document which constitutes a penetrating criticism of past performance, and by directing major reforms, overhaul, and a new approach for the future.

It is now three years since Secretary Stewart L. Udall received the historic Leopold Report, so named for Dr. A. Starker Leopold, the distinguished wildlife biologist who served as chairman of the Advisory Board. It is two years since Secretary Udall ordered the old Branch of Predator and Rodent Control (PARC) to be renamed the Division of Wildlife Services and to have its functions recast. But is it that simple? Can deep-set prejudices be reversed, and political opposition overcome by an executive order? If we have been damaging the natural resource for half a century and longer, can we stop overnight or will it take another half century?

I have been pondering these questions and asking them of scientists, sportsmen, stockmen, state fish and game directors, and federal officials, and have covered the range of interested organizations from Defenders of Wildlife to the National Woolgrowers Association. Above all, one conclusion stands out: Indiscriminate trapping, shooting, and poisoning have reduced some of the rarest, most beautiful, and superbly adapted species of our wildlife heritage to the brink of extinction, although they constitute a resource that could be enjoyed and harvested by sportsmen under good management practices. The

war on predators has been waged with little scientific knowledge of their beneficial roles in the biotic community, with the moral or ethical consideration
for man's responsibility in conserving natural life as an integral part of the
environment.

Predator control is often seen as an issue stirring emotion and controversy. It should be. The true wolf is virtually gone except in Alaska, Isle Royale
National Park in Michigan, and Minnesota's Superior National Forest. The
puma, the mysterious big cat known variously as panther, cougar, and mountain lion, once found in every state except Alaska and Hawaii, and the grizzly
bear are so rare they require nearly complete protection in national parks,
national forests, and the public lands. The coyote and bobcat are in danger of
vanishing from portions of their range even where there are no sheep to demand control. Yet there is no one to deny that the sight of a grizzly conjures
the image of daring and primitive times, that a coyote's song lends excitement
and a dimension of natural truth to a still desert evening, that the bobcat does
more good in killing rodents than harm in killing a few game birds.

Poisoning, in particular, whether by accident or deliberate design, has
taken a heavy toll of many of the flesh-eating mammals called predators. The
virtual disappearance of the black-footed ferret, now considered the rarest
American mammal, must be credited to poison programs aimed at the eradication of prairie dogs and other rodents in the Great Plains and Rockies. The
harmless, beautiful kit fox and ringtail cat may be nearing the end of the line
in their native habitat, from poison baits set for coyote.

If one decides to place blame for this unfortunate travesty, there is plenty
of blame to go around. "Federal predator control is perpetuated by misguided
ranchers and Congressmen," William A. Towell, executive vice president of
the American Forestry Association, declared three years ago when he was
director of the Missouri Conservation Department and setting a pace for the
nation in enlightened wildlife management. Mr. Towell was right, as far as his
statement went. The sheepmen and the legislators they influence are responsible, but only partly so. Some federal officials themselves have been zealous
in perpetuating the bureaucracy. It is much easier to start a program at taxpayers' expense than to end one. For example, the old-time government trappers, according to Paul Maxwell, of Grand Junction, Colorado, who was one
of them, would ask their superiors, "Why carry on a campaign against the bobcat when it is a proven fact they never kill lambs?" "We know that," the
supervisors would reply, "but don't tell the sheepman. Keep him thinking
the bobcat is as much a killer of lambs as any other predator."

There are still other forces. Many federal programs start when states hope they can get something for nothing. The states have the legal right over resident wildlife, yet they relinquish too willingly the right over predators, on the grounds they are non-game species, to the federal government. Further, some of the state legislatures throw good money after bad on control, either by contributing so-called "cooperative funds" to the federal agency or by running programs of their own, or doing both, often against the best advice of their state game directors, who regard wholesale predator control as a poor wildlife management practice.

Basically, the blame lies deep in the national conscience. Since pioneer days, agricultural and sports thinking has been aimed at extermination of all competitors: the "varmints," the grizzly, timber wolf, cougar, golden eagle, bald eagle, fox, hawk, owl, badger, mink, various snakes, and the alligator. Consequently, the federal programs were conceived in the dark ages of management, at a time when life-history studies of wild animals in their environment and in man's were first dawning. It was an age when the bounty was in flower, a terribly fraudulent, wasteful system, biologically unsound, ineffective, costly and corruptible, an instrument of getting money from the state house into the counties, a system which lingers to this day out of biological illiteracy and political expediency.

It was normal in those days for sportsmen and naturalists to assume that the meat-eating mammals were the main cause of certain seasonal and cyclical variations in the numbers of animals which man may have wanted for his own enjoyment and profit. The key to successful game management was thought to be elimination of the species which preyed on the game. Thus, Theodore Roosevelt, the hunter, conservationist, and President, understandably described a cougar treed at the rim of the Grand Canyon as "a big horse-killing cat, the destroyer of the deer, the lord of stealthy murder, facing his doom with a heart both craven and cruel." Such thinking led to establishment in 1906 of the Kaibab Plateau, on the north rim of the Canyon, as a national game preserve. It was an area that had been inhabited for centuries by a herd of some 4,000 deer, together with a balance of mountain lions. When the preserve was established, however, deer shooting was terminated and government hunters were ordered to clean out the predators. Within twenty-five years, the kill was reported at 781 mountain lions, 30 wolves, 4,889 coyotes, plus an untallied number of eagles.

The deer grew, as expected. By 1924, the total herd had reached 100,000. Then came the inevitable and unexpected: deer perished by the thousands, while the survivors ate every available leaf and twig, destroying almost 90 percent of the range. Though hunting was resumed and a thousand animals taken annually, the numbers still declined. By 1930, there were 20,000 deer left, by 1940 only 10,000. It was a tragic, costly mistake repeated in parks and forests all over the West.

In Yellowstone, with cougar and wolf eliminated, the coyote reduced, and ancient winter migration routes cut off by human settlements, thousands of elk, following their population explosion, starved and reduced the range to a point from which it will still take decades to recover. The lessons learned were simple and direct: A given range will support only a certain number of animals, whether game or domestic. Predators take only small numbers from the animals they prey upon and are probably essential to maintenance of a healthy, virile population.

These lessons are emphasized in a study of recent years conducted at Isle Royale National Park under the leadership of Dr. Durward Allen. The moose had reached that remote island in Lake Superior early in the century and by the mid-thirties had increased to between 1,000 and 3,000. The food supply dwindled rapidly, the moose depleted the browse (as the deer had at Kaibab), and many died. The cycle repeated itself a few years later. Then, in the winter of 1949, a band of timber wolves crossed the 15-mile icy stretch from Canada, opening a new era. Dr. Allen and his associates observed that the wolves claimed the old, the diseased, the heavily parasitized, and the weak young among the moose, hardly ever those between the ages of one and six. As a result of natural selection, the closely cropped herd of 600 today is healthy, among the most productive on the continent, bearing a high proportion of twin calves. The wolves, moose, and browse have achieved a balance.

Isle Royale may be isolated, but most principles learned there apply to predator-prey relationships all over the world. Hunting plays an important role by helping to remove excess population but, unlike natural predation, hunting does not necessarily select the weak unhealthy specimens. When the predatory population is excluded from a natural community the weaker members remain, weakening future generations of the species. But natural predation keeps the old and weak individuals to a minimum, benefitting the hunter as well as the herd. . . .

Despite the laws of modern wildlife biology and management, federal predator control has been going strong for more years than we care to remember. The total kill in a year's time is almost 200,000 animals, half of them coyotes. The remainder are lesser numbers of lynx and bobcat, bear, mountain lion, wolves, plus thousands more of badger, fox, opossum, porcupine, raccoon, skunk.

Most of the Fish and Wildlife Service in the Department of the Interior is concerned with protection, perpetuation, or management of birds and animals. But one branch, PARC, has made its way by following the paradoxical course of extermination and by providing a special service to a commodity-producing, profit-making industry.

After fifty years, livestock growers have come to expect total protection, as a substitute for their own effort. Predators do cause damage; those of us who prefer natural ways have no more right to deny that individual cougars, coyotes, and bears kill sheep, and occasionally calves, than stockmen have the right to accuse the entire species. Where economic liability is clearly demonstrated, the owner is justified in protecting his interests. Where problems are acute, government advisory service is reasonable. But we now have the major responsibility assumed by tax-supported agencies, serving a privileged segment of the public, rather than the entire public. In many areas, special levies are assessed against livestock on a per-head basis. But these rarely cover 25 percent of the cost. The rest comes from county, state, and federal funds, and much of it is paid by sportsmen.

The bulk of these activities are centered on the national forests and public lands of the West. Not only has there been an abrogation of responsibility in diverting public funds to serve a special interest, but that interest, the sheep industry, has caused more damage to the land through the years than any other force. Overgrazing, first at lower elevations, now on alpine meadows, has ruined millions of acres, removing plant cover, disrupting animal communities, and devastating the watershed.

The statement is often made by the cracker barrel and barbershop experts that predation, not the starved-out range, makes sheep raising impossible. But Durward Allen points out that "overgrazing sets vegetation back to early stages of succession, and hence ground squirrels, pocket gophers, woodrats, hares and rabbits are most plentiful on misused land. Likewise, more of such prey species may well contribute to coyote abundance." Or as Dr. Raymond Dasmann writes, "Monoculture over broad areas favors irruption of pests, as does any land use which greatly simplifies natural communities. For some of the more serious pests, such as ground squirrels and jackrabbits, habitat destruction often means simply protection of the land from overgrazing. A first step in any control is thus good land management." And good land management is a way of life which sheepmen, as a class, are just beginning to appreciate and accept.

One could take this a step further in an ethical review of history. Even after bison were eliminated from the plains to make way for domestic stock, the mountains could have provided a refuge if grazing had not become such big business. Should wolves, coyotes, and cougars be destroyed on public land so sheep may graze safely and the sheepman, a guest on the land, profit thereby?

Or to put it another way, had cougars remained to concentrate on their favorite prey, deer and elk, they would have left a part of the carcass for coyotes, bobcats, bears, and other meat-eating scavengers. These leftovers might have eliminated, or at least reduced, their need to make fresh kills in the barnyard. Or, to quote A. D. Coleman, of the Colorado Fish and Game Department, "Trapping and poisoning of the so-called predators for monetary gain, whether bounties to individuals or appropriations for officials, has been a racket for many years. With carnivores like bobcats, coyotes, foxes, and badgers killed off, rodent populations flourish and multiply, ruining untold acres of grasslands. The results are large rodent and grasshopper poisoning programs, and appropriations of more millions to control these real pests."

Predator control agents have been able to utilize a wide variety of weapons. They have dispatched the enemy with both sophisticated and guerrilla warfare: shooting from planes; hunting and gassing dens; actual physical strangulation (sometimes called "gopher choking"); chasing down the quarry with cars and dogs; setting steel traps (which the Leopold Report called one of the most damaging techniques since many animals besides the offender are likely to take the bait); setting cyanide guns, or "coyote getters," which shoot poison into a predator's mouth (or any other mouth, including a human's) when he touches a bait, and scattering suet pellets impregnated with strychnine over the countryside like wheat seed.

Poison has long been a special favorite. Strychnine, the old reliable, was first used in the 1850s when fur hunters turned to wolves and coyotes after decimating the beaver resource. A special trick in modern control is to inject strychnine into hens' eggs to catch coyotes and sometimes, by mistake, raccoons. Then came thallium, a highly toxic material developed by the Germans during World War I, guaranteeing a slow, agonizing death. For twenty years it was the main instrument in the arsenal of chemical warfare against predators.

The death toll rose; there must have been consciousness in control techniques, as biologists charged, but field men were eager to make their quotas and to qualify for elite "200 Clubs," reserved for those who could claim 200 coyotes to their credit.

The pinnacle of refinement, Compound 1080, sodium fluoracetate, was developed during World War II when red squill, or rat poison, was hard to get. It is tasteless, odorless, colorless, particularly lethal to members of the canine family; but man, too, is highly susceptible and it has caused human deaths—there is no known antidote.

The sequence in deploying 1080 against coyotes is as follows: first, the compound is dissolved in water and injected into a freshly killed horse, and is carried by the still active blood system through the entire carcass. Then, large chunks are placed at likely "stations" in the wilds during the late fall, presumably to be picked up in the spring, unless picked up earlier by the intended victim. The animal may go as far as 10 miles before dying. Any other which feeds at the dead carcass also becomes poisoned; it affects as many as five or more animals in a continuous chain reaction, including game species, in its toll. In this manner, predator control strikes not only its own target but the resource which sportsmen seek to conserve.

"Far more animals are being killed than would be required for effective protection of livestock, agricultural crops, wildland resources, and human welfare," the Leopold Report declared. "Control has developed into a semi-autonomous bureaucracy whose function in many localities bears scant relationship to real need and still less to scientific management."

This was no instant revelation. "I found out while writing my book," J. Frank Dobie, scholarly Texan and biographer of the coyote, warned years ago, "that the hierarchy of 'Control' care nothing at all except to keep killing and to keep increasing their jobs." Equally blunt are the words of Dean Coleman of Colorado: "In the wake of Compound 1080's dramatic discovery has followed widespread tragedy to wildlife, and almost unbelievable official incompetency, complacency, and concealment."

Now we have the "new look" in control. But how good is it? On the face of things, changes have been made for the better. The director of the new Division of Wildlife Services, Jack Berryman, is a respected biologist with a background of conservation activity in Utah, and a tough row to hoe in Washington. When the Interior Department endeavored to reduce the expenditure on control, the sheepmen's lobby in Congress restored it. When a regulation was announced

calling for a written justification wherever it becomes necessary to take a bear or
lion threatening livestock, an uproar of objection erupted among sheepmen
and politicians in Colorado, Utah, Wyoming, and New Mexico.

Nevertheless, advances are evident. Berryman has begun a program to
reeducate the field men. He has demoted some die-hard personnel and fired
others for continuing the indiscriminate control practices and for promoting
their services to state, county, and stockmen's associations. He has hired
college-trained biologists for work in Washington and in the field. In trying to
shift the agency's base of activity from predator control to wildlife in general, he
has taken on new responsibilities for habitat enhancement on Indian lands and
military reservations, and participates in surface mining studies and pesticide
surveillance. These programs are promising and deserve encouragement. . . .

The program, according to a recent statement of policy issued by the
Bureau of Sport Fisheries and Wildlife, will be directed "to insure the maintenance of the varied wildlife and wildlife habitats of the United States." It will
endeavor "to reduce animal depredations as selectively as possible, and to
direct control at the depredating individual or local depredating population . . .
when and where there is a demonstrated need." Above all, "Ecological principles must guide those situations where animal numbers must be regulated
or managed."

Unfortunately, the word is easier than the deed; there is no simple, sure
way of reshaping an old line agency in which concepts of "good" and "bad"
animals are deep-rooted, and extermination of the latter was given priority
status.

For example, according to James T. McBroom, Assistant Director of the
Bureau of Sport Fisheries and Wildlife, "It is a fact that coyotes kill sheep sometimes more than they can eat. This is the nature of the animal." Unquestionably
this is the nature of certain coyotes in certain circumstances; there are coyote
outlaws as there are human outlaws. But by failing to recognize variations, Mr.
McBroom perpetuates the ancient indictment of an entire species.

The same philosophy is found in the field, where the work is done. At a
hotel in Portland, Oregon, a promotional display selling the Division activities to the public showed a bobcat attacking a turkey; a coyote gloating over a
dead calf; a badger eating birds' eggs, and a farmer terror-stricken by a rabid
fox. For an agency presumably concerned with spreading ecological enlightenment this was a horror show.

What might have been shown?

Perhaps a healthy calf, with its mother nearby, having little or nothing to fear from coyotes. Most cattle ranchers, in fact, forbid predator hunters to operate with poison on their ranges; they want the coyotes left alone to clean up the carrion, and prevent over-abundance of rodents and rabbits that compete with stock for forage.

Perhaps the bobcat, timid and inoffensive as far as man is concerned, controlling gophers and mice, while the poultryman takes precautions in his physical setup to prevent intrusion from semi-wild dogs and cats, as well as wild predators.

The badger could be depicted by its new federal champions as an interesting and harmless creature, not only feeding on rodents but aiding soil formation by its burrowing. And the odds of a human catching rabies from foxes could be shown as one in a million, with insects, domestic and semi-domestic animals far more potent transmitters of the disease.

Above all, if the federal government is truly determined to set an example in proper management, in behalf of all the public, there should be no apology for the existence of predators in this civilized age. Nor of predation. We are all, in some sense, predators, from the pitcher plant feeding on insects, the lark devouring grasshoppers, the bass swallowing minnows, up to the higher mammals and man himself. Predation is an essential instrument in the harmonics of all living things; even more, predation is a beneficial instrument, a management tool, as man has learned by using predation of sport fishing and sport hunting to manage the numbers of animals and improve the species in the process.

The federal agency is much too committed to the principle of mechanical control. "We live in a synthetic environment, modified by the most complex civilization in the history of man," according to Jack Berryman. Therefore, he downgrades the balance of nature on the grounds that there is nothing left of the original balance. However, even before man touched America there was no status quo, or real balance, considering the effect of glacial ages, causing vegetation shifts and forcing animal species to adapt to new environments. "Balance" fluctuates as conditions of climate, soil, water, and other factors change their influences.

In its statement of policy, the Bureau of Sport Fisheries and Wildlife pledges to conduct studies in "animal ecology and life history biology, seeking alternate methods of control." But the reliance on poison continues and the research seems directed toward devising a better coyote-getter and coyote birth control chemicals, rather than toward habitat management or securing the place of all animals in the total fauna.

There is still, after all, the old urge to furnish a special service to a special-user group. So Bureau officials speak of the national parks as "reservoirs of predation," requiring extra control measures around their borders, instead of as laboratories of predator-prey relationships deserving buffer zones where predators are not subject to systematic control. The pity is that the National Park Service lacks the courage to stress enhancement of ecosystems with wide-scale reintroduction of predators into their native habitats. The wolf and mountain lion should be restored in fitting numbers to Yellowstone and Glacier, vast areas buffered by surrounding national forests. Certainly both these fascinating animals are needed to play their roles in management of the overstocked Yellowstone elk herd.

But officials and agencies are inclined to move slowly, rarely with daring. Reforms in predator control have come as the result of public pressure, rather than official initiative. That Forest Service and BLM land managers now have the authority to approve or reject proposed poison campaigns is not in itself impressive, considering that for years many of them, with notable exceptions, have abdicated their responsibility for wildlife habitat by accepting these campaigns. How they express their authority in the future is another question. Will they challenge each proposed bait station or trap until the need is clearly and fully demonstrated? Will they think of the short-range interest of the commodity user or long-range values of predator management and recreational potential?

In the Pacific Northwest today, both the BLM and the Forest Service have accepted widespread use of 1080 in timber country in order to kill mice, squirrels, and chipmunks that feed on seeds. This is the easy way. One land manager I know, however, has banned poison in his district; he prefers more predators not only to control rodents but to help harvest the surplus deer that browse and destroy young trees.

The Forest Service has cooperated with the states of Oregon, Idaho, Montana, Wisconsin, and Michigan in reintroducing the fisher, a weasel-like animal as large as a fox, decimated years ago by the fur hunters. It did so to provide a natural predator on the tree-girdling porcupine (though other reasons should have been present). Since most foresters consider the porcupine a major pest, the cougar's role should not be underestimated, since in many areas the porky ranks second to deer in that animal's food supply. It is perfectly true that the cougar is capable of inflicting serious damage on a band of sheep, but predation is usually confined to individuals, not the species. Even so, where sheep are grazed on public lands that are prime cougar habitat, in the name of multiple use and public interest should the cougar or the sheep be moved?

It is obvious that the nation needs both a new definition and a new evaluation of predation. We need to tear loose from the past with all its prejudice and seek a new yardstick. There is no doubt that the taxpayer has spent far more for predator control than he has received in economic benefit, but this isn't the point. We must measure benefits in terms of recreation, natural beauty, human integrity, and responsibility to resources of the American earth.

The sheepmen are incredibly ill-informed and backward on this question. They grasp at any straw to hold back the great movement toward morality. "As ranchers and farmers, we are basically conservationists, custodians of the land," James L. Powell, of San Angelo, Texas, a vice president of the National Woolgrowers Association, said to me in offering an explanation of why predators should be controlled. "Therefore we must see to it that wildlife doesn't overpopulate." I venture that some sheepmen haven't the foggiest notion of the fundamentals of animal behavior, though they have lived in the company of animals all their lives.

When Dr. Stanley A. Cain, one of this country's foremost ecologists, now Assistant Secretary of the Interior, and previously a member of the Leopold Board, appeared before the last convention of the Woolgrowers, he declared that "the livestock industry, with few exceptions, has not seen fit to invest in research and development." For his troubles he was greeted by a spokesman for the diehards, who said, to much cheering, that he would like to put a rope around Dr. Cain's neck and string him up.

But the fact is that neither the sheepmen, the Division of Wildlife Services, nor anybody else knows how many sheep are killed by predators, or what the cost-ratio of control may be. The best available figures on predator losses are maintained by the Forest Service in its annual grazing statistical report. But Dr. D. L. Rasmussen, director of the Forest Service's Division of Wildlife Management, admits, "It is a poor report at best, based on information from herders and owners, as well as observations of the rangers themselves. We need more objectivity."

No one can deny that lambs are taken by individual coyotes, mountain lions, and bears. However, it is sometimes difficult to tell the difference between a dog kill and a coyote kill. Coyotes are scavengers and will eat a stillborn animal or an afterbirth. Lamb losses occur from weather, disease, inadequate forage, a variety of causes; all of these are apt to be blamed on the sheepman's hated enemy, the predator.

But even sheepmen, or at least the more progressive and practical of their number, are capable of opening their minds to new ideas. They must realize that the politics of conservation are against them, that they are no longer alone on the public lands, that the day of enlightened management will dawn with or without them. As a result, the National Woolgrowers Association, despite the reception given Dr. Cain, supported its leadership and adopted resolutions favoring better research into predator-prey relationships. Even more, the Woolgrowers, who for years have been clamoring for the death of every eagle, entered into an agreement with the National Audubon Society, the defender of eagles, and the Bureau of Sport Fisheries and Wildlife for a joint $28,000 study into the movements and variations of eagle population and to lamb and kid losses resulting from their predation. The object of this study is to provide a scientific basis for whatever controls may be necessary. And there are sheepmen who would like to extend this cooperation into other areas. Who can tell, they may even take the next step and recognize the value of stability to the grazing range, where habits of wild animals can be predicted.

The states contributing to federal predator control, for one political reason or another, could insist that their money also be applied for research instead of poisons. South Dakota gives $121,000, Oregon $40,000, Nevada $40,000, Idaho $25,000 (with a stipulation that none of it be used for 1080)— good money that could hire biologists to improve wildlife habitat. Now, the states make cooperative grants to the federal government for predator control, but perhaps it would be more logical to reverse the procedure, considering that the states have responsibility for jurisdiction over all resident, nonmigratory indigenous wildlife.

The federal government should restrict itself to furnishing advice and leadership. This approach is provided in a bill presented to Congress last year by Rep. John Dingell, of Michigan, which would declare a national policy recognizing the wolf, coyote, mountain lion, lynx, bobcat, bear, and other large carnivores known as predators to be among "the wildlife resources of interest and value to the people of the United States." It would establish in each regional office of the Bureau of Sport Fisheries and Wildlife a position of "extension mammal-control agent" to provide advice and demonstrations to state-employed specialists in methods of instructing farmers and ranchers on how to prevent depredations.

The Dingell Bill is patterned after a system used in Missouri for twenty years with undeniable success. It began after the state had tried the federal trapper approach. During that period Missouri learned the best results came from trappers responding to requests of farmers with specific problems. These men were able to halt damage by catching the individual coyotes and other predators that were guilty of killing livestock. Losses over the years have declined dramatically; there are no longer loud complaints from any corner of the state. Farmers without damage do not waste their time chasing down imaginary or harmless predators. The system operates with one full-time control agent, a trapper and teacher, not a poisoner, who responds to requests from landowners for training assistance in eliminating guilty individuals. It is an efficient, economical system.

Most important, the Missouri Wildlife Code makes no distinction between predators and other forms of wildlife: the word predator is not mentioned. Control is conceived as a part of management to help the landowner solve his own problems through sound conservation practices. Publications and films explain predation as a necessary, beneficial part of life. The federal government has no documents like these.

The nation has a long way to go toward developing sound management of its predator resource. Research will prove a step in the right direction. Acceptance of the Missouri system by other states and a prohibition by law against the use of poisons with chain-reaction effects would be other positive steps. Placing sport hunting and trapping of predators on a sustained-yield basis could be a highly desirable form of resource use, certainly to be preferred over wholesale killing by professional hunters and waste of usable fur.

There is no single rule in predator control. As Dr. Durward Allen writes, "The answer is sometimes (locally and temporarily) yes, but more often (and in the long pull) no." The soundest rule will be written, of course, when the nation achieves a mature ethical, moral, and scientific evaluation of the predator's rightful role in its wildlife heritage.

The Most *Horribilis* of Them All

Defenders of Wildlife
February 1976

The grizzly bear has lately been elevated to a new status in modern society. The big bear of the West is now officially recognized as "a threatened species." This should come as welcome news to those who love wildlife for its own sake, since it means the bear is warranted federal protection under the Endangered Species Act.

But hold on here. Before rejoicing that all is well and the grizzly's future finally is secured, let's look closer and delve deeper. Maybe I'm just naturally suspicious, but studied observation over the years has raised serious doubts in my mind about the efficacy of agencies and officials in charge of wildlife policies and practices. Protection of species in need is somehow not an overpowering drive.

According to the Interior Department announcement designating the grizzly as a threatened species, old *Ursus arctos horribilis* is "an aggressive animal that is highly intolerant of man." It's this kind of prima facie assumption that disturbs me deeply. In behalf of the bear, I resent it. As the *Ursus* family knows too well, man is the most *horribilis* of them all. Man is the aggressive critter intolerant of absolutely anything that gets in his way.

From all I've read and reviewed, a bear rarely attacks unless wounded, provoked, or startled, or if it thinks its home, food supply, or family is in danger. When bears aren't bothered, they are less dangerous than most other animals. They prefer to avoid man.

Of course, any person who has traveled much in wild country has learned that every bear will act differently under different circumstances. They are never to be fully trusted since they are wild, but they certainly ought to be fully respected on their own terrain. Unfortunately, agencies and officials now presumed as grizzly guardians have long been involved in grizzly eradication rather than respect. But more of that later.

Once about 1.5 million of these giants roamed across the West, from the Mississippi River to the Pacific Ocean. Now there are no more than a thousand in the United States south of Alaska, likely only 600 to 700. There are several thousand still remaining in western Canada and Alaska, but within ten years, or even five years, it may be another story. Change is coming on very fast in those regions: with the encroachments of oil and gas pipelines, strip-mining and clearcut logging, the bear will have no place left.

During the early stages of contact in the nineteenth century, grizzlies were not hostile. So long as men exercised caution and restraint, and treated the grizzlies with respect, they would be safe. This was not to last, however. In the 1830s and '40s, the celebrated beaver trappers served not only to clear out the beaver, but to clean out the grizzly country as well. The Jim Bridgers were crude forerunners of civilization, making the West safe for wagon trains and the cities to follow. With repeating rifle and trap, they ended the saga of the great bears, those intelligent, powerful creatures, un-challenged monarchs since the Ice Age when they roamed the West with the mastodon and saber-toothed tiger.

In the 1830s, grizzlies in California numbered about 10,000. Then the slaughter began. A group of five professional hunters killed 700 grizzlies in a single year. One hunter alone killed 200. In the early 1920s the last grizzly was seen, and then there were none. This suggests to me that once the num-bers of the species are low, then total collapse is apt to follow quickly. Cer-tainly such tragedies have been proven in the history of other species. Insofar as the grizzly is concerned, my intuitive thought is reinforced by the warnings from Dr. Frank Craighead and Dr. John Craighead, the noted natural scien-tists and conservationists who probably know more about the grizzly than anyone else alive today.

"In two years, 1971 and 1972, we have recorded ninety-one grizzly bear deaths from all causes within the Yellowstone ecosystem. The death rate ac-cording to our data has been more than double the birth rate," John Craighead reported three years ago. "Our conclusion is that this population is in very serious trouble and a change in management practices is strongly indicated."

My theory of resource management is that the conservative approach is always best. If a respected authority, or a responsible segment of public opinion, raises some significant doubt or challenge, whether about clearcut logging, strip-mining, grizzly bears, or what have you, then the resource manager is well advised to take heed and follow the cautious, conservative approach to protect the resource. Let man's needs wait.

In the case of the grizzly, man's needs apparently cannot wait, not even in the age of endangerment. In Yellowstone last year, the park superintendent,

Jack Anderson, declared: "We're finding grizzly. My concern would be that because of a low sub-adult mortality the numbers might get too high." Numbers of grizzly bears too high? Too high for what? For human use and enjoyment of Yellowstone, of course.

The Interior Department responded to the Craigheads' plea by sponsoring a short-term review by the National Academy of Science. The subsequent report (August 1974) seemed to me inadequate, scarcely distinguished. The Academy committee found no evidence that Yellowstone bears are in "immediate danger of extinction," which made me wonder whether immediacy begins before or after the last bear is hung. The committee recommended prompt and adequate funding for a comprehensive research study on the grizzly by qualified independent scientists, a commendable idea in itself, though not much aid to the bear in the meantime.

The vestigial grizzly bear population is concentrated now in the wild rugged mountain country of the national forests and national parks of the northern Rockies. Three years ago the Forest Service furnished me with a rough estimate of 763 grizzlies in 16 national forests of Idaho, Montana, and Wyoming. The largest numbers are in the north-south corridor extending from the so-called Bob Marshall ecosystem, covering three million acres and embracing Glacier National Park at the Canadian border and the neighboring Bob Marshall Wilderness, down to Yellowstone and Grand Teton National Parks and the surrounding national forests. By far the greatest concentration is in the five-million-acre Yellowstone ecosystem, embracing the largest of our national parks, plus five bordering national forests (Gallatin, Shoshone, Custer, Teton, and Targhee). Here lies the grizzly's last major stronghold.

The trouble is that neither agency really has the protection of grizzlies as its mission or on its mind. The Park Service is in the business of serving people, not bears. So is the Congress to which the agency is responsible. This explains why there are now 25,000 snowmobiles roaring across the Yellowstone wildlands during a winter season, a traffic cloverleaf at Old Faithful, and an airport expansion under way in the heart of the Grand Tetons.

You may recall the twin tragedies of 1967 at Glacier National Park, when two campers were pulled from their sleeping bags, dragged off into the woods, and killed by grizzly bears. The consequence was the summary execution of two bears, alleged to be responsible and found guilty and executed without significant evidence against them. There were really no declarations from administrators that man is more dangerous to bears than bears to man, or that national parks are really wild places, and not manicured zoos.

The Forest Service controls the overwhelming abundance of grizzly habitat. This agency employs a number of biologists, but they exercise little authority as compared with the production-oriented foresters who run things. In modern forest management, wildlife come in last; thus, one grizzly area after another has been roaded and logged, destroying the bears' isolation and disrupting their food sources.

The Forest Service fought establishment in 1971 of the Lincoln-Scapegoat Wilderness in west central Montana, a 240,000-acre sanctuary of high mountain snowfields, rushing streams, and narrow valleys carpeted with wild flowers. The agency ignored the need to protect such rare and vanishing species as native cutthroat trout, wolverine, bald eagle, grizzly bear, and mountain lion that are wholly dependent on the wilderness environment. Instead, the Forest Service sought to develop the area for combined timber production and intensive recreational use, despite the steep gradients and shallow soils that should never be intensely developed.

Although citizen conservationists successfully pressed their case for wilderness in the Lincoln-Scapegoat, the Forest Service failed to learn its lesson. Even now, while Montana conservationists, supported by national organizations, have proposed establishment of the Great Bear Wilderness, in the Flathead River drainage of northwestern Montana, an unprotected vital link between Glacier National Park and the Bob Marshall Wilderness, the Forest Service is still unresponsive. John McGuire, chief of the Forest Service, has designated a part of the area for wilderness review as one of the "new study areas," but the acreage listed is minimal and much potential wilderness omitted.

The high, rugged backbone of the Rockies, characterized by steep slopes and erodible soils, should never be logged, mined, or roaded; such areas should not be grazed either. Wildlife habitat protection and wilderness recreation are compatible. Conservationists have urged the establishment of a new and independent agency, to be called the United States Wilderness Service; perhaps now is the time to bring it into being, with these critical wildlands under its administration.

It's very difficult to place one's trust or faith in the Department of the Interior, whose agents in the predator control division have, over the years, slaughtered bears by the thousands. From 1970 through 1973, according to the

Department's own figures, these agents killed eleven grizzlies in Montana alone, and five in Idaho. I have requested figures on possible killings elsewhere but cannot obtain them. . . .

Under the Endangered Species Act it is now unlawful to kill, capture, harm, harass, or export a grizzly bear anywhere in the lower 48 states, or to sell any parts or products of this type animal in interstate or foreign commerce. Such is the theory of the law. In actual practice, the rules promulgated by the Interior Department do indeed permit grizzlies to be taken "anytime they pose a threat to humans." The old predator control agents and state officers are authorized under terms of the rules to take bears when they consider it necessary "to prevent significant depredation on lawfully present livestock."

The emphasis is plainly on the protection of the commodity values implicit in the livestock, rather than the ethical, ecological, and scientific values in the grizzly. There is no differentiation as between depredations on public or private land, though it seems to me there should be absolutely no reason to kill a threatened species on public land except where there is an immediate threat to human safety or life.

It is utterly ludicrous to countenance sport hunting of a species at a time when it is considered to be threatened. Yet such is the case. Under the Interior regulations, grizzly hunting is permitted to continue in northwestern Montana so long as the total number of bears killed in a given year does not exceed 25. Most ludicrous of all is the official justification, as follows:

Permitting a small number of grizzlies to be hunted each year keeps such livestock predations and human confrontations at a minimum. It is essential for the continual survival of the grizzly bear species that it maintain its fear of man and thus its distance from man and never become accustomed to human activity.

Not a word there about keeping man, and his livestock, reasonably distant from bear activity. And needless to say, hunting in the remote wild areas is likely to put bears on the run, driving them into the settled areas where deeper trouble awaits them. Unfortunately, the concept of protection is sheer anathema to many a game biologist and manager. I was at a meeting of the Grizzly Bear Committee of the International Association of Game, Fish, and Conservation Commissioners in Portland, Oregon, in July, 1972, when several attendees threw up their hands at the very idea. As Don Brown, then director of fish and game in the state of Montana, declared, "This species could be 'protected' into extinction." His very words.

The grizzly bear is in grave peril, notwithstanding the promise of the Endangered Species Act; only the alertness of Americans who care, and of committed organizations like Defenders of Wildlife, can save it.

Federal and state agencies must be encouraged to fulfill their obligations to protect the great bear and its habitat. Under terms of the Endangered Species Act, public agencies are explicitly prohibited from taking any action (including issuance of leases and permits) that might lessen a threatened species' chance for survival. Destruction and encroachment threaten virtually all the national forests where the grizzly is found—destruction from copper mining, oil and gas exploration, logging, grazing, and road building—but the Forest Service needs to feel public pressure to fully apply the Endangered Species Act in the grizzly's behalf.

Moreover, there are large wilderness areas secure from drastic influences by man presently unoccupied by grizzlies but containing suitable habitat to meet their needs. According to Interior, bears are often difficult to remove or transplant. Maybe so, but serious efforts have not really been made. Reestablishing grizzly populations in remote areas where they once were indigenous in such places as Idaho, Colorado, Oregon, Washington, New Mexico, and perhaps others deserves high priority.

Here is one of God's creatures that runs like the wind, fishes better with bare teeth than any man with rod and reel, and roars like distant thunder. The grizzly is the embodiment of natural dignity. Let us set aside man's need and greed for a while and save the great bear. Surely, it has as much right to its place on this planet as have we.

Who's Managing the Managers
While They Manage the Wolves?

Defenders of Wildlife
June 1979

Professional wildlife managers have been vigorously complaining that their good works are simply not appreciated by uninformed "protectionists" among the public. The latest basis for their distress, of course, is the refusal of the unenlightened to appreciate all the benefits to man and beast of the infamous wolf "control" project in Alaska. Somehow, folks just won't understand.

The basic question as I see it is not one of hunting versus anti-hunting sentiment, as the wildlife management establishment would have it appear, but one of scientific management and resource husbandry versus unsound, politically directed, or politically acquiescent, pseudo-management clothed in mumbo-jumbo.

Consider the United States Fish and Wildlife Service: a weak, inbred bureaucracy that gave its blessing to and was ready to contribute federal funds for the extermination of Alaskan wolves. Yes, there are fine people in the FWS ranks, but almost all, or at least all that I know, are frustrated individuals, frustrated because of institutional ineptness, the unwillingness and incapability of the agency leadership either to chart a courageous, pro-wildlife course or to come to grips with environmental issues.

Yet FWS recently issued a brazen statement to the media through its Great Lakes Region, headlined "The American Hunter Is Hauled Into Kangaroo Court." The following excerpt represents the essence of this shockingly partisan outburst injected by a federal agency into an area of public controversy:

> *The great debate to kill or not to kill is the issue. A heritage and philosophy are systematically debased but not by evidence or fundamental common sense. Rather, the hunter hears a strange naiveté characteristic of ill-informed individuals trying desperately to rewrite their own history centuries after their origin as meat eaters.*

Officials in the top leadership control of the Fish and Wildlife Service and of many state game agencies are essentially narrow in vision, superficial in outlook, oriented to production of target species rather than to protection of life systems. They profess to represent the interests of hunters but do little to encourage true sportsmanship. The hunter is actually an exploited victim, encouraged to kill more game animals so the fish and game agencies can sell more licenses to meet rising operating costs.

Game commissions often are composed of political hacks and cronies, bearing little in common with the outdoorsmen they are presumably charged with serving. It doesn't take a Ph.D. in wildlife sciences to qualify for membership on a fish and game commission, but rather an appreciation of the outdoors and genuine concern for the resource, which one could expect from the true sportsman. Often, alas, appointments are passed around as political payoffs to those without valid background or interest who want something special for themselves. Commissioners are supposedly free of politics, but when the governor tells them what position he favors on an issue they generally take it. In such a climate the interest of the hunter is forgotten. The department itself is sorely deprived of sound public policy in a position of weakness rather than of strength.

The management syndrome can be used to cover a variety of sins. In the case of the proposed hunt at the Great Swamp National Wildlife Refuge in New Jersey, challenged in court before it was finally conducted, the Fish and Wildlife Service insisted there simply were too many deer for their own good. As the refuge manager declared in 1973, herd reduction was "fundamental to the preservation of the pristine uniqueness and natural beauty" of the designated wilderness in the heart of the refuge and to furnishing "suitable habitat for optimum numbers and variety of migratory birds and other wildlife." The words sound so—well, so professional. But, in fact, had the hunt been allowed to proceed as originally planned there would have been no centralized control over the age, health, experience, competence, and method of selection of the hunters; nor over the age, sex, and health of the deer selected to be shot. In short, no guarantee of culling the old, crippled, and unfit, or of sound management worthy of a wildlife sanctuary.

Too many managers do not deal in ecosystems, but rather in deer, moose, rabbits, or waterfowl. Their objective is to sustain or, better yet, to increase the "take." Once an ecosystem is impacted by man, it thus becomes justifiable to promote manipulation of plants and animals for the production of target species. The emphasis is placed on manipulation within an increasingly artificial environment, rather than on protection or restoration of a natural environment. It's this overpowering commitment to sheer consumptive use of nature that enmeshes management in so much public difficulty.

Such is the case in Alaska. According to the current policy on wolves of the Alaska Department of Fish and Game (ADFG): " . . . whenever substantial conflicts arise between humans and wolves over the use of prey the wolf population will be managed to minimize such conflicts." The prey refers to the moose, of course, and wolves are "managed" by reduction of their numbers. Over the past several years, the moose declined because of severe winters and hunting pressure, including hunting by snowmobile, an unsportsmanlike intrusion into nature. But apparently the idea of restricting snowmobiles and insisting that hunters prove themselves as sportsmen was not worthy of consideration.

Wildlife populations are under terrible duress in Alaska from highways, timber crews and foresters, pipelines that take precedence over everything, work camps, and planless growth for the profit of Alaska's budding economic power structure. With boomers anxious to build new cities, the elimination of the wolf is an issue of practical value. As Rep. Don Young, of Alaska, declared in their behalf in Washington: "Alaska is not a national possession to be managed by short-sighted outside residents with guilty consciences, but an autonomous state capable of handling its own affairs." Mr. Young marches behind the same banner that Western politicians have carried for years in order to insure preemption of the public rangelands by domestic livestock.

But why in the world should a wildlife resource agency fall in line and single out a particular species as the scapegoat for human mismanagement? Particularly in a land where wolves and moose have existed for centuries to the benefit of both? Sound wildlife management demands that control of predators be based on the evidence of specific predator pressure, rather than being conducted over a wide area without proven data. This principle was enunciated in the 1964 Leopold Report to the Secretary of the Interior and reinforced in the 1972 Cain Report to the Council on Environmental Quality and the Secretary of the Interior. And yet the ADFG is proposing wolf extirpation this year in three game management units covering over 10,000 square miles. It makes little sense and I should think wildlife professionals everywhere would object.

Such an unsound approach sets a poor precedent for game management throughout Alaska and elsewhere. It could mark the beginning of a long period of wolf hunting by air as a "management tool" and trigger demands for "control" wherever there is local feeling that deer herds are depleted. Already

Robert Henning, publisher of *Alaska Magazine*, one of the boomers of oil pipelines and like blessings, has editorialized as follows:

> *For the first time in Alaska game management history, to our knowledge, there are areas closed to the taking of deer this year. Two bad winters and wolves are the cause, each to varying degree, but cold logic tells us there were simply too many wolves to permit a weather-decimated deer herd to make its traditional rebound.*

For good measure, Mr. Henning added that in Southeast Alaska, when mountain goats have been driven by severe weather to feed and shelter at sea level, "the wolf takings of goats have been almost carnage." Actually, the "wolf takings of goats" would be peanuts compared to the killing of caribou along Alaska highways during migration. This kind of talk recalls the days early in the century when it was normal for sportsmen and naturalists to assume that the meat-eating mammals (called "predators") were the main cause of certain seasonal and cyclical variations in the number of animals which man may have wanted for his own enjoyment and profit. The key to successful game management was thought to be elimination of the species which preyed on the game. . . .

Moreover, it is basic biology that predator populations fluctuate behind those of the species they prey upon. If the moose population has been declining for several years, then the wolf population also must decline proportionately, with a small time lag. This biological control is automatic with many wild canids, and is affected by increased fighting both within and between packs, reduced birthrate, and reduced survival of pups. When conditions are right and the prey population increases once more, this will be followed by an increase in the predators. It seems logical to me that Alaska Fish and Game would first try to remove as many as possible of the other depressant influences on the moose population before turning to wolf control. There is no evidence that this has been done, or for that matter suggested by the U.S. Fish and Wildlife Service.

Part of the projected aerial extirpation of wolves in Alaska has been described and defended as a research effort. ADFG wants to kill off the wolves, then observe the effect on the moose. Research, in theory, is based on scientific method, but there is precious little science implicit in the ecologically disruptive Alaskan approach. Research at its best does not take into consideration politics, special customs or local hunting attitudes, but I fear these are precisely the vital considerations in Alaska today. Research biologists should feel free, and be encouraged, to express their findings fully and frankly, but I cannot believe, based on my personal experiences and acquaintanceships in Alaska, that this is the kind of "control" in the guise of research that ADFG field biologists really care to undertake.

On January 19, Lynn Greenwalt, Director of the Fish and Wildlife Service, suspended federal-aid funding of the Alaska wolf annihilation in a portion of "game management unit 13" until the requirements of the National Environmental Policy Act could be met and further studies made. This could have been a reluctant action on Mr. Greenwalt's part, induced by the pressures on the Interior Department by Defenders of Wildlife and other concerned citizen organizations, and by the wiser judgment of his superiors. Until then, FWS seemed perfectly content to ride along with the State of Alaska, without even serious question.

This in itself is disturbing. It makes one wonder who is minding the store in doling out to the states the millions of dollars provided by the Pittman-Robertson Act (the Federal Aid in Wildlife Restoration Act of 1937). According to the text of an expensive four-color brochure published last year by FWS titled "35 Years of Shared Wildlife Management," every project is scrutinized "to make sure that it fits within the carefully designed limits of approvability before a survey line is drawn and any Federal Aid dollars are spent." I can't imagine anyone of any competence critically reviewing the Alaska wolf control plan and then approving a single farthing of federal funds.

This isn't the first time I've had occasion to question the outlay of Pittman-Robertson money. In 1973, I went to Oklahoma in behalf of *Field & Stream* magazine to investigate the dismissal of three research biologists employed by the fish and game department of that state. They had been studying the status, habits and needs of deer, small game, waterfowl, and upland birds. Their recommendations, based on the best available biological data, were rejected by a provincial, politicized and unprofessionally run department. And the biologists were fired.

In behalf of the three biologists, the Oklahoma Wildlife Federation sought an expression of concern from the Fish and Wildlife Service, considering that the federal agency was providing funds for this state-conducted research project. At first, a regional FWS official indicated that $74,000 might have to be returned by Oklahoma if the research conducted by the three biologists could not be completed. But this viewpoint was not sustained in Washington. Theoretically, such underwritten research must be professionally sound and administered by competent individuals; in practice, this was a carte blanche grant to Oklahoma. And I daresay the same applies in Alaska.

Something is seriously wrong throughout the entire wildlife management establishment. The basic principles may be valid, but the practices have gone awry and the practitioners are hiding behind the technical jargon of their profession. For instance, the National Wildlife Federation declared its support of the Alaska aerial wolf hunt as sound research to establish management programs "designed to bring wolf and moose into a state of dynamic equilibrium." Balderdash. Then there is the fact sheet titled "Wolves in Alaska," now being disseminated by FWS Washington headquarters, which begins as follows: "The wolf is an important part of our country's native fauna. The Fish and Wildlife Service believes that all necessary steps should be taken to ensure its continued survival." The words sound right, but I know of no steps the agency is taking anywhere in behalf of the wolf.

The wolf is, in fact, a native American to be proud of, an integral part and symbol of our natural heritage. The wolf is an animal of endurance, courage, wisdom, and passionate loyalty to its own kind. This largest member of the dog family is not unfriendly to man and certainly it has important lessons to teach us, if we are willing to learn. With or without the support of the wildlife management establishment, concerned Americans hunters and "protectionists" alike are determined to save the wolf to demonstrate our worthiness as caretakers of the American earth.

Aldo Leopold defined game management as "the art of making land produce sustained animal crops of wild game for recreational use." On this basis, management may be regarded as the production of a game crop through manipulation of animals and vegetation. But this is only part of the game manager's role. "What he really labors for," wrote Leopold, "is to bring about a new attitude toward the land." When they concentrate on cultivating this new attitude, the game managers will no longer feel so overlooked and misunderstood.

Safeguarding the Greatest Concentration of Eagles on Earth

Los Angeles Times
September 16, 1979

To watch eagles perched in trees, sitting on rocks along the beaches or riding the winds in flight is one of the thrills of anybody's visit to southeast Alaska. But for how much longer?

There are five times as many eagles in this one region, known as the Panhandle, as in all the Lower 48 states combined. These great birds comprise a treasure that enriches Alaska and the entire nation. But for how much longer?

Alaska's Department of Natural Resources, the agency responsible for managing state-owned lands, has elected to launch a large-scale, long-term logging project across the heart of the scenic Chilkat Valley, one of the most unusual of all eagle areas.

This one section, of 7 or 8 miles along the Chilkat River, attracts the greatest concentration of eagles during fall and winter of any place on earth. At any given time there may be as many as 3,000, possibly even more, grouped in spectacular masses of 50 to 100 per tree.

By the time the logging is completed in 25 years, the eagle legacy will have been decimated, if not destroyed. It will doubtless rank as one of the major wildlife tragedies of history, all the worse considering the consequences are plainly known in advance.

The political leaders of Alaska, including Governor Jay Hammond, have criticized pending congressional legislation designed to protect vast areas of Alaska's wilderness frontier, arguing that the state can properly manage its own resources. But the Haines-Skagway Area Land Use Plan, one of the first such plans adopted by the Department of Natural Resources, hardly offers evidence to support the claim.

This plan provides for logging of a minimum of 10.2 million board feet a year. It commits virtually all available spruce and hemlock, requiring that significant watersheds now in natural condition be logged and roaded.

Although small tracts are reserved for "critical eagle habitat" and "public recreation," other tracts adjacent are to be sacrificed to logging. Biologists warn that eagles cannot be restricted to such man-made boundaries. Even at best, the sales contract stipulates that the state must meet its annual timber commitment, regardless of reservations for scenic purposes or habitat protection.

Alaska has been a long time in learning to appreciate its eagles. In times past the mighty raptor was damned by salmon fishermen who thought it preyed on their spawning fish and cursed by trappers and fur farmers who felt it dined too frequently on mink and weasel stocks.

Between 1917 and 1952 a bounty on eagles, ranging from 50 cents to $2 a bird, was claimed 128,000 times statewide. More than 100,000 birds were killed in southeast Alaska alone. In 1952 the territorial legislature terminated the bounty, but it wasn't until 1959 that the bird received the protection it had earlier won in the Lower 48 with the 1940 Bald Eagle Protection Act.

As many as 15,000 eagles live along the Panhandle's 30,000 miles of coast. There are nearly 7,000 nests, some 3,000 in use at once (compared with 800 known nests in the Lower 48). The eagle nest, or eyrie, built with endless additions of sticks and grass, must be in a sturdy old tree because it often measures 5 feet across and 10 feet deep. Once seen, it's a sight never forgotten.

The highest known density of eagle nests is on Admiralty Island, now to be protected from logging as a national monument administered by the Forest Service. About 1,100 nests, averaging almost two nests a mile, shelter an estimated 2,500 eagles.

What, then, makes the Chilkat Valley special? The eagles arrive in late fall, apparently drawn by the late salmon run on the ice-free waters of the Chilkat River. They roost and perch in the trees, and feed on spawned-out salmon long after other rivers are frozen. Most are drawn from nearby, but others arrive from as far off as Puget Sound, so the loss of the area would have far-reaching effects.

Alaska's naturalists and conservationists have pleaded with Governor Hammond to intercede, urging that he overrule the Department of Natural Resources and save the Chilkat Valley. They reason state-owned lands should be managed for the benefit of all Alaskans, present and future, and that consideration must be given to recreation, tourism, and commercial fishing (which depends upon clean water for salmon spawning and raising).

The object of the land-use plan presumably is to stimulate commerce in Haines by reviving a sawmill that hasn't been operating for more than two years. However, it denies consideration of other values and resources, such as Chilkat State Park, 5,400 acres of scenic beauty just coming into its own; the fabulous *Fairweather*, the new day-time cruise ship running on the Lynn Canal between Juneau and Skagway; and the history-rich Haines trading post noted for totem carving and Chilkat Indian ceremonial dancing.

Such places and activities are compatible with standing forests and roosting eagles. They complement each other, aesthetically and economically, instead of competing and dominating, as does intensive logging.

Alaska's officials would be well advised to review their position in advance of potentially harsh judgment by the nation and the world.

Owls, Logs, and Ecology

Defenders of Wildlife
May 1989

When a federal judge in mid-March ordered a halt to tree-cutting in parts of Washington State and set a June trial date, a headline read, "Loggers Feel Threatened by Spotted Owl." One might almost think the rare little night owl of the Northwest, *Strix occidentalis caurina*, the culprit in the case. That headline, after all, was followed by grim warnings from the timber industry and its political allies that 20 sawmills would close with a terrible loss of jobs—10,000 or 15,000, or even more considering the ripple effect extending from sawmill workers to shopkeepers and gasoline station attendants.

The spotted owl, however, is not on trial. The environment attorneys arguing on its behalf are not responsible for whatever plight, real or illusory, may befall Oregon and Washington loggers and their communities. On the contrary, defendants before the broader court of social justice are the timber tycoons who deserve to be tried and judged for undiluted corporate greed.

But they should not stand alone, any more than should Exxon for the catastrophic oil spill of late March in Prince William Sound. Big Oil and Big Timber both exemplify the basic design of 20th century industry to maximize profits. They may speak of community responsibility and environmental respect, but profit-making will always come first. On the other hand, government is equally culpable. Elected officials and administrative personnel answer in theory to a different board of directors. In practice, however, they align themselves with the principle that what's best for big business is best for America.

That principle doesn't work. Business wants to take everything now. But Gifford Pinchot early in this century gave the clarion call for higher goals. "Conservation is the foresighted utilization, preservation, and/or renewal of forests, waters, and lands and minerals, for the greatest good of the greatest number for the longest time," he said. "No generation can be allowed needlessly to damage or reduce the future general wealth and welfare by the way it uses or misuses any natural resource."

America has forgotten the message. Oil and timber resources would not be so heavily exploited if they were not so heavily consumed. "We are, after all, responding to market demand," timber and oil will plead in their own defense. And that is not an easy line to refute.

The spotted owl reminds us of the need to change direction, or at least slow down and review the options before plunging onward. Judge William L. Dwyer in Seattle, in ordering the U.S. Forest Service to halt all timber sales in 18,000 acres of owl country in Washington and Oregon for three months, served as the messenger of reason. He declared: "It's obvious that once habitat is destroyed, it cannot be replaced in any time frame that our generation can deal with. That, of course, demonstrates a form of irreparable harm. The trees in question have been growing for hundreds of years, and they will still be available for logging."

The spotted owl needs the old-growth forest, but little remains after a century of cutting—no more than 30 percent, perhaps as little as 10 percent. These ancient forests of the Cascades and Olympics, the forests of giants, are still the wonder of the Northwest. But they are largely within the federal timber reserves called national forests, public lands generously made available for private profit. The pace of destruction is quickening. At this rate, scarcely any old growth will survive for the next generation.

Enter the northern spotted owl, a relative of the eastern barred owl and the tawny owl of Europe, inhabiting mixed forest dominated by large conifers. In 1969 Eric Forsman, then a young technician working for the Forest Service, heard a pair of owls calling at night from the woods near his remote guard station. He became interested and learned to lure the shy birds by imitating their call. Later, as a graduate student at Oregon State University, Eric conducted scientific research funded by the Forest Service and designed to answer three questions: What are the spotted owl's range and habitat requirements? What is the effect of forest management? How can the species be perpetuated? Over a two-year span, Eric learned that spotted owls maintain and utilize the same roosting trees year after year, requiring terrain with mature forest dominated by Douglas-firs 200 to 600 years old—a dense multilayered forest with a canopy of old-growth foliage at the top and layers of shade-tolerant trees and other plants underneath. He recommended a staggered rotation of long cutting cycles to assure diversity of plants and perpetuation of old-growth timber.

The Forest Service did indeed make some effort to protect the spotted owl, but it was simply not enough. At best, by the admission of its own analysis (in an environmental impact statement), the chance of maintaining population viability over the next 50 years would be "moderate" and after 150 years "poor." The Forest Service designed a fragmented habitat for the spotted owl, somewhat like its approach of 20 years ago to the eagles of Admiralty Island in Southeast Alaska, which it proposed to protect by setting aside the specific trees in which eagles roosted with an acre or so around them, while logging everything else. That was another poor scheme, easily rejected.

Thus the spotted owl stands in the way of timber production—a blessing in the spirit of genuine multiple use, if you ask me. When the Forest Service says up to a third of its timber harvest in the Northwest could be halted, I suggest it's time to cheer. Unfortunately, the U.S. Fish and Wildlife Service (FWS) ignored its own scientific findings and decided not to place the spotted owl on the endangered species list. That is an especially sordid side of the story, which came to light with a report issued in February by the General Accounting Office (GAO), an investigative arm of Congress. As the GAO revealed, scientists of FWS (which determines the animals and plants requiring designation as threatened or endangered) had concluded that the spotted owl faces serious survival problems as a consequence of large-scale logging. But that portion of the report was deleted, evidently on direct orders of higher-ups at the Interior Department in Washington, D.C. It was a case of political interference in a decision supposedly based strictly on biological considerations. Judge Dwyer gave FWS until May 1st to explain in detail how it decided not to list the owl as endangered.

But there's still more to it. Rolf Wallenstrom, West Coast FWS regional director, was fired from his position. He went out with a blast, charging the Watt-Hodel crowd at Interior with punishing him and others for doing their jobs as wildlife professionals. Then James Cason, one of the political middlemen at Interior, was appointed by President Bush to become Assistant Secretary of Agriculture in charge of national forests. Wallenstrom let loose another blast, fingering Cason as one of the figures who pressured FWS not to list the spotted owl as endangered.

Little has changed, I fear, since Ronald Reagan and the Sagebrush Rebels rode into Washington with fire in their eyes and determination in their hearts to dismantle federal resource programs. Still, they have the courts to deal with. In addition to rulings involving the national forests, a court decision has halted logging of old-growth forest administered by the Bureau of Land Management in southern Oregon.

Yes, there are problems in sustaining employment in logging and sawmilling, but the spotted owl and its advocates are not responsible for them. For one thing, although timber companies like to talk about "meeting the wood needs of the nation" and providing housing for the urban needy as though public service were their mission, the truth is that they are feverishly shipping raw logs to Japan and elsewhere. While our mills here at home are scraping for leftovers, decks at Japanese mills are piled as high as Mt. Fuji, and those mills are running around the clock.

Federal law prohibits export of unfinished logs from federal forests. Consequently, the timber companies have cut everything on both their own lands and state lands for the overseas trade. In Washington State, the Department of Natural Resources takes the highest price for logs on extensive state-owned lands because the money helps finance public school construction—without a word on how the future is being denied its heritage.

Politicians conveniently ignore the facts and get carried away with the frenzy of mill closures. The Republican-controlled state senate adopted a resolution saying in effect, "Owls be damned, log the national forests." Democratic Governor Booth Gardner responded with his own proposal to increase federal timber harvests, at least until state-owned and private forests grow back. But they are not going to grow back in this century, and probably not in the 21st century, and maybe never, given the inclination of large timber companies to convert their cutover lands into subdivisions and real estate.

The small mills, meanwhile, unable to match the bids of foreign log buyers, are forced to close down or to depend wholly on national forests for their supplies. They in fact joined with conservationists in denouncing a proposal by Ronald Reagan, just before he left office, to permit the export of raw logs from the national forests.

The timber industry of the Northwest isn't what it used to be. Increased automation and mechanization in the woods and mills have taken away timber jobs that won't be restored no matter how many trees are cut. But the need to save the ancient forests is more critical than ever, not simply as habitat for the spotted owl or the other old-growth-dependent species, but as a testament of the maturity of the human species.

Places of scenic beauty are not increasing but are being reduced in number and diminished in quality. Our responsibility is to see that future generations enjoy the same opportunity for solitude and the same sense that nature, rather than humankind, prevails. I remember when I was a kid singing the lovely anthem that includes these lines: I love thy rocks and rills, Thy woods and templed hills. Consequently, I feel the responsibility of protecting whatever is left. The vestiges of God's Cascades and Olympics, indeed of the original America, are pretty darned puny. And God isn't making any more of them.

I recently rediscovered a meaningful and challenging statement by Charles Evans Hughes, then governor of New York and later chief justice of the United States, made at the dedication of Palisades Interstate Park early in this century. "Of what avail would be the benefits of gainful occupation, what would be the promise of prosperous communities, with wealth of products and freedom of exchange, were it not for the opportunities to cultivate the love of the beautiful? The preservation of the scenery of the Hudson is the highest duty with respect to this river imposed upon those who are the trustees of its manifold benefits," he declared.

Yea verily, we need beauty as a principle, to be advanced through the body politic, through public and private institutions and the professions, so that life may be more elevating and Americans may love their country more devotedly. Yes, I can adapt that idea into the practical. "Reasonable land stewardship includes the protection of soil, water quality, and fish and wildlife habitat," F. Dale Robertson, now chief of the Forest Service, declared in 1974 when he was supervisor of the Siuslaw National Forest in the Northwest. "Short-term economics will not override long-term needs of high-quality land management," he predicted.

We wait, along with the spotted owl, for that to happen. Let us work for it as well, through the many channels available in the democratic system, and by all means consuming less and saving more of the earth's resources along the way.

Vindication of the Craigheads

Defenders of Wildlife
July 1984

When someone says, "Oh, he's controversial," what is meant? Is this a way of discounting credibility, of suggesting someone is not to be trusted fully?

Having been labeled controversial myself a time or two, I can tell how I see it. I consider it my responsibility to lay the facts before the public without fear or favor. When those facts stir objection from authority or some powerful interest, then I am apt to become controversial.

Biologists involved in research and wildlife management should not be frightened or intimidated by controversy. They have a clear obligation, by the nature of their training and missions, to furnish the best available professional data and recommendations for decision-making. That is what they are paid to do—not to play politics or knuckle under to entrenched bureaucracy. Unfortunately, many of them are willing to shelter the facts while rising up the ladder as "team players."

The Craigheads, Frank and John, are the most controversial biologists of our time. To my knowledge, they never have compromised principle or taken the easy way out. Much has been written on the Craighead controversy and I don't mean to pursue it here, or to argue whether or not the garbage dumps in Yellowstone should have been closed. Even more important to me are the personal integrity and independent professional expression which Frank and John personify.

It was they who alerted the American people to the onrushing catastrophe of the grizzly bear. They noted in the early 1970s that the death rate of the bear in Yellowstone was running way ahead of the birth rate and warned: "The present management program, if continued, will very probably exterminate the Yellowstone grizzly population in about 20 to 25 years."

On the other hand, the National Park Service, its prestigious advisory groups (generally composed of experts who steer clear of controversy) and its parent the Department of the Interior insisted that the Yellowstone situation was not critical. On November 16, 1973, Assistant Secretary of the Interior Nathaniel P. Reed wrote me: "The grizzly bear population appears to be healthy and viable and maintaining itself in a wild, free-ranging state independent of garbage as a food source. Also, reproductive success was reported to be very good this year as compared with previous years."

That was the official position until August 1982, when Roland Wauer of the Park Service, chairman of the Interagency Grizzly Bear Steering Committee—one of those committees and commissions that seem interminably to deal with wildlife problems yet never solve them—issued a surprising memorandum. He completely reversed the official line. Echoing the Craigheads' warning of ten years before, he grimly predicted the bear's disappearance from Yellowstone unless major action was taken on its behalf.

Dr. Maurice Hornocker, my colleague at the University of Idaho who served for five years as a member of the Craighead research team in Yellowstone, was moved by the Wauer memorandum to write in *The Wildlifer*, organ of the Wildlife Society:

The Craigheads stuck to what they believed and paid a very dear price. Their research was stopped. A large segment of the profession ostracized them. They were criticized by many. Yet, on principle, they endured and never faltered in their position.

Many of the lasting contributions in biology and wildlife management have been made by individuals willing to endure criticism and hardship for what they believed. They have been capable of rising above professional jealousies, conflicting personalities, opposing agency positions, and non-support from their own organization or agency.

These individuals have placed the resource itself uppermost in their work and in their recommendations, regardless of any "agency" position. They have been men of principle, and because of this the rewards of their profession have been denied them. Yet most of us are employed by public agencies in which "going along" is rewarded far more frequently than any stand on principle. This is a sorry state of affairs.

Downright dismal, I would call it. Of course, an employee should be loyal to his employer, but how far must loyalty extend into one's own convictions and conscience? A biologist has the responsibility to stick to professional standards—that is what professionalism is about. Scientific data and valid research should never be withheld, distorted or suppressed, and certainly not to satisfy politics or bureaucracy. The welfare of wildlife depends on trained professionals willing to say what they believe.

Public confidence in the wildlife profession depends on willingness to speak out; so does public confidence in the federal and state agencies charged with protecting our wildlife heritage. As in the case of the Yellowstone grizzly, the truth ultimately must come out and the record written as it should be.

In 1973 during the height of the grizzly controversy, one of those "blue-ribbon" committees, this one representing the National Academy of Sciences, went to Montana. A Park Service scientist (name withheld, since he still works for the agency) addressed an earnest plea to the committee chairman, Ian McTaggart Cowan:

Your focus of interest is on the true status of the grizzly bear, but the magnitude and character of the controversy which you seek to resolve has evolved primarily because of the inability of the National Park Service to deal openly and honestly with viewpoints which conflict with those internally espoused by the agency. Such a situation will destroy not only the relationships between scientists and the National Park Service, it will continue to subvert the freedom of legitimate scientific investigation and the rational management of important natural resources.

In recent years there has been an increasing tendency on the part of the National Park Service to harass and eventually eliminate from the parks those whose data or interpretations of data do not coincide with those of the agency. The "manipulation" of data has become commonplace in some areas. In Glacier National Park, e.g., grizzly death statistics used by the park include only those bears killed within the park rather than a consideration of the ecosystem within which the bears operate. Grizzlies from the park are killed each year outside in the North Fork area and West Glacier area. Whether these losses are significant or not is not known, but they are real and should be considered rather than administratively excluded. False information on grizzly management actions within the park has been deliberately released to the press for the purpose of "good pubic relations."

I don't mean to single out the Park Service, though Yellowstone, Glacier and their environs are the keys to grizzly survival in the lower 48 states. There is plenty of responsibility to go around. Federal and state officials attend meetings of interagency committees and issue reports to show all they are doing, when very little, if anything, changes except on paper.

The Hornocker statement in *The Wildlifer* was followed by one from Robert B. Finley, Jr., now a research associate at the University of Colorado Museum. Finley was a section chief in the U.S. Fish and Wildlife Service's

Denver Wildlife Service Center from 1972 to 1974, during the period when the Interagency Grizzly Bear Study Team was established.

As Finley noted, a biologist in his section, Bob Phillips, was the Fish and Wildlife Service member of the team. But it quickly became apparent that the team leader was expected to run things in a way that gave support to the policies of Yellowstone National Park. Views of other team members were overruled or ignored, and Phillips was unable to get access to original data on which the Park Service claims were based.

When Finley wrote to the park superintendent attempting to win some loosening of restrictions, Phillips and other dissenting agency biologists on the study team were excluded from working in the park. In August 1973, Finley himself was removed from supervisory responsibility over Phillips, who thereafter took his orders from Washington. This led Finley to declare: "My efforts to promote a sound research effort convinced me that the Department of the Interior was more interested in suppressing disagreement than in finding the truth or in saving grizzlies. I agree that the Craigheads have been vindicated, but I am not so sanguine as Hornocker when he says, 'Now, presumably, the Craigheads' recommendations will be followed.' My experience indicates that research is likely to be mismanaged until the last bear has been counted."

That must not be. The public has shown its concern over the future of the grizzly bear and all wildlife, creating a climate favorable to biologists with commitment and conviction. We need wildlifers ready and able to communicate with a constituency more than willing to support them. Chances are it would lead to controversy, but it might also save the wildlife. Isn't that the role professionalism claims to play?

Wolves Make Whole the Family of the Land

Defenders of Wildlife
May 1983

When the first Europeans arrived, wolves lived everywhere in North America, from the polar regions to the tropics of Mexico. They were most numerous where sources of meat were plentiful, particularly in the deer forests and on the buffalo plains. Daniel Boone noted wolves in his native Yadkin Valley of western North Carolina, where he also saw panthers, wildcats, and even a few buffalo.

In barely three centuries, the abundant and varied wildlife of the New World has been sharply reduced, with many species gone forever or at the brink of oblivion. To observe living panthers, wildcats, and buffalo, most Americans must visit unnatural settings called zoos. There it is also possible, of course, to see wolves, those intrepid travelers of the wild, restricted to caged journeys to utterly nowhere.

Few timber wolves remain in natural environments anywhere in the United States, probably fewer than 1,300 outside Alaska. The smaller red wolves, which a few years ago appeared to have a chance in southern states, are now listed by the federal government as extinct. Significant concentrations of wolves in the lower 48 are found only in Isle Royale National Park in Lake Superior and the Superior National Forest in northern Minnesota. Wolves in appreciable numbers are found in Alaska and Canada, but they are increasingly subject to the stresses of civilization. More than 1,000 wolves are killed yearly in Alaska, including those taken by the Alaska Department of Fish and Game to curb alleged depredation of big-game. Many Canadian provinces conduct regular wolf control programs. A few years ago, in fact, I saw photographs of dead Canadian wolves in massive piles.

I am writing of wolves now because our generation has the opportunity, as well as responsibility, to make restitution for mistakes and sins of the past. There are wolves or a potential for wolves in areas other than those mentioned. Under the Endangered Species Act of 1973, tentative first steps have been taken to provide some small sanctuary. These steps need encouragement and support, particularly in the West, where the wolf has its best chance.

Wolf hatred is deep-rooted, and that is the problem. The dog is called man's best friend, but man detests the dog's wild cousins. It was the "wicked wolf" that ate Red Riding Hood's grandmother and the "big bad wolf" that tried to eat the three little pigs. The coyote has been labeled cowardly and cruel. The sounds and songs of a wolf family have been called "blood-curdling," shrill, the "menace of a howling pack," when they are none of these. Such terms of superstition and fable are born of misunderstanding, prejudice against the unknown, and sheer ignorance.

When the tide of the nation moved west, wild animals stood in the path of settlement. Certain species were useful, but others, such as the coyote, wolf, grizzly, wolverine and badger, new and strange to pioneers, were considered vermin or varmints, to be eradicated whenever possible.

The wolf—well, the wolf kills for food. That is its crime. It uses its teeth, the instruments nature designed for it, and does the killing itself, close to the heart of nature. We kill for food, too, but conveniently have someone else at the slaughterhouse do it for us. Wolves are not generally hostile to humans, despite endless unsubstantiated myths about attacks on children and the like. They were domesticated by the Indians, serving as sled dogs and beasts of burden. Adolph Murie, the noted biologist, once tried a singular experiment in the Alaska wilds. He crawled through the entrance tunnel of a wolf den and tenderly withdrew a pup while its parents stood back and watched. I've often thought that a wolf passing my tent in the woods would be less likely to attack than some stranger on a city street.

The male of the species is renowned as one who mates for life and as a devoted provider. When he disgorges food from his stomach to feed his pups, it is almost in the same condition as when he swallowed it. It is one of nature's wonders. No one knows how the wolf can stop its digestive process while bringing home a meal.

Before the white man arrived, wolves fed on a variety of animals, ranging from large ungulates such as elk, deer, moose, and caribou to mice and rabbits. They all played their roles in nature. But the cowman, sheepman, buffalo hunter, bounty hunter, and trader in skins marched across the continent, leaving destruction in their path. Native wildlife was slaughtered by the millions, yet the wolf was denounced as "the beast of waste and desolation."

Deprived of natural food sources, the wolf turned to prey on domestic stock—horses, cows, and sheep—and thus became an object of intense western hatred. Professional "wolfers" spread strychnine across forests and plains in meat baits. Bounty hunters pursued one of the greatest rackets in history, collecting as much as $200 per animal, even when substituting dog scalps for wolves' and selling the same scalps over and over.

Then came an even bigger racket, the federal predator control bureaucracy. Sordid techniques devised by government agents included staking out a wolf reared in captivity to attract a wild one and spreading baits containing the chemical thallium, which caused a slow, agonizing death.

Taxpayers everywhere contributed unknowingly to the war on wolves and all the other predators, though it served only the interest of a few stockmen, principally sheep growers. Wolves, in fact, might have survived in the West's wilderness if sheepmen had not moved in. Though targeted for extermination, wolves did much less damage to the resource than the vast roving bands of sheep stripping the protective layer from the soil.

Now the public has the chance to define a new priority. The Northern Rocky Mountain Wolf Recovery Team has identified the three key areas where wolves can still make it. One is in northwestern Montana, centered on Glacier National Park and bordering national forest wilderness areas, where wolf activity has been detected for many years. Second is central Idaho, where national forests have been the scene of continued wolf sightings in recent years. Third is the Yellowstone ecosystem, embracing the great national park and surrounding public lands. Despite no recent evidence of wolf presence, this area is considered a logical first choice for transplanting.

Tradition dies hard, and the idea of giving the wolf a break has stirred some local opposition. A few hunters complain that wolves as well as grizzly bears threaten deer and elk herds, though enlightened sportsmen know better. Loggers don't like to recognize that multiple use of national forests involves yielding here and there for wildlife, all kinds of wildlife. Stockmen fear for their investment.

Through the influence of these groups, Senator James McClure of Idaho tacked an amendment onto the Interior Department's appropriation bill during the waning days of the last Congress. The amendment provides that critical Idaho habitat identified for wolves must be within the boundaries of central Idaho wilderness areas. Fortunately, this will only affect wolf studies in Idaho during the fiscal year covered in the bill.

These actions demonstrate the need for educational activity and expression of other viewpoints. But there is more reason for hope than despair. Referring to the stockmen's apprehension over wolves, Bill Geoffroy, an outdoor columnist of the *Lewiston* (Idaho) *Tribune*, writes: "This is probably a justifiable concern. If wolves trespass on private land and in the process kill cattle or sheep, there is no question in my mind that they should be dealt with like any other marauding predator. On the other hand, when we're talking about public land, national forest land, I feel certain that the wolves have as much right to be there as privately owned cattle or sheep. I would rather have wolves on my share of the forest."

Geoffroy also wrote, "The possibility of wolves adds a new dimension to the back country." That is true. Wolves make whole the family of the land and demonstrate an ethical approach. Just as a drained pond cannot support fish, a disturbed wilderness cannot support wolves. How fortunate we are that wild places remain where wolves can play their role in balance with elk, deer, moose, and other animals. How foolish we would be to miss our opportunity and responsibility.

The wolf is an animal known for its endurance. It expresses the living history of the continent. During the 19th century wolves were unwary and easy to trap and poison, for they were unafraid. I've read that they trusted man. Now in the 20th century it is time to justify their trust.

CHAPTER IV

HOW MUCH IS ACCOMPLISHED BY SO FEW

An Associated Press dispatch of October 10, 1972 cited a statement presented to the seventh World Forestry Congress in Buenos Aires by three American conservation leaders of that time—William E. Towell of the American Forestry Association, Daniel A. Poole of the Wildlife Management Institute, and Thomas L. Kimball of the National Wildlife Federation—charging that uninformed "extremists" harm the environmental cause more than they help it. They declared jointly:

> *Our new generation of city-raised young adults is running on the land*

*they have not known and claiming it as their own. Few understand the
dynamism of living things and seek to arrest natural succession.*

*Most oppose hunting, mining, tree cutting, recreational-vehicle use, live-
stock grazing or the use of any renewable resource, for that matter.*

They're entitled to their view, but experience has taught me that what they
derided as extremism, or what I call citizen activism, is absolutely critical to the
environmental cause. Hunting, mining, tree cutting, recreational-vehicle use,
livestock grazing, all those *need* to be challenged by a caring, concerned public,
whether by individuals or collectively by groups. But then, in my years in
Washington, D.C., I knew Towell, Poole, and Kimball as old-guard conserva-
tives who hewed to the status quo and had little actual contact with ordinary
citizens in the communities and at the crossroads of the country.

Yet the fundamental issues are at the community level. I've watched
democracy start with community action, scarcely ever with answers from above.
True enough, the environmental crisis is global, which means that government
must have a role, along with universities, the media, science, and organizations, but the critical role belongs to people exercising citizenship. Government has a way of beguiling communities and their citizens into believing
they are being protected, into thinking they have a say in the process. Business interests usually have the larger say by far, but government has become a
self-sustaining entity of its own, apart from people. Scientific experts, educators, the media, large environmental groups, and others help prop up the
structure, when the whole system needs changing. Institutional change begins
with the people directly affected. Community involvement enables people to
analyze problems, test ideas, learn from the experience of others, and feel
empowered. That is the best way.

I remember that Towell was executive vice president of the American
Forestry Association while Charles Connaughton, regional chief of the Forest
Service in the Northwest, was president of the association. When Connaughton
retired from federal service he found new employment as vice president of the
Western Wood Products Association (WWPA). This led Brock Evans, Northwest representative of the Sierra Club, in a personal letter to me to comment
as follows:

*His record here was one of the utmost contempt for environmentalists
and environmental values. He only kept one appointment with me in all the
years he was here, and canceled many others at the last minute. He rejected*

appeal after appeal from us on timber sales in such critical areas as French
Pete Creek and the Mt. Jefferson area. He traveled around the state saying
that he was "not about to preside over the demise of the national forests"; at
the same time he bent every effort to accelerate the rate of logging, even in
critical areas.

WWPA is probably the most virulent and anti-wilderness of all the
forestry industry lobbying associations, and is one of our prime opponents
out here.

Organizations and associations ranging from Western Wood Products and
American Forestry to the Sierra Club and Earth First! may vary widely in their
goals, but they still share essential characteristics. All are based on membership
and a structure of one kind or another, and all, even volunteer groups, need
to pay their bills. The larger they grow the more complex they become, their
defined principles apt to be clouded by factors of finance, personalities, and
politics. It's another story with individuals, especially with individualists, who
intuitively answer to their own conscience.

Such people make a difference, rising above themselves, and above institutions, challenging an entrenched system without hope or design on their
part for material reward. Over the years I've been blessed with the opportunity to observe and record the efforts of unsung heroes and heroines, often
timid or frustrated at first, but emboldened by commitment and belief.

For example, one day about thirty years ago, Ed Chaney came down to my
house outside of Washington, the same Ed Chaney who in recent years has been
fearlessly leading the fight from Idaho to save the endangered salmon. I don't
mean that he used to be timid. In those days he was doing an excellent job as a
writer for the National Wildlife Federation. He told me of his discontent with
the lack of conservation consciousness around him at the federation, and he
cried, a great big guy in tears. He said he didn't believe anybody working in the
conservation movement should make more than $20,000 a year.

I thought of Ed while writing the piece which in this book I call "The
Environmental Movement at Midlife" (*Western Outdoors* titled it "Fat Cats
Among the Conservationists")—maybe now he would tolerate salaries of
$60,000. I would allow a little more, but I see no rationale in the environ-
mental movement for salaries much over $100,000. What can those people
do with their money, except practice conspicuous consumption in safe, sani-
tized suburbs? When Jay Hair precipitously departed the National Wildlife
Federation in mid-1995, following a stormy showdown with federation

directors, he was making considerably more than the figure I quoted, yet left the federation at a lower point than he found it. The rationale that "We need to pay more to get good, qualified people" is sheer myth.

Environmental professionalism ought to be more a cause than a career; it should be practiced by men and women who have risked and sacrificed, who have listened and learned on the ground, where the issues are found and fought. I respect the "nationals"; they have their place and we need them, but whenever I go to Washington to make the environmental rounds, I find the large groups to be institutionalized, staffed by bright young people from our best colleges and universities, where they have been properly prepared by lessons in objectivity and how to get ahead. I also see evidence of cynicism, jealousy, snobbery, and mean-spiritedness among people presumably working toward common goals. It isn't right for those trying to save the world to think hurtfully or condescendingly of others.

It isn't that way with the unsung heroes. Gordon Robinson, for example, to my knowledge was the first forester to break ranks with the prevailing position of his profession regarding clearcutting. Because he challenged the validity of clearcutting and warned the public against it, he was roundly detested and treated like a pariah. Still, there was nothing mean about him. For twenty-seven years, from 1939 to 1966, Gordon managed 730,000 acres of land-grant forest for the Southern Pacific Railroad, relying on the practical forestry principle of sustained yield and earning a fair profit for his employer. Then, as staff forester for the Sierra Club, he felt blessed to discover the work he should have been doing long before: studying and commenting on forest plans, testifying at public hearings, teaching citizens the ways of "excellent forestry." Little wonder the timber-first foresters despised him. In a correspondence dated September 17, 1971, he wrote:

> *Most unfortunately, public inspiration and enjoyment of a walk up Redwood Creek is today seriously marred by logging. All three of the major timber companies that own land in Redwood Creek outside the Redwood Park are conducting clearcutting operations and are heavily engaged in the most destructive logging operations that have ever occurred in human history.*

Gordon was creative and talented. For years he was a wine maker at home across the bay from San Francisco. He studied art, producing paintings that are soft, gentle, free-flowing, spirited, much like Gordon himself. In the book *Sterile Forest,* largely about a celebrated 1976 trial over clearcutting in the Texas national forests, Ned Fritz wrote:

On the stand, Robinson looked less like a forester than an artist: a little aesthete with a flowing white beard, big tummy and cultured voice.

And earlier (while plans for the trial took shape):

As Gordon conversed, I realized that while this man used the words of a forester, he was different from all the foresters I had known. His voice was cultured. He backed up many of his statements with references to articles in professional journals. He often pointed out the argument on the other side.

That trial was something special in itself. Ned Fritz was a Dallas lawyer who felt a void in the established environmental organizations so he founded the Texas Committee on Natural Resources, which became the plaintiff in the case (suing the Forest Service for clearcutting in a wilderness study area). Fritz brought as expert witnesses Gordon Robinson and Charles H. Stoddard, former director of the Bureau of Land Management, two of the few foresters of their time who dared to break ranks over clearcutting. Actually, there isn't anything of consequence in the current "new forestry" and "ecosystem management" that they weren't advocating then. The citizens won the case in federal district court, but then lost in the appeals court.

Gordon went around the country working unpretentiously with local groups and individual citizens. He wrote a book, *The Forest and the Trees*, to encourage practical public input in decision making. Gordon followed his conscience until he died in 1994, but individuality and personal freedom were clearly at the root of it. Once he shared with me a letter he wrote to the San Francisco papers during the McCarthy witch hunt era:

To sign a loyalty oath or to salute a flag or recite a creed is not a demonstration of loyalty but an act of submission; free people just don't submit.

And again, on what he really learned from art:

I found that the self esteem, and the courage to be, that arose out of becoming an artist, carried over into everything else I do.

Maybe exercising the courage to *be* is what it's all about, rather than attaining something demonstrable or tangible. Society has a long, long way to go to appreciate all that we have to give to each other and to learn from each other. That is true, but resentment leads only to frustration and the yielding of power to another. On the other hand, working to make a difference, in a positive way, helps us to understand that efforts and energies are rewarded, that trying in itself makes a person whole and worthy.

Beulah Edmiston, who lived in Southern California, was that way. Nothing could stop her once she took on the cause of the tule elk, smallest of the

North American wapiti. Once thousands roamed the central and coastal valleys of California, but with the gold rush their habitat was invaded; the dwarf elk were shot for food and fun and were virtually eliminated. When Edmiston entered the scene in the 1960s, the remnant elk were reduced to their last refuge in the Owens Valley, east of the Sierra crest. They were subject to continual harassment, including legal slaughter designed by state game managers to keep their numbers down to 300. In her efforts through Friends of the Tule Elk, Edmiston challenged trained professionals and demanded they grant as much consideration to the wild wapiti as to domestic livestock on the same range. Through force of will, she stirred public support, stopped the slaughter, and ultimately won protection in various parts of California for 2,000 tule elk.

Charles S. Watson, Jr., is another example. In 1995 Charlie was probably the best known and most effective environmentalist in Nevada, living in a trailer in Carson City, from which he conducted the affairs of the Nevada Outdoor Recreation Association (NORA). NORA has a board of directors and actual dues-paying members, but essentially it's the vehicle through which Charlie has fought long and lonely wars against political giveaways of the public domain administered by the Bureau of Land Management, for which he once worked. In the early 1970s, he fought the Reagan-Watt Sagebrush Rebellion. In June 1994 he testified in Reno at a Department of the Interior hearing on what it called "Rangeland Reform '94." In NORA's quarterly newsletter, he reported:

Not one Nevada organization came to urge the abolishment of the cows [removal of livestock from the public range]. The true issue with us was meaningful reform. NORA testified that it was tragic for an advanced nation like America to have allowed desertification to run rampant over our native grasslands for over a century.

We called desertification a rank insult to any self-respecting fiscal conservative. Low fees, we said, have actually helped exacerbate U.S. deficit spending while at the same time encouraging welfare ranching.

In 1995, after congressional Republicans introduced legislation to yield control of 200 million acres of BLM and national forest land to livestock grazing permittees and to transfer designated BLM wilderness to the states, Charlie wrote in the newsletter: "We've been warning everybody about this for the last 19 years."

Alaska has had its share of unsung heroes, who warned everybody for years. You'll read in the following pages about Karl Lane, the big-game guide, and his defense of Admiralty Island. Others I knew were Jack Calvin of Sitka, who saved the Chichagof Island wilderness, Harry Merriam, the state game biologist who was punished for his professional view (later wholly validated) that clearcut logging would destroy the old growth that Sitka deer need in winter, and Bob Baade, the state fisheries biologist who showed me logging devastation that wiped out fishing environments on Prince of Wales Island. Baade felt the displeasure of his bosses for the activities of his wife, Dixie. As a public health professional at the government laboratory at Ketchikan, she became concerned in the 1950s over pollution caused by the pulp mills and later was instrumental in gaining designation of Misty Fjords National Monument, one of the marvels of this continent. In those years there was little organized effort to protect the environment in Alaska, largest and last of the frontier states. It's amazing to me how much of what is now taken for granted by so many was achieved by so few.

Those people, and many more like them throughout the West, have learned there's no limit to what an individual can accomplish as long as he or she doesn't care who gets the credit. The great calamity is not to have failed but to have failed to try. Some of the national organizations conduct leadership training programs, which is all to the good, yet they need to emphasize the qualities of humility and humor, of leading by example, the example of commitment and caring, free of vanity, always trading in hope, never in despair, sticking to issues without getting involved in the pettiness of personalities, concern with purpose rather than professional recognition or payroll benefits and perks. The citizen activist spends his or her own money in the effort and never thinks a thought about it because it's not a job but an opportunity for fulfillment.

Brandy, Preaching Power to the People

Sierra Club Bulletin
March 1978

You may find it hard to believe, based on present performance, but sound forestry began in America as part of the muckraking, trust-busting social crusade of the early years of this century. Gifford Pinchot, pioneer forester and close ally of Theodore Roosevelt, foresaw conservation as the foundation of a national destiny of freedom and brotherhood. Sound forestry was to be not a technical end in itself, but a wedge in the fight "against the control of government by Big Money."

This kind of life was made for Guy M. Brandborg, a two-fisted populist if ever there was one. In 1914, at the age of 21, he joined the Forest Service. At that time the fledgling outfit was loaded with Pinchot's disciples, a breed of idealists determined to halt destruction of the forests by free-wheeling timber barons and to rescue the grasslands from cattlemen's anarchy. Imbued with the idea that all wealth comes from the earth, Brandborg committed himself through 40 years in the Forest Service and retirement thereafter to leaving the land and its resources in better condition than he found them.

"Brandy" departed this world in March 1977 with little baggage. His body he willed to medical research; his ideals which he had drawn from Pinchot, to disciples of his own. He was an absolute original among foresters and grassroots activists, and his kind of inspiration never dies.

For twenty years Brandy was supervisor of the Bitterroot National Forest, and when he retired in Hamilton, in the heart of the valley, he could view the results of this work with pride—that is, until the Forest Service shifted gears from resource protection with conservative use to intensive exploitation without protection. Nowadays a supervisor spends only two or three years in charge of a forest, so he doesn't have the sense of belonging or of lasting responsibility for his actions.

Brandy exercised amazingly wide influence from his own country corner. He raised a son, Stewart, who became executive director of the Wilderness Society and is now an official of the Interior Department in Washington. Sierra Club staffers such as Gordon Robinson, Brock Evans, and Doug Scott

came to western Montana to counsel with the old sage as well as to see the
Bitterroot through his eyes. Folks in his own state—in the Montana Wilderness Association, the Wildlife Federation, faculty and students at the University (50 miles north at Missoula), public officials and thoughtful people all
over Montana—looked up to Brandy with admiration and warmth.

Brandy also had an uncanny touch with writers. Among these were Bernard DeVoto, who first visited in the late 1940s for his "Easy Chair" column
in *Harper's*, correspondents for the *New York Times, Washington Post* and
CBS, who came twenty years later for Brandy's views on clearcutting in the
Bitterroot.

In my own case, his ideas run like a thread through columns I wrote in
American Forests and *Field & Stream*. From one end of the country to the
other, everywhere I looked in the 1960s and early 1970s, the Forest Service
was on the wrong side of environmental issues—from Admiralty Island in
Alaska, down through the redwoods and Mineral King in California, Big
Thicket in Texas, Bitterroot in Montana, to the Monongahela in West Virginia. Brandy helped me to evoke forceful protest against squandering the
heritage of our forest for greed and gain. Though I lost my columns one after
another, it was well worth the fight.

Brandy had a way of linking little issues to big ones and particular contro-
versies to principles of social and economic consequence. He was a mover
who got things done. The fight he sparked over the Bitterroot led to an investigation by a committee of the University of Montana Forestry School (at the
request of Senator Lee Metcalf) and subsequently to the 1971 Washington
Senate hearings on clearcutting. Even near the end he was brewing a new plan
to bring President Carter face to face with the continued mismanagement of
our public forests.

He was never vindictive, never personal, never (to my knowledge) pessi-
mistic. Despite harsh treatment by the Forest Service leadership—which tried
to dismiss him as "a disgruntled ex-employee"—workers in the ranks cheered
him, hoping he could get the old outfit back on course.

Like Pinchot, he believed that exhaustion of resources leads nations to
poverty and war—and that protection of the land and its resources makes for
peace and begins with the forests. Both saw forestry as the leading activist
edge of social reform.

Brandy was a born-again evangelist of our time, preaching that society too must be born again, out of an economy based on exploitation into an economy of conservation.

Pinchot said: "There is no reason why the American people should not take into their hands again the full political power which is theirs by right and which they exercised before the special interests began to nullify the will of the majority." G. M. Brandborg believed in power to the people. He had lofty visions and left us challenges that give purpose and meaning to life.

Horace Looked For and Found the Good in People

Foreword to *The Conservators of Hope: The Horace M. Albright Conservation Lectures*. University of Idaho Press, 1988

The genius of Horace M. Albright was in his human touch. I saw this manifested over and over again. In his lifetime he received abundant awards and accolades, even including the Presidential Medal of Freedom and, as late as 1986, the John Muir Award from the Sierra Club. But he never lost the touch. In retrospect, I see the human touch as his strength and his power, derived perhaps from his roots in the Owens Valley of California, but even more from his belief in his fellow men and women. He looked for and found the good in people, individually and collectively.

Horace Marden Albright did more to advance the cause of national parks on behalf of the American people than any individual of any period of history. Because of his years in the mining industry, following his government service, he also had an intimate understanding of the viewpoint of the resource producer. He is the symbol of sound, progressive conservation in its very broadest sense.

"Please don't call me Mr. Albright. Call me Horace," he said when first we met many years ago. Modesty was a basic trait. Horace didn't have to act important to command attention and respect. He was the sort who can move into any circle and be heeded. I've always felt that he generated a sense of warmth and the idea that here, now, is someone worth listening to and who, in turn, will prove to be a good listener.

This reminds me of a funny story. Before going to the University of California at Berkeley to deliver the 1984 Albright Lecture on Conservation, I stopped to visit him at the convalescent home in Los Angeles. Despite his years and physical frailty, Horace was in superlative spirit. He'd been writing letters that day on his trusty old portable typewriter. For a period of five years starting in 1977, when I wrote a column each Sunday in the *Los Angeles Times*, I was privileged to receive a letter from him once every week with my column enclosed. I remember that I wanted to provide him with stamps, but he wouldn't think of it.

During the course of that 1984 visit he was expounding on his meetings with Harold L. Ickes, the Secretary of the Interior during the New Deal. It was all very vivid—Horace would bring the past to life as though it were yesterday—and I was delighted to hear it. I interrupted him, pointed to a door in the room, asked if it led to the bathroom, and if I might use it. "Why, I'd be honored if you would." That's vintage Albright.

My friend Horace lived into his ninety-sixth year. He became a legend in his own lifetime to park professionals and to citizen conservationists. He seems to have explained himself in referring to the works of another American: "I do not believe they could have been done at all," Horace wrote of someone else's accomplishments, "without the basic human compulsion to save what we prize for our fellows and for our children. He brings to the problems of conservation a natural love of the beauties of nature, an alert inquiring mind, a realistic sense of pace and appropriateness."

With these words he was describing John D. Rockefeller, Jr., who for thirty-five years relied on Albright's advice and judgment in spending countless millions to safeguard precious lands for public purposes. Without this relationship, it is highly unlikely that certain national parks would exist at all, not the Great Smoky Mountains of Southern Appalachia, nor the Grand Tetons of the Wyoming Rockies, nor the Virgin Islands in the Caribbean, nor portions of other parks. The beautiful gorge of Linville Falls in North Carolina was purchased by Mr. Rockefeller for $100,000 to be included in the Blue Ridge Parkway, virtually on Horace's say-so.

The protection of scenic beauty in national parks, however, represents only one phase of his career. The Albright touch is felt in regional and city planning and in the movement to preserve and restore historic places. Few men, if indeed any, have exercised a longer or more profound influence over the destiny of treasured American lands and landscape.

A lot of things about Horace Albright are unknown, too little known, or too soon forgotten. I had always thought that his role at Colonial Williamsburg, the Rockefeller restoration project in Virginia, was more academic than active. He served on the board of directors almost from the very start in the 1920s. During a visit to Williamsburg in the 1960s, I learned from Edwin Kendrew, the senior vice president of Colonial Williamsburg, of the part Horace played there. As Mr. Kendrew told me:

> *Getting Williamsburg going was daring in its way, like ploughing new ground. There was nothing like it in America, nor dreamed of. Mr. Rockefeller was not interested in restoring a single building in inappropriate*

surroundings—his objective was to revive an entire segment of the past or none at all. He was reticent, cautious, and kept largely to himself. But Horace Albright was able to penetrate with sound advice in particularly trying areas of principle, policy and ideals, and of spending money in the right places.

Looking back, it is difficult to define Horace Albright's precise role at Williamsburg. He was helpful in zoning and city planning in our painstaking, slow endeavor—the battle to turn back the pages of history with authenticity. He supported the architects and other professionals in matters which some considered visionary. One was the instance of setting the new hotel well back from the street. Or, he would tell Mr. Rockefeller that detailed research into the shape and substance of original buildings might be costly but was essential. He championed purchase of land not only for restoration but for protection of the area from encroachment. "It will never be any cheaper, you know," he would suggest to Mr. Rockefeller. When it was proposed to intrude on history with modern streetlights, he insisted that one concession would only lead to another. "Instead of giving the visitor convenience," he would say, "we should give him a street map."

He would make his points stick, at Williamsburg and elsewhere, because he had a love for people at all stations, for a carpenter or a gardener no less than for Laurance Rockefeller, whom he influenced deeply to take up his father's work in conservation. In time when Congress passed the Historic Sites Act and the Park Service undertook its own restoration work, Washington people would say, "Let's go down and see how the experts do it at Williamsburg." That fine rapport was his work.

For years Horace served the government on committees, commissions and boards. Members of Congress counted on his wisdom and judgment. I remember attending a testimonial dinner in Washington in 1963 for Senator Clinton Anderson of New Mexico, and hearing the leading conservationist and champion of wilderness legislation name Horace Albright among a half-dozen or so who had been most helpful to him over the decades in Washington.

When he retired from the mining business in New York, he and Mrs. Albright lived within a long stride of the UCLA campus in Los Angeles, partially because of his activities on the Council of the Friends of the UCLA Library. I recall visiting him with a mutual friend, Patrice Manahan, editor of *Westways Magazine*. Books were clearly a passion, filling shelves from floor to ceiling in almost every room, including the basement, an amazing collection, carefully arranged to reflect the study of his special interests: the life and times of Theodore Roosevelt, mining, forestry, wildlife, the national parks, the California story. A prize package if ever there was one.

His daughter, Marian Albright Schenck, continues to maintain and collect valuable Albright materials. She knows him better than anyone and is ever determined to keep the record straight. Marian and her husband, Roswell, were central figures to Horace and to his friends; their home provided the rendezvous when old colleagues came to southern California to visit him in the last years.

"I have been submerged in correspondence," he wrote to me while he was in his seventies, scorning the temptations of age to live at ease. "I do not expect to be in the east anytime soon. Normally I would be there in October for the meeting of the directors of Resources for the Future, but Mrs. Albright and I are planning a trip to Nairobi, Kenya, for the International Union for the Conservation of Nature." And another time, "We have lately been to Owens Valley, where I was born and reared. As a trustee for the National Trust for Historic Preservation, I was asked to make the address at the annual dinner of the Eastern California Museum Association. So we went up there and stayed a few days to enjoy the beauty of the mountains covered with a mantle of snow."

In this appreciation of a great man's career, it should be noted that he has not always been above criticism. In the early years of the national parks he supported public feeding of grizzly bears at Yellowstone and the "Rock of Ages" singing at Carlsbad Caverns, which verge more on entertainment than park conservation and are no longer practiced. Perhaps they were right, or at least righter, in the context of their time, when parks were new and "ecology" a word still unknown.

But that's not the point. I think of Horace Albright's own words that the mission of conserving the best of America takes many forms of expression in different individuals, and that the real requirement is "wider support from more citizens who will take the trouble to inform themselves of new needs and weak spots in our conservation program." No man has done better to show the way to his own generation or done more to inspire a succeeding generation. And that's what counts.

Karl Lane, the Big-Game Guide, Stands Up for Admiralty

Western Outdoors
May 1985

The best part about returning to Alaska, which I've been lucky to do at least every other year for the past 20 years, is renewing friendships with people like Karl Lane, master guide and outfitter. The last time we had been together was in 1972. We traveled from Juneau, his home base, to Admiralty Island, one of the most fabulous wildlife areas in North America and stronghold of a thousand brown bears, Sitka blacktail deer, more than 60 salmon streams, a thousand bald eagle nests, plus whales, seals and sea lions in the saltwater bays and inlets.

In those days Karl was in the thick of the fight to save Admiralty from being sacrificed to misguided timber-first forestry. Merchants in nearby Juneau figured it would be great for business to cut down the trees, and never mind the wildlife. When Karl joined the Sierra Club lawsuit to block the big timber sale, one of the merchants threatened him. "Go ahead," invited Karl, "you reach for it and it will be the last time you do." That ended that.

We sat on his boat, the *Heron*, a comfortable, diesel-powered cruiser, when I was in Juneau last summer and talked about how things were, and how they've changed and what the future is likely to hold. Having been an Alaska guide for 35 years (and before that in the Okefenokee in Georgia), Karl has developed a perspective of human relationship to the natural environment.

"I used to go on a spring bear hunt and in a week's time I might see another guide and possibly an occasional fisherman," he recalled. "You never saw anyone from the Forest Service. Admiralty and other islands looked and felt like wilderness without being called that name. Now people are all over. Everybody and his brother has either a boat or plane. Biologists, recreation technicians and other federal and state personnel are studying everything. Most of Admiralty is now classified as wilderness with a capital 'W,' but with all those people the spirit and challenge of the wild are gone."

Admiralty is an island I've known and known of for years, particularly through the time I spent with *Field & Stream*. Frank Dufresne, legendary in

Alaska wildlife management, long before I joined the staff, had written stirring articles urging that Admiralty be safeguarded for its wildlife. His pleas
were followed by those of Ralph Young, big-game guide and author, and close
friend of Karl Lane. Ralph played a pivotal role when he wrote such powerful
lines as these:

> *Alaska is my home. I shall live here until I die. And when I die I have
> willed that my ashes be scattered on Admiralty Island that I may be part of
> the land I love so long as the grass shall grow and the sun shall rise.*

Then there was my sidekick, Dick Starnes, a two-fisted journalist and
outdoorsman who showed revulsion for the logging blight he found. His classic article, "Night Comes to Admiralty," shook up a lot of folks. Bureaucrats
and loggers knew they were being watched and proceeded very cautiously.

In 1901, President Theodore Roosevelt proposed that Admiralty, Baranof
and Chichagof Islands be protected as brown bear refuges. Instead, these
islands and virtually all of southeast Alaska, the long, indented panhandle
stretching 500 miles from British Columbia to Glacier Bay, were established
as Tongass National Forest. In the early years some trees were cut, but only by
local loggers for local needs. For the most part, foresters were resource stew-
ards, consciously conserving 16.9 million acres—the largest national forest
anywhere—a complex of misty fjords, glaciers, rocky peaks, rain forests of
Sitka spruce and western hemlock sheltering varied wildlife. The undisturbed
streams provided habitat for five species of Pacific salmon and supported a
major commercial fishery and sport fishery as well.

The big change came following World War II. The Forest Service felt a
new obligation to promote a large-scale timber industry, with two huge 50-
year sales: one to Ketchikan Pulp (later Louisiana-Pacific), the other to Alaska
Pulp at Sitka, representing Japanese interests. A third contract, pending to
Champion International, would have taken virtually everything growing on
Admiralty.

"When I first came to Alaska in 1946," Karl recalled, "there were small
logging operations selling to sawmills, without much effect on the country.
They could have had logging forever—real multiple use—but they chose the
path of big operations, too big for the land, destined to tear up everything.

"I had worked in the woods. That was how I came here. I started in Ohio
where I was born and became interested in hunting as an archer at the age of
five. Later I moved to Okefenokee and then worked as a logger felling timber
in California. Even while logging in Alaska, I did not believe in clearcutting

the valley watersheds to the detriment of fish and wildlife. I saw most other islands heavily roaded, subject to large block cutting of a thousand acres or more. I felt that Admiralty, at least, should be spared."

The Sierra Club and Karl Lane, the big-game guide, jointly brought suit in 1970 to block the proposed sale that would have been the largest and longest in U.S. history—spanning 50 years and 1 million acres, designed to allow Champion International to harvest almost 1 billion board feet, enough timber to build a plank road from the Arctic Circle to the tip of South America— though virtually all for shipment to Japan. The litigants cited, among other things, the fact that only a small portion of Admiralty consists of economically accessible commercial forest, while the better timber zones at heads of bays and along valley bottoms are critical for brown bear, eagle and salmon.

The whole idea of the sale wasn't too sound, which is why other large companies had looked it over and declined to bid. Ultimately Champion withdrew before the case went to trial.

One of the major lessons I've learned from associating with people like Karl Lane and from being in the wild places is the connection of all life in natural form to our benefit. In spring, for instance, Karl guides his hunters to sheltered bays of Admiralty, Baranof and Chichagof. With Boston Whaler skiffs they hunt tidal flats and beaches where the brown bears feed. Then in the fall, hunters head inland for the salmon spawning streams, fishing for salmon and trout during the day, hunting bear in the early evening. They can follow bear trails to gravel riffles where salmon dig their beds in which to lay and fertilize the eggs of a succeeding generation. It's the abundance of salmon, based on conditions of ideal habitat, that has made Admiralty the "fortress of bears" and brought to it the highest density of bald eagles anywhere in the world.

Down through the years wildlife biologists and the Alaska Fish and Game Department urged the Forest Service to safeguard the salmon streams in its trust. Their pleas were lost in the scramble to build a timber industry, supposedly "to aid the economy of Alaska" but actually hurting it. Under the present monopoly control, there is no open market for logs. Instead of small mills cutting lumber and manufacturing wood products, Alaskans must go to Puget Sound to meet their consumer needs.

In 1980, Congress adopted the Alaska National Interest Lands Conservation Act designating 14 wilderness areas in the Tongass National Forest, covering more than 5 million acres. Two areas, Admiralty Island and Misty Fjords, already designated as national monuments by presidential order, were confirmed in the act. That sounds like a lot of turf set aside for scenery, wild-life and recreation—most of it, however, is sheer rock, ice, muskeg and outer coast, without much of the old-growth forest essential to fish and wildlife habitat.

The productive forest was targeted for other purposes: Congress gener-ously provided a timber supply fund of $40 million per year—"or whatever the Secretary of Agriculture finds necessary"—to produce 4.5 billion board feet per decade, or 450 million board feet annually.

All indications suggest the so-called "450 cut" is wasteful and destruc-tive, and that it should be revised and down-scaled forthwith. State Fish and Game, for instance, warns that the programmed timber harvest represents "a major impediment to meeting its mandated responsibilities to manage, pro-tect, maintain, improve and extend fish, game and aquatic plant resources of the state." And the Southeast Alaska Conservation Council is promoting development of a scaled-down regional timber industry that does not domi-nate other resource values and the protection of key fish and wildlife habitats.

Those goals make sense to me. For they would not only safeguard species of wildlife, but also endangered individualists like Karl Lane and Ralph Young, who embody the spirit of Alaska and who have enriched the lives of those who experience it with their guidance.

The Environmental Movement at Midlife

Western Outdoors
May 1985

The large national conservation organizations are always asking for money to carry on their crusades. They do considerable good, to be sure, but I have watched them in recent years bog down in their own bureaucracies, complete with high-salaried executives, petty personal jealousies and rivalries, and a shift in direction from issues of principle to promotion of business.

When friends ask my advice on where to give their contributions, I caution them as follows: Think twice if the only time you hear from an organization is when it wants money. Consider donating most of what you have to spare to some local or regional feisty, hungry, grassroots outfit which is really in need.

Jay Norwood "Ding" Darling was my kind of conservationist—a fighter, mover and shaker. He was renowned first as a newspaper editorial cartoonist, who then turned his talent and his energy to the protection of wildlife and natural resources. He was one of the early supporters of the migratory bird hunting stamp program. Though personally a Republican, he was appointed by Franklin D. Roosevelt to be chief of the Bureau of Biological Survey, where he did a superb job in just a short time.

In 1936, Darling sparked organization of the General Wildlife Federation, which subsequently became the National Wildlife Federation. He wanted a grassroots action organization, but he watched the federation become anything but.

In 1946, he wrote: "I don't see how the federation can go on justifying its existence just by selling stamps and having a few executives in their home office and not making a campaign among the states which might organize and contribute to a national organization."

Those words are equally valid and challenging today. I recently read an article in the *Los Angeles Times* by Robert L. Jones, a perceptive environmental reporter, about the imminent change in leadership in three major national organizations, the Sierra Club, National Audubon Society and Wilderness Society. Jones wrote that he found the environmental movement "at midlife," facing a marked transformation—from volunteer effort to multi-million-dollar business enterprise.

Sierra and Audubon, he continued, have taken lessons from corporations and hired professional search companies to find new executives. "The list of qualifications handed to the professional searchers looks more or less identical to that required for the head of a division at, say, General Motors."

That, in my humble judgment, should never be. The article quoted Michael McCloskey, executive director of the Sierra Club, who is being kicked upstairs, as follows: "We're looking for a person who is strong in finance and budgets, who has a track record in management, who is alert to changes in the marketplace." And that should never be, either.

A friend sent me a copy of a letter dispatched widely by the chairman of the search committee at the Wilderness Society. That organization, the chairman explained, is looking for a chief executive to represent it effectively with funding resources—a fund-raiser. The searchers want someone who understands the political system, is dedicated to conservation and public service. But substantive knowledge of public lands issues is secondary.

Well, I don't feel it is secondary, I believe it is critical and foremost to the making of an effective environmental leader.

It takes that kind of awareness based on experience, plus sensitivity to nature and deep concern for its future, but what the organizations are looking for are management experts and fund-raisers. And at high prices. According to the article, the new executive directors at Sierra and Wilderness each will be paid between $70,000 and $90,000 annually, while at Audubon the salary could go above $100,000.

I have no objection to a living wage in an age of high prices, and I don't begrudge anything to the well-paid executive of some profit-making enterprise. But when an ordinary fellow advances up the ladder to the affluent level, his outlook, interests and motivations change. He loses touch.

The same goes for crusading organizations as they become institutionalized in midlife. "I had hoped the federation would be the crowning achievement of my devotion to conservation," wrote Ding Darling in 1955, seven years before his death. "It is, instead, my greatest humiliation."

What would he say today? The National Wildlife Federation is big business. It employs about 500 people, many involved in mail order and merchandising, not in conservation. The salary of the executive head of the federation, Jay

Hair, was not included in the article, so I inquired. "It's our policy not to give out salary information," a spokesperson at federation headquarters in Washington told me.

From other confidential sources I learned that Jay Hair, executive vice president of the National Wildlife Federation, is paid annually in the $120,000 range, plus a $15,000 expense account, plus a car and auto expenses, plus a fully furnished apartment in Washington, which allows him to spend most of his time at home in Raleigh, North Carolina.

That amount of money could sure do a lot of good for groups like the Idaho Sportsmen's Coalition, which Steve Hall, Jack Trueblood and other stalwarts organized last year in order to demonstrate that hunters and fishermen care more about protecting national forests than politicians realize. The coalition has been raising nickels, dimes and dollars to get its message across. Such, of course, may be the fate of the missionary, but I'm sure that Ding Darling would be proud.

He would be proud, also, of Don Aldrich, who for years was executive director of the Montana Wildlife Federation; Bill Meiners, the sparkplug of the Idaho Federation; Mort Brigham, of the Idaho Environmental Council; Dick Carter, of the Utah Wilderness Association; Cliff Merritt, who left the Wilderness Society to form the grassroots-based American Wilderness Alliance, headquartered in Denver; and Tom Bell, who left the Wyoming Fish and Game Department years ago to organize the Wyoming Outdoor Council. These people are in the Darling tradition.

"The great irony," one of my friends said to me, "is that national environmental leaders mirror the foxes they have been chasing." I wouldn't put it quite like that. I have known many outstanding, highly principled people in the environmental movement. But if the national organizations insist on being run by fund-raising management specialists, they ought first to send them to the hinterlands to learn what the environment, and humility, are about.

State of Mind, Way of Life

Western Outdoors
Fall 1986

Conservation of natural resources certainly represents one of the great challenges of our time, which is why we expect government to solve it for us. While laws and regulations and agencies to carry them out have a place, it strikes me that conservation should first be a state of mind and a way of life. It starts with thee and me.

I admit that I am part of the problem. I think of it when driving my car, flying in an airplane, or purchasing some particular luxury item to demonstrate affluence in this age of conspicuous consumption. I may complain that consumer demand is contrived, stimulated artificially by clever merchandising; in the case of transportation, I may cite the absence of energy-efficient trains or streetcars. But the truth is that I don't have to drive two blocks to the supermarket.

What is conservation that makes it critical to us? Gifford Pinchot answered it this way:

> *From birth to death, natural resources, transformed for human use, feed, clothe, shelter and transport us. Upon them we depend for every material necessity, comfort, convenience and protection in our lives. Without abundant resources, prosperity is out of reach. Therefore, the conservation of natural resources is the fundamental material problem.*

Pinchot, forestry pioneer and close collaborator of President Theodore Roosevelt in the conservation crusade of the early 20th century, based his creed on a simple, straightforward proposition: "No generation can be allowed needlessly to damage or reduce the future general wealth and welfare by the way it uses or misuses any natural resource." Thus, he said, conservation means the wise use of the earth for the lasting good of humankind.

This concept allows for cutting of trees, extraction of minerals, and the utilization of living animals and plants. In the most primeval society, with or without humans, species serve each other, virtually by design. The earth is a mechanism powered by many internal parts. Conservation is based on respect for these natural systems, without using more than is needed, and without waste.

[169]

In our brief modern era, technology and super-civilization have advanced so rapidly that the connection with nature is scarcely recognized or understood. Our entire course of growth has been based on the principle of resource luxury—of limitless land, forests, water, soil and air. Waste is the offspring of an *overdeveloped* society, in which people are prone to devour endless quantities of "disposable" products with little thought of where they came from or where they must go, without inclination to save, or repair, anything older than yesterday.

It may be helpful, now and again, to look back to the time before machines replaced functions of body and brain in the name of convenience. This thought came to me while rereading that classic novel of the Southwest, *Death Comes for the Archbishop*, by Willa Cather. Though published in 1927, it reflects the New Mexico frontier of the mid-19th century.

I was especially taken with the episode when Father Latour, the pioneer bishop, was traveling from the Navajo country on horseback with his Indian friend, Eusabio. It took them almost two weeks, between blinding sandstorms and brilliant sunlight, to cover the 400 miles to Santa Fe.

Riding with Eusabio was like riding with the landscape made human; he accepted chance and the weather as the country did. When they left the rock or tree or sand dune that had sheltered them overnight, the Navajo was careful to obliterate every trace. He buried the embers of the fire and the remnants of food, unpiled the stones he had piled together, and filled the holes he had scooped in the sand. It was the Indian's way to pass through a country without disturbing anything; to pass and leave no trace, like fish through the water, or birds through the air.

It was the Indian manner (as Cather wrote) to vanish into the landscape, not to stand out against it. Hopi villages were set upon rock mesas to look like the rock, imperceptible at a distance. Navajo hogans, among sand and willows, were made of sand and willows. None of the pueblos would have glass windows in their dwellings. The reflection of the sun on the glazing was ugly and unnatural to them—even dangerous.

Why did they cling to their ways? Cather explained it in her own sensitive style:

> It was as if the great country were asleep, and they wished to carry on their lives without awakening it; or as if the spirits of earth and air and water were things not to antagonize and arouse. When they hunted, it was with the same discretion; an Indian hunt was never a slaughter. They

ravaged neither the rivers nor the forest, and if they irrigated, they took as little water as would serve their needs. The land and all that it bore they treated with consideration; not attempting to improve it, they never desecrated it.

That is conservation, as a state of mind and a way of life. Later in the book, when the bishop was dying, Eusabio came to see him, this time arriving by train, that new miracle. "Men travel faster now," the Navajo observed, "but I do not know if they go to better things."

As with the Indian settlements, the goal of early monasteries was self-sufficiency, to manage the land to supply the food and clothing, retaining productivity despite intense cultivation. The architecture of the padres was functional, suited to the country in which they lived. Those who came to California built their missions of earth and seashell, mortar and reeds, wasting neither land nor materials.

Yes, there is a price tag to progress. Many cities, large and small, still cart their waste to blighted eyesores called city dumps. They're told they can do a better job through incineration, composting and landfilling—but landfilling, for one, claims marshes valuable for wildlife, birds and fish, and for open space recreation.

I believe that true sportsmen are conservationists by the nature of their activities. They use a resource, but with respect and responsibility. They are neither gluttonous nor wasteful. They go to the out-of-doors to find harmony with an outer landscape and spiritual recreation within themselves. They are models of conservation as a way of life and state of mind.

In years past I, like many others, decried "slob hunting," but I don't do it any longer. The slob hunter is trying, in his own way, to find the path. The mature sportsman can serve as a role model, demonstrating the pleasure and fulfillment derived from self-restraint and consideration for the environment.

Individual responsibility doesn't meet the whole challenge, but it marks the starting point from which people can work together, with mutual trust and understanding, to explore what seem to be larger issues. If, as I wrote above, I am part of the problem, then surely I will be part of the solution to it.

"To Wake My Neighbors"

National Parks
May 1986

I am glad that in recent years I have taken to teaching, for in the class-room I learn a great deal. Most especially, I discover hope and heart in young people. When I ask them to join me in a commitment to protect and perpetuate our most precious heritage, America's lands, students' faces brighten with ready response.

I try to merge history, science, philosophy, and art, citing the lives and works of individuals I admire, such as Loren Eisley, who wrote: "Only in acts of articulate compassion, in rare and hidden moments of communion with nature, does man briefly escape his solitary destiny."

Taken a step further, we must save the resource, the earthly wildness, that ensures opportunities for those rare and hidden moments—and not just for ourselves alone. The great use of a life is to create something that outlasts it; thus, the most significant gift of our generation will be a record of not selfishly devouring the earth for our own satisfaction, but of leaving nature as we found it, to the future.

It won't be easy; but, then, it never has been. History books, after all, are records of events and the doings of individuals who didn't go with the flow. Henry David Thoreau is a prime example. I love *The Maine Woods*, his book on his time spent there, which makes that northeast corner more than a place but a symbol with calling and meaning for people everywhere.

Thoreau has been reduced to scholarship by scholars and to literature by litterateurs, yet he has given us a battle cry rather than a lullaby. His standards are clear and consistent:

If a man walks in the woods for half of each day, he is in danger of being regarded as a loafer, but if he spends his whole day as a speculator, shearing off those woods and making the earth bald before her time, he is esteemed as industrious and enterprising.

Thoreau personifies independence. In 1849, he refused to pay his taxes to protest the U.S. war against Mexico. For his action, he was jailed. Emerson, his close friend, wanted to pay his taxes for him, but Thoreau refused.

There must be some little bit of Thoreau in all of us, an urge to be proud and free as he was. With Thoreau as your companion, there is no loneliness, only a challenge to rise above the mediocre.

In class I cite Thoreau and others, particular heroes of mine, who have contributed to the cause of conservation and human progress in the face of opposition and adversity. My heroes include Stephen T. Mather, Horace Albright, Newton B. Drury, Gifford Pinchot, Robert Marshall, Aldo Leopold, William O. Douglas, Adolph and Olaus Murie, John and Frank Craighead. All of them may now be recorded in the books as "achievers," but they did a lot of rowing against the tide.

That's what it requires to make the difference. Each national park, starting with Yellowstone, came into being only through public will and desire. Someone had a dream, a vision, then rallied others to make it come true. Our generation is programmed to taking rather than giving, to "success" measured in a material way. But those motivated by caring and sharing, by love of the earth, know that success comes from within, that only self-realization is success.

In many cases a particular cause may seem hopeless; the odds never appear to be on the side of angels. But when there is something worth saving one must never give up, certainly one must never give up hope. As long as there is a cadre of people, or a single individual, with commitment and conscience to stand in defense of nature, hope and the dream still have a chance.

Yes, there is a lot of risk and challenge in activism. I see so much to be done and few who are doing it. Lots of bodies are rattling around drawing paychecks; good people are lost in large institutions. Movers and shakers are rare. That's understandable, considering that action can change one's life—in a complete, sometimes devastating, way—though often the change is uplifting and fulfilling.

It may be that nobody will say that he or she saved that stand of virgin forest, or that marsh for water birds, or that last wild stretch of stream, or that urban park, but the reward is there, in the knowledge that a fragment of the land is preserved through human concern.

Consider the case of the Boundary Waters Canoe Area in northern Minnesota. When Arthur Carhart worked as a Forest Service landscape architect between 1919 and 1923, he was sent to that region with directions to prepare a plan for recreation development.

Carhart recognized that the area could be "as priceless as Yellowstone,

Yosemite, or the Grand Canyon—if it remained a water-trail wilderness." His bosses thought that was wild talk; they favored a master plan to build roads to every lake and to line the shores with thousands of summer homes. But Carhart persisted. Ultimately, he won support for his concept and laid the basis for what is now called the Boundary Waters Canoe Area.

After Carhart left the region, Sigurd Olson arrived on the scene. Over the years, Olson would stand in meeting halls urging that natural values be protected from assorted mining, dam-building, logging, and motor boating interests. It wasn't easy, and sometimes he was treated to hoots of scorn and derision.

Years later, Carhart paid tribute to Olson for leading a small group that held, as Carhart said, "a thin line of defense protecting this exquisite wilderness until help could rally to save it." How fortunate we are that Carhart, Olson, and their collaborators identified this treasure of the North Country and defended it from becoming just another parcel of exploited American earth.

From my own life, I know that individual commitment to nature works. That I should have uncensored outlets for my writing, that I should have a platform from which to lecture, that I should have direct access to young people for open dialogue on the process of decision-making—these give me faith in myself and the American system. The only trouble with democracy is that we take it for granted.

Producers of commodities know full well that land is wealth. They measure resources in specific terms, as timber, forage, minerals, or real estate. I don't deny them their right or society's need of such materials; but waterfalls, mountain meadows, and the chorus of thrushes are critical to the human spirit.

I value the earth for its own sake, rather than for its utility. My earth is living poetry, music and art. Or, as Emerson wrote, literature, poetry, and science all are the homage of humankind to the unfathomed secrets of nature.

"I do not propose to write an ode to dejection," Thoreau advised the world, "but to brag as lustily as a chanticleer in the morning, if only to wake my neighbors." Well, Thoreau is always in style.

I don't think he would mind my adding this exhortation: Whether young or old, set aside fear and apprehension to chart a destiny with mission and purpose. Be brave, bold, determined, and dare to unlock your dreams.

CHAPTER V

THE PLACE, TOO, HAS ITS SOUL

The American West has forever been a magic part of the universe, rich in diverse miracles of nature. Long before the advent of civilization as we know it, humans paid homage to these wonders and considered them sacred—the mesas, canyons, badlands and grasslands, deserts, geysers and glaciers, snow-covered volcanic domes, rushing rivers, surf-pounded rocky coast and the massive mountains of rock that form the backbone of the continent, thousand-year-old redwood forests, and the even older bristlecone pines growing in their separate environments where other trees cannot make it.

Just as humans modify places, places influence people, how they view themselves, the earth and each other. The child who grows up in the out-of-doors will have a different worldview than the child of the inner city. In *The Vanishing American*, Zane Grey's hero, Nophaie, loved most to be alone, "listening to the real sounds of the open and to the whispering of his soul." "For all the toll the desert takes of a man it gives compensations, deep breaths, deep sleep, and the communion of the stars," wrote Mary Austin in *The Land of Little Rain*. And she concluded that "Go as far as you dare in the heart of a lonely land, you cannot go so far that life and death are not before you."

Trouble is there's not much left of the lonely land. Places have changed, and people with them. I remember once, more than forty years ago, driving cross-country with three friends. Heading west beyond Cheyenne, Wyoming, we ran out of gas. The very first fellow to come by stopped to help. Then he drove forty miles to the nearest town and returned with a can full of gas that he insisted on paying for. That doesn't happen much any more, in an increasingly crowded world, where cities and suburbs and freeways and malls look alike and could be anywhere, and good people are strangers instead of neighbors.

Some places in the West have been impacted more seriously than others, wounded deep into the soul. Before World War II northern New Mexico was largely self-sustaining, a composite of distinctive ancient Native American and Hispanic communities living on agriculture and ranching, out of touch with the modern world. Then the sacred lands of the San Ildefonso pueblo were preempted by the government to become an important and secret scientific laboratory: The sole purpose at Los Alamos was to develop and produce a weapon with great destructive capability. Initially the new age of the atom and uranium appeared to bring good things to people of the Southwest as well as to the nation, but history has shown otherwise.

Uranium mines first appeared in central New Mexico on the Laguna and Acoma pueblos and the lands of the Navajo Nation in the 1950s. The communities were not informed of the dangers; no one spoke of the radiation that results from mining and milling, nor of where and how to dispose of the radioactive waste. In due course Native Americans were left with contaminated land, unsafe drinking water, people sick and dying of cancer. Although the opportunities that seemingly began for Native Americans at Los Alamos have turned to ashes, pressure on the communities continues. The Western Shoshone have been resisting for years Nevada's designation as the nation's nuclear dumping ground. In January 1995, in a historic tribal referendum the

Mescalero Apache people of New Mexico voted 490 to 362 to refuse the "privatized" nuclear waste of Northern States Power. In a second vote they accepted privatized waste, 593 to 372, but the issue is far from concluded.

The Native American experience embodies lessons for all. Consequent to the destruction of most of their traditional culture, chronic welfare dependency, illness, unemployment, alcoholism, and other addictions have become an everyday part of life. How far behind, I ask, is the place where I live? Or Seattle, San Francisco, Cheyenne? Yet the earth provides so much that is enriching and elevating, that engenders love of home, of a particular place, and love of inner self as well.

I observe Native Americans, for all their travail, still honoring the earth and life as divine gifts. On the Northwest Coast, native peoples cherish the giant cedar, hemlock, and Douglas-fir of the cold rain forest, not simply for canoes and longhouses but as source of a sacred state of mind where magic and beauty are everywhere. They want to be part of a modern world, while kindling and rekindling an earth-based tradition and culture. But then, all religions emphasize God's gifts of earth, sky, water, and life, the unity and wholeness of creation. Starting with a compatible worldview, it takes no effort to see a cohesive landscape in which each place merits respect and care.

In Moscow, Idaho, the Outlook Differs

Palouse Journal
Winter 1984

I came to Moscow in 1982 for what I expected would be a one-year stint at the University, which might account for the fact that people were nice to me. I mean, I was invited out, and was interviewed here and there, and lectured, and was made to feel like a small-scale celebrity, or at least a personality.

So I opted for another year, during which time I was invited out, and was interviewed, and lectured. I was still more or less of a personality but always a person. That is to say, virtually anywhere I went I would be treated courteously and helpfully. I dread the notion of wearing out my welcome, like the man who came to dinner and seemingly stayed forever, but here I am into my third year. I feel almost as though I am settling in, which I had never intended in the first place, and am not at all sure I want to. Still, the quality of life here is appealing and enriching, at least to me, for now.

"Come steelhead fishing with me," a friend will say. "Have some mushrooms I picked in the woods back of my cabin," offers another. Or, "Can you use another zucchini or two?" One day in October when I went to my favorite garage on Troy Highway to have my car serviced, the place was closed and everybody was gone—for the first day of elk hunting, of course. I approve of that, of people who take the time to enjoy their environment and with inclination to share what it gives them, rather than allowing themselves to be smothered and rendered selfish by it.

My dentist is a wiry long distance runner and mountain climber who likes his work and doesn't take vacations as such, but only a couple of days off now and then to enter a road-race or do another climb of Mount Rainier. Besides being a very constructive influence on my dental health, he and I talk about general fitness and conditioning. As it happens, my strong suit is in push-ups.

"You mean, you really do 75 push-ups?" he asked one day while working on my teeth. And a few minutes later, "Do you do those push-ups at one time, without stopping?"

He was dubious indeed, considering that he, the figure of fitness, and younger than me, could manage by his own admission only 20 or 25 push-ups.

In that case, I said, what if I do 50 push-ups for you right here as soon as you're through with my teeth? He liked that idea and I performed in his waiting room to his satisfaction and the pleasure of waiting patients.

That sort of thing happens in little old Moscow. It tells me about the place and people. Another time I was playing racquetball with my friend and mentor, Jim Tangen-Foster. He is the same age as my son, but I never think of him in that context. Jim has taken two courses with me (and done very well both times), but it's hard for me to think of him as a student, since I have derived so much of value from him.

On this day two teenagers appeared at the court; they wanted to play but had to wait patiently until we were through. Meantime, they saw me take a hard whack when the ball struck the back of my leg. When we finished our game and yielded the court, one of the boys said something like, "I hope you're okay," or "I hope it doesn't hurt." I laughed a little and told Jim, "In a city they probably would have heckled us and then exclaimed, 'It's about time you got off the court!'"

The outlook on life is different in little old Moscow. Last June I went back to Washington, D.C., where I spent 35 years. As a journalist I was in the swim of things. This time I spent part of a day at the Senate Office Building, which seemed to be crawling with people, more than ever, most working in cubbyholes and scurrying down corridors, highly compartmentalized in their functions yet each convinced that he or she must be doing something absolutely critical to the fate and future of the Republic.

Washington is the kind of place where people forget who they are. New York, too, or almost any large city. Moscow provides a reverse stage set, where people can play honest roles to discover who they are. I love it for the lack of pretension and put-on, the reflection of a democratic society that Thomas Jefferson might approve.

It isn't quite all that way in Moscow. A few do take themselves, their status and their talents too seriously. One evening last summer I went to a dinner party of about ten or twelve, all well dressed and quite cultivated, bright people with a lot to say. The trouble was they all had to show how bright they are. Everybody talked, mostly about himself or herself, while hardly anybody listened. It reminded me of the world I left behind back East. I thought also of a seminar I once attended on "The Philosophy of Silence," and of the benefits of letting up on show and soliloquy, now and then, to learn from someone else.

The Moscow I prefer is social at a sociable level. Potluck is a fine art and cultural expression that should be memorialized alongside the old Northwest Indian potlatch. I've experienced some of the finest cuisine I've ever tasted at Moscow potlucks. And some of the best company, individuals of all types of backgrounds, cross-fertilizing sound ideas and wild notions, dressed in whatever style they wish without clue to success or failure, and lots of kids who rarely are in the way or pesky.

Now and then I travel elsewhere. Even without that new airport terminal somebody thinks is desperately needed, it's no strain to fly to Seattle, Portland, California, Denver or back East. I do my business, have drinks or dinner with old friends and playmates and am glad to return here. Some friends can't understand it, but that's their problem.

If I were living in Boulder, Colorado, or Jackson, Wyoming, a couple of classy places, they might think otherwise. Little old Moscow has class, quality and character as I measure them. I still have to make it to the Clearwater for steelhead and, who knows, maybe sometime the fellows at the garage will ask me to go out with them for elk.

Pinyon and Juniper:
The Landscape, Legend, and Life of the Southwest

American Forests

September 1968

One of my trusted agents has written me from the West in behalf of the so-called "dwarf forests" of pinyon and juniper, which are derided in some circles as being scrubby, unspectacular and generally more of a nuisance to humankind than they are worth.

My correspondent protests this harsh dismissal of tenacious life forms. If the pinyon-juniper vegetative type is so useless, he inquires, why is it spread across such large portions, some eighty million acres, of the Southwest? Why are pinyon and juniper found on rocky points, exposed bluffs and dry foothills, where most trees are unable to exist, as well as on more favorable settings along ravines and in sheltered canyons? And why should we persist in efforts to eradicate them, contrary to the laws of nature?

Our viewpoint of the pinyon-juniper "woodland" (a term which tends to distinguish it in technical thought from the commercially worthy "forest") is shaped in part from the same background as our view of the desert. Seemingly endless and useless, the desert until recent times was regarded as sheer wasteland on the face of America. But, as the desert has shrunk in size and man's appreciation of his environs has grown, we have begun to recognize the desert as a national asset, a marvelous community of minerals, vegetables and animals capable of maintaining its own balance in the face of much sun and little rain, and a decidedly pleasant place to live. We have not yet reached the same level of understanding of the pinyon-juniper country.

Pinyon and juniper are hardy and gnarled evergreens which grow slowly and rarely very tall. They cannot provide the livable habitat for millions of Americans as do the central and northern hardwoods, nor are they as valuable for recreation as the superb alpine stands of the Rockies or Cascades, and it seems almost sacrilege to speak of them and redwoods in the same breath. But they are part of the landscape, the legend and the life of the Southwest.

The pungent, crisp aroma of pinyon and juniper smoke is deep in the memory of Southwest villagers, be they Indian, Spanish-American, or Yankee. The oil-rich pinyon nut once was a staple item in the fall and winter diet of Indian and Spanish American and even now is a source of income in many villages, when the crop is good. The pinyon nut is really a large wingless seed, a delicacy with birds, wildlife, Indians and Easterners who call it the Indian nut. It reaches us via traders who buy it from the pickers by the bushel and ship it east by the ton.

The berries of the juniper have their values, too, being eaten by the Indians, either fresh or ground and baked into cakes, and also by a variety of birds without elaborate preparation. Adobe roofs, found in ancient ruins and still used on many modern homes, rest on juniper logs, which shows how the tree has been utilized through the centuries. It is hardly likely that we could have conquered the Southwest without cutting railroad ties of pinyon and driving barbed-wire posts of juniper during the days when cattle was king.

The livestock economy has had much influence in our view toward the pinyon-juniper. In the massive overgrazing that began in the 1880s, millions of head of cattle, then of sheep, devoured grass and edible plants. By the turn of the century the grass was gone, replaced by desert shrubs, invading juniper and great gullies draining away the water.

The livestock economy manifested its influence again in the 1950s. The Bureau of Land Management and the Forest Service both recognized there were too many cows grazing on the range. My impression is that both followed the path of history in an effort to create more forage for the stockmen. They resorted to chemical spraying, fire and the use of heavy ship anchor chains stretched between tractors to uproot pinyon and juniper, then followed with seeding of crested wheat grass.

Certainly much value has been derived from the extensive seeding, fencing, development of watering places and such efforts to restore large areas of sterile soil to usefulness and productivity. But productivity for whom? The chaining of pinyon-juniper, I fear, has been in many places a single-purpose program designed simply to furnish more food for cows.

Our friends, the land managers, may insist that game is also, and always, considered, that some patches are left untouched to provide good concealment and cover close to the grass. But the fact is that they are now, after harsh experience and due criticism, chaining smaller areas to insure cover and habitat. Certainly there was an important lesson to learn in this regard during the severe winter in Arizona last year when antelope moved into the unchained area to find food and protection. It is also interesting to observe the healthy shift in seeding to one-third grass, one-third legumes, and one-third browse, designed to provide a better balance for game.

But I wonder whether this is the right answer. Is such management furnishing game for hunters today and tomorrow rather than conceiving of wildlife—of all forms, game and non-game, predator and prey, reptile, bird and mammal—as part of the long-range life community of the land? It seems to be part of our concentrated attention on profitable payoff. We may accomplish the narrow objectives, but failure to anticipate the consequences may lead to unexplored side effects and irreversible changes in the environment which we may later regret.

It seems to me a better practice to integrate our practical sciences such as forestry and range management with the ecological way of looking at nature and with a humanistic, cultural way of looking at land. It is encouraging to hear more technicians use the word "esthetics" and grope for its meaning (I mean beyond the painfully contrived "beauty" of clearcutting the forests).

As for the future of the pinyon-juniper country, I recently discussed it with an able federal official, William J. Sauerwein, regional forester in the West of the Soil Conservation Service.

"We haven't really begun to be concerned with or to manage this resource the way it could be," he conceded. "Properly coordinated, there can be good conservation and utilization of this vast soil and plant resource based on sound multiple-use principles—for wood products, grazing, wildlife, recreation and, yes, even esthetics or natural beauty, or whatever you choose to call it.

"Not long ago I visited Mesa Verde National Park with some of our plant and soil resources people making a study of the potential of such lands. I was amazed to see a dense stand of pinyon and juniper with a good understory of grass. There were abundant big-game in the area, but no domestic livestock. Our range conservationist felt it could be carefully grazed without destroying the forage resource. Our woodland conservationist felt that selective cutting of the mature trees would benefit the stand and leave adequate reproduction and young trees to keep the area productive. These could be done in a way to enhance big-game habitat and not grossly affect esthetics. Certainly it would look better than an anchor-chained landscape."

Investigation discloses that some efforts are being made to encourage management of these lands—BLM and Forest Service in their management plans and Soil Conservation Service through cooperation with soil and water conservation districts and private landowners—but these efforts have been small and often ineffective. What is needed is public awareness of the value of the native landscape and insistence on better alternatives to its use and management. Planning is done by people. This means that people must insist on a great variety of factors in land-use planning, along with sheer technology, economics and politics of the prevailing power structure. It is not too much to hope that BLM and Forest Service may administer significant pinyon-juniper natural and wilderness areas.

Chaining may have its place, but the place should be limited to restoration of land destroyed by the abuse of overgrazing, not as the means of perpetuating the source of the abuse. If the bigger concept is understood and accepted, the roles of chain and 'dozer will find their own small levels.

Pinyon and juniper with their stocky, bushy outlines are a joy to behold in the landscape of rough draws, canyons and foothills. Recognition of their usefulness, both actual and potential, would be a proper measure of maturity by the national viewer who beholds them.

I'd Rather Crawl Than Ride a Machine in the Desert

Los Angeles Times
August 20, 1978

I feel pretty small in the desert, not simply because of the quality of space, but of time as well.

It took 60 million years of evolution, according to Dr. Kenneth Norris of the University of California at Santa Cruz, to assemble and integrate the life of the California desert into what we know today.

Yet, as Dr. Norris warns, in a tick of that time span we are witnessing whole areas such as Johnson Valley (southeast of Barstow) in wreckage, desert intaglios rutted with wheel tracks, prehistoric pictographs desecrated and the natural life systems disrupted in ways we scarcely understand.

"Who can tell what happens to animals that spend most of their lives buried under shifting sands when a 500,000-person day occurs at the Yuma dunes?" demands Dr. Norris. "Viewed in this context, it's all too easy to expect that many of the natural things of the desert will vanish unless prompt action is taken to stem the tide."

The course for such prompt action, quite possibly the only course, is in the wilderness review process being undertaken by the Bureau of Land Management in compliance with federal legislation. The first phase, the preliminary inventory of study areas, is underway. Then, suitable areas will be selected and recommended to Congress for inclusion in the National Wilderness Preservation System.

The wilderness potential may exceed 6 million acres, or roughly half the public domain lands in the California desert. It includes a few huge areas, such as the Eureka-Saline Valleys, embracing more than half a million acres east of Death Valley, and others such as Amargosa Canyon north of Baker, with colorful canyon scenery, historic and archaeological values and year-round water supporting abundant wildlife.

Opposition to wilderness designation, however, is intense and vocal, mostly from off-road vehicle (ORV) groups, as well as from mining and other commercial interests.

While a series of public hearings on wilderness was conducted earlier this year by BLM, a cadre of ORV enthusiasts issued a flyer denouncing the "wilderness plague" they claimed would close 98 percent of the California desert and turn it into a "red desert." That, of course, depends upon how you see it.

Feelings among the ORV set were so high, with nearly 1,200 of them turning out for the Anaheim meeting alone, that wilderness advocates chose the better part of wisdom and stayed away. "We are threatened by boos, catcalls, and bodily harm," Harriet Allen, president of the Desert Protective Council, told me. "We want to inventory wilderness and develop a sound desert plan, but seem pitted against those who want to keep good planning from taking place."

On the other hand, groups such as the California Association of Four-Wheel Drive Clubs consider that land-use planning is aimed at restricting off-roaders, that BLM is overly sensitive to scientific data, that the proposed wilderness is much larger than necessary.

There are ten desert sand dunes of significance, of which seven and four-fifths are open to ORVs. With due credit to those who enjoy motorized recreation, this hardly conserves the dunes for future generations. Wilderness designation is a better way.

"In dry soil, direct mechanical erosion by ORVs is most evident as dust, especially as generated during major ORV events," the Geological Society of America reported in a classic study, "Impacts and Management of Off-Road Vehicles," issued last year.

"One such event," it said, "the 1974 Barstow to Las Vegas motorcycle race with its 3,000 riders, produced more than 600 tons of airborne particulates, a quantity 10 times greater than that raised by a single severe dust storm from the barren floor of Owens dry lake in California.

"Damage by ORVs in even the least vulnerable areas will require periods for recovery measured in centuries or millennia. Losses of soil and changes in the land surface will be long-lasting, and certain natural life systems will never recover from the intensive ORV impacts already sustained."

Now that I've been in the California desert and seen the damage in Johnson Valley and Jawbone Canyon and Great Falls Basin above Trona, I'm glad I walk. Truthfully, however, in these fragile places if I had to ride a machine, I'd rather crawl.

In Western Canada There Is Still Hope to Save the Best

Defenders of Wildlife
July 1989

The earth's largest ocean, the Pacific, used to sweep the purest salt water onto the world's cleanest beaches along the wild coast of British Columbia. Those coastal waters were a paradise for migrating gray whales and for sea otters and seabirds.

Another paradise lay a few hundred miles inland in the alpine ranges reaching to endless horizons along the boundary between British Columbia and Alberta. This paradise was for grizzly bears and woodland caribou, for wolves and eagles and elk, and for tall trees and wildflowers growing in high meadows at the foot of living glaciers.

Certainly western Canada has been richly endowed, and the people of Alberta and British Columbia have been singularly blessed. The rest of us have shared in the treasures. British Columbia invites visitors with advertising describing itself as "Super, Natural." No fewer than seven national parks—Banff, Jasper, Kootenay, Yoho, Waterton Lakes, Glacier and Mt. Revelstoke—are accessible to visitors here in the heart of the Rockies.

Maybe that's the trouble. The remotest places on earth are now too readily accessible and too often abused. Where isolation once protected parcels of paradise, civilization in our time has caught up fast and hard. Thus the renowned wonderlands of western Canada are victims of the war against the environment waged by reckless, wasteful technology in the service of corporate profit, with scant responsible defense by government.

Consider the disastrous oil spill that hit the west coast of Vancouver Island last January. Two days before Christmas, an oil barge was punctured off the Washington coast when a tow cable broke in high seas. In consequence of the uncontrolled leak of heavy black bunker oil, more than 6,000 dead and dying seabirds washed up on Oregon and Washington shores. The oil drifted northward, but Canadian officials didn't want to believe it would hit their coast and failed to prepare a cleanup plan. Hundreds of volunteers—Canadians who care—worked to save what birds they could along remote beaches while the provincial and federal governments delayed action and haggled over responsibility. And when they did come, government ministers helicoptered around, getting in the way of volunteers.

Those volunteers, working from dawn to dusk on wintry sands, found tangled among seaweed and oily debris a heartbreaking spectacle: hundreds of tar-coated corpses of deep-diving seabirds. They could tell that crabs and shellfish had been killed. And it was feared that more tragedy could be in the offing. The director of the B.C. Fish and Wildlife Branch warned that such an oil spill could easily wipe out the province's 400 reintroduced sea otters. There is also concern that this summer bottom-feeding gray whales may pick up tar-like residue that could affect them adversely. To be sure, as I write, only one otter death from the spilled oil has been documented in British Columbia, and while three dead oiled otters have been found in Washington, the exact cause of their deaths is not known. But there is no question about the hazard oil spills pose for marine life.

Despite this hazard, offshore oil drilling is being considered seriously by the B.C. government. I find this hard to believe, considering that British Columbia has one of the stormiest coasts in the world. The B.C. government, unfortunately, appears hell-bent on destroying its "Super, Natural" image. The notorious campaign of recent years to annihilate wolves in the name of game management provoked revulsion among enlightened people everywhere. And now grassroots citizens are fighting to save Carmanah Valley, jewel of the Pacific Coast rainforest on the southwestern coast of Vancouver Island, from certain ruin by clearcut logging. MacMillan Bloedel, the corporate timber giant, would reap the profits, but the basic responsibility belongs to the provincial government of Premier William Vander Zalm, the willing peddler of public lands. . . .

Forestry practices in western Canada are very poor. Overcutting, with immense clearcuts, has caused extensive soil erosion, washing natural beauty into rivers and the sea. In 1975 Ted Young, then chief forester of British Columbia, wrote: "Logging should only be permitted on those areas where we can guarantee regeneration without loss of productivity. Liquidation cuts, unless specifically approved for a particular reason, should be rejected regardless of the pressure in the name of economics." But his warning has been ignored.

In neighboring Alberta, the provincial government has committed over half of the province's northern forests to the primary production of pulp fiber. This was done without public hearings or independent and scientific environmental assessment. Citizen groups such as Friends of the Athabasca have challenged the government's giveaway, warning that dumping toxic chemicals from Kraft bleaching mills would ruin the Athabasca River and other beautiful clean streams of northern Alberta.

Even areas presumably saved are not very safe. Albertans like to note that Canadian national parks are almost as old as ours. That's quite true: Yellowstone was established in 1872 and Banff, in the Canadian Rockies, in 1885. But Banff administrators in recent years have favored tourism development over resource protection. When grizzly bear habitat stands in the way of a proposed downhill ski project or construction of new lodging, the bear and its habitat are likely to give way. On a recent visit I was astonished at the degradation of the town (or townsite, as they say) of Banff. Though it is within the boundaries of the park, planless growth—thoroughly unworthy of the natural setting—prevails. Banff, I fear, is on the way to becoming another tourist ghetto.

Alberta has been one of the natural glories of North America. Virtually the whole province until recent years was like a great natural preserve of varied landscapes, from grasslands and badlands to mountain marvels, with abundant wildlife roaming free. Yet at the recent annual meeting of the Alberta Wilderness Association I heard repeatedly of the priority being given by the provincial government to oil and gas drilling, logging, roading, dam building, livestock-grazing—everything but responsible resource conservation.

The manifest failure of the governments of Alberta and British Columbia is not unique. Governments at all levels and everywhere in the world are out of touch with the needs of the age. I wish statesmen of high principle were leading the way toward a peaceful green planet, rather than petty politicians pursuing business as usual on behalf of corporate rule and technological ruin. The lesson of the 1980s is that we are all in this together and that people must reach out to cooperate where governments miss the mark. Canadians and Americans share the same acid rain, the same ozone, and the same need to do things differently in the 1990s.

Thus I'm glad to cite the emergence of the transboundary Alliance for the Wild Rockies with its focus on the "Crown of the Continent," including portions of Montana, Idaho, Wyoming, Washington, Oregon, British Columbia, and Alberta. The alliance envisions a North American Serengeti, comprising the wildest land outside Alaska, a preserve for caribou, eagles, grizzly bears, wolves, mountain sheep, and other species. The truth is that we haven't done well on our side either, with millions of acres unprotected because of the influence of corporate timber, mining, oil and gas. We have allowed land-use decisions to be made by each state's congressional delegation, although these are federal lands belonging to all the people and deserving a national and, better yet, international approach.

We can still save the best. May the 1990s be the decade of determined change and of cooperation among peoples, with Canadians and Americans showing that it can be done.

Climb to the Summit of Mauna Loa

Defenders of Wildlife
October 1986

The paradox of abundant blessings mingled with inescapable blight struck me forcefully last summer while I was climbing to the summit of Hawaii's Mauna Loa. For one thing, there I was on the world's largest volcano, a mountain built by layer upon layer of lava, rising from about 20,000 feet below the sea to 13,677 feet above. I thought of the early Hawaiians making their way to the top without shoes, backpacks, or freeze-dried food, perhaps without warm clothing, living close to nature and free of the artifices that clutter our advanced civilization.

My companion and I hiked upward through a forest of ohia, the pioneer tree of fresh lava flows. "The invincible ohia," Mark Twain called it after observing its trunks emerging like spears of grass from volcanic crevices. Growing to a height of 80 feet or more, the ohia has been useful to humans. Hawaiians of other days fashioned spears, mallets, and bowls from its hard wood. Considerable quantities were cut and shipped to mainland America for railroad ties. In fact, the celebrated golden spike connecting the transcontinental rail lines in 1869 was driven into an ohia tie from Hawaii.

We hadn't heard many sounds since starting from the trailhead. Suddenly we became aware of a whirring of wings. We stopped and stood very quietly. Joe, a Hawaii Volcanoes National Park ranger, said it was an apapane, the most common surviving species of Hawaiian honeycreeper, flitting from one tree to another in the forest canopy to feed on nectar from ohia blossoms. This striking bird, known for its deep crimson body feathers and black wings and tail, declined to reveal itself. We were lucky enough, at least, to hear its rambling, rolling song, the high melodic passages contrasting with occasional harsh and raucous notes.

Everything natural and native about Hawaii—its birds, insects, plants, ferns, and trees—seems so distinctive and luxuriant, yet it is all acutely vulnerable. Of the 70 bird species found nowhere else in the world, 29 are on the threatened or endangered list and at least three are close to extinction.

Why should this be? Andrew J. Berger, the retired chairman of the University of Hawaii's zoology department, is the foremost authority on Hawaiian birds. His credentials include many field trips across the Hawaiian chain from the "Big Island" to Midway, 1,600 nautical miles westward in the Pacific. In his definitive book *Hawaiian Birdlife*, Dr. Berger traces the evolution of species and the influences of civilization leading to their decline. In the beginning, after the volcanic islands emerged from the sea, life forms arrived, adapted and evolved. Like the finches Charles Darwin found on the Galapagos Islands off the coast of South America, Hawaiian honeycreepers developed in their various niches as seed eaters and nectar feeders, one with a bill like a woodpecker's, another with a parrot-like bill for crushing seeds, and still another with a downcurving bill to suck nectar from a particular flower.

Polynesians came a thousand years ago bringing domestic animals that destroyed bird nests and preyed on eggs and nestlings. The new Hawaiians used birds for food and feathers for capes and headdresses for their chieftains. European settlers, following Captain Cook's exploration of 1778, converted forests into plantations and pastures for goats, sheep, cattle, horses, and pigs. Exotic species such as the mockingbird, meadowlark, cardinal, house finch, and California quail were introduced. Bird diseases came with them.

Dr. Berger brings credit to ornithology by refusing to hide behind scientific jargon, instead placing blame where it belongs in language anyone can understand. As he relates, in the 1950s the Hawaiian Division of Forestry and U.S. Forest Service promoted destruction of native Koa forests in order to plant pines. "Until recently," he writes, "the board-feet-oriented federal foresters referred to the endemic Hawaiian ecosystems as 'decadent forests,' consisting of 'weed species' and 'unproductive forest land.' Consequently, state forestry plans have continued to place emphasis on planting exotic trees."

Little wonder that of the 23 species and 24 subspecies of honeycreepers identified during the nineteenth century, most are now threatened, endangered or extinct. Only three of the islands—Kauai, Maui, and Hawaii, the Big Island—have forest birds in any numbers, and these live on extremely small parts of each island. I first visited Hawaii as a World War II navigator; each time I return, I see its rare and lovely qualities more exploited and disfigured—by unrestrained tourism, transportation, energy production, construction, commerce of virtually any kind.

Dr. Berger's assessment of the situation is bitter and unequivocal: "That the Hawaiian biota should have been raped, ravaged, and devastated during the nineteenth century was regrettable even though understandable, but that this rape has continued not only into the twentieth century but even into the eighth decade of that century is a sad commentary on man as an animal species. Man is, indeed, a disease on the planet earth."

I hope not, even though the visible record of our time, in Hawaii as elsewhere in the world, is clear enough to support the charge of rape, ravage, and devastation. Luckily there is still time to undo damage and reverse course. I thought about it at length while Joe and I made the long, rough climb up Mauna Loa. Following the trail marked by stone cairns called ahus, we walked over lava flows of the 1984 eruption, raw and black, glistening with gold or silvery tint. The upper slopes, high above any vegetation, were stark and bare. For all the scientific studies of earthquakes and the movement of magma, the source of that molten rock deep below the surface remains a mystery.

The 220,000-acre Hawaii Volcanoes National Park reaches from the sea through forest and desert to the summit of Mauna Loa. National Park Service efforts to eliminate free-ranging goats and pigs are encouraging, even though it may be centuries before habitat for forest birds is restored. Moreover, historic and prehistoric features, including petroglyphs, rock carvings, graves and Hawaiian sacred shrines, the heiaus, are being preserved.

The trouble is that the integrity of Hawaii Volcanoes, as of all national parks, depends on conditions beyond its borders. On one slope of Kilauea just outside the park, ohia has been clearcut from a key native rain forest held by one of Hawaii's fiefdoms, the Campbell Estate, presumably to furnish the chips to fuel electric generators and to "provide new jobs." But the mainland firm operating under Campbell Estate lease left in failure, with a trail of unpaid bills, penalties, and fines.

Now the Campbell Estate is involved in a proposed 9,000-acre geothermal energy complex along the park border, designed to tap volcanic steam with drilling rigs, roads, pipelines, wells, cooling towers, and power plants. Never mind the honeycreepers and ferns or inevitable noxious gases when volcanic steam can be exploited for commercial gain. Never mind, either, the classification of Kilauea as a conservation district under Hawaii's land-use legislation of the 1960s. That problem was casually resolved by legislatively designating a "geothermal subzone" in 1984.

The Park Service wants to acquire the Campbell land as an addition to the park and shift the geothermal project to another site. That would help, I suppose, but only to a limited degree. Something more fundamental is needed. Native Hawaiians speak of "Aina," the traditional love of land or reverence for life. Their poetic oli, or chants, and the hula recount stories and traditions of humankind woven into the natural universe. The summit of Kilauea is considered sacred, the palace of the goddess Pele. As daughter of Earth Mother and Sky Father, Pele came to Hawaii in flight from her cruel older sister, the goddess of the sea. She found her refuge at last in the volcano, where she has prevailed ever since as goddess of fire. This view may be dismissed as superstition or respected as reverence for life. Science, after all, may increase knowledge, but scientific data can't be equated with feeling that derives from the heart and soul.

Both science and spirituality are needed to solve our environmental problems. At a 1984 symposium at Hawaii Volcanoes National Park on Hawaii's terrestrial ecosystems and how to protect them, scientists Alan Holt and Barrie Fox said: "If a thousand years from today there are large areas of native landscape in Hawaii, it will be because the people cared enough to save them, cared enough to keep natural areas protected even in the face of other potential uses of these lands. The long-term success that we all hope for depends on the people's appreciation of the land. The best prospect for making that future happen is to show today's people the value of our natural heritage and to show them how to care for it."

These are words to remember. I can't conceive of a better prescription, not simply for Hawaii but for everywhere, a prescription that overcomes despair with opportunity and hope.

Rebirth in Yellowstone

Defenders of Wildlife
November 1988

One morning late last summer, I was hiking the trail from Jenny Lake up Cascade Canyon in Grand Teton National Park. The monumental wildfires burning in Yellowstone not far north clouded the skies and covered the lake, rather like a shroud of gloom. My two companions and I talked of smelling the smoke, of feeling it on our clothes.

Such was the morning scene. Heading back down the trail in the afternoon, however, the world turned around. A fair wind blew off the smoke. The peaks of the Tetons shone against a clear blue sky, while Jenny Lake became its old self, reflecting the glory of the earth around and above it. The change in a few short hours lifted our spirits. I felt a lesson in the experience: a reassurance that all would be well, in Yellowstone and in our lives, if only we would be patient, allowing nature and time the chance to heal.

Since then I've thought considerably about the fires, talked with experts and tried to digest assorted published materials, reviewing them all in the context of time rather than only of the moment. Soon after the fires, for instance, while at a conference in Washington State, I met my friend Russell E. Dickenson, a former director of the National Park Service. "The Yellowstone you and I knew for those many years," he said ruefully, "will never be the same." That is true, but the more I weigh the evidence, the more I look forward to the new, different Yellowstone. For there is life after fire—fire marks a rebirth, the continuation of a life-cycle founded on time, patience and harmony.

Forces like blizzard, cold, drought, earthquake, fire, flood, heat, hurricane, storm, volcano, and wind are beneficial as well as inevitable influences on the planet. They are the architects that shape and reshape the land into landscape and that continually recast form and function of all the creatures, whether plants or animals, growing upon the land and in the water. They are nature's art and poetry and dance and music, the genuine originals that spark creative inspiration in the human soul.

The damage to Yellowstone was unquestionably extensive, but more

commercial than ecological. "Let it burn," urged the scientists and park preservationists. "Fire will benefit the park in the long run." But commercial interests
operating inside the park and in nearby communities complained, "Fire is bad
for business," leading the politicians to insist upon suppression. The fires became a new source of headline-hunting, with assorted charges generously disre-
garding history and the best interests of the park as a natural life community.

Senator Malcolm Wallop, running for reelection in Wyoming, called for
the removal of William Penn Mott, director of the National Park Service, charging
that Mott had not been sufficiently aggressive in ordering that the fires be fought.
Bob Barbee, superintendent of Yellowstone, was ridiculed by Wallop as Bob
"Barbecue." The Secretary of the Interior, Donald Hodel, vowed that if the
Republicans were reelected, the government would really crack down on
national park fires. Governor Cecil Andrus of Idaho on national television
denounced the Republicans for allowing "a disastrous fire season in Yellowstone,"
leading Hodel to countercharge that Andrus as Interior Secretary had encouraged the policy of letting fires burn.

In such shallow, self-serving debate the wonders and welfare of Yellowstone
are obscured and forgotten. I think of Yellowstone as a particular treasure deserving better, to be safeguarded rather than exploited for profit or politics. I perceive Yellowstone as the last great stronghold of the grizzly bear, elk, bighorn
sheep and bison, whose interest is ignored in the fire-related hysteria. And so
too for the majestic winged animals: the bald eagle, trumpeter swan, raven
and great gray owl, which have long lived with fire and never complained, and
which ask our dominant human society to grant them this sanctuary, without
complaining. . . .

Fire has been part of Yellowstone and of the West since long before the
first explorer. Fire swept through periodically, releasing nutrients such as nitrogen, calcium, phosphorous, and potassium that come from burned wood.
These mixed into the soil to fertilize new growth. Fire opened the cones of
lodgepole pine trees, raining seeds on the ground. Most fires killed some
trees, but those left, free of competition for nutrients, light and water, grew
stronger and healthier.

Many Indian tribes considered fire a friend rather than an enemy, just as
primitive peoples and farmers in various parts of the world even to this day set
fire to "green up the grass" and stimulate new growth. But as a consequence
of wildfires devastating to valuable commercial timber forests, American public policy for the last century has been designed to suppress all fires. So the

national parks were managed, although their forests are not intended to produce timber. In 1972, natural regulation, or "let burn," at last became the policy, allowing natural fires, such as those caused by lightning, to run their course except when threatening human life or property.

That policy worked, reinforced by research showing that the vast majority of wildfires die on their own, seldom burning more than 100 acres. Then came last June, when lightning danced in Yellowstone skies. Severe drought had turned trees into tinder; dead litter on the forest floor, untouched during years of fire suppression, made it worse. The fires took off. A carelessly tossed cigarette butt set off a massive new blaze in July.

In early September, when I was in the Grand Tetons, the first snows fell on Wyoming. They helped to extinguish the fires. The tourist industry of the region, looking toward its own future, was the first to proclaim that damage, while serious, really wasn't all that serious. None of the main attractions along the loop road were affected; wildlife was affected only lightly; plenty of old-growth forest remains untouched; and wildflowers and grasses are springing up from nutrient-rich ash. As the Wyoming Travel Commission advised, "New national park exhibits and interpretive displays will be in place by the spring of 1989 to provide visitors with a better understanding of the unique role of fire within a natural ecosystem."

That statement is to the good as far as it goes, but the Wyoming Travel Commission, its business constituents and the politicians who speak for them need the "better understanding" more than park visitors do. Yellowstone must be treated more as a national ecological preserve and less as a national playground. The wolf must be restored to the habitat from which it was wrongfully removed. The Yellowstone ecosystem must be perceived and administered in larger terms than the park itself, with clearcut logging and oil and gas drilling eliminated from bordering national forests.

If Wyoming and the other bordering states, Idaho and Montana, join with the rest of the nation in moving toward these goals, the 1988 fires will have served an important educational purpose. For now, I can hardly wait to revisit Yellowstone and find new meaning in its changing landscape.

A Treasure in the North

Defenders of Wildlife
February 1992

In 1956 the Murie party headed for the Arctic north, the barely known, little charted top of the continent. The small group of scientific explorers was committed to a single mission: to collect data "to push a movement to establish a large permanent reserve in the Brooks Range region extending perhaps across the border into Canada."

Their efforts then and thereafter led to establishment of our country's largest national wildlife refuge. Together with an adjacent Canadian national park, it constitutes an international wilderness sanctuary of dimensions and values scarcely matched anywhere on earth. This is a rare American treasure in our trust. I think of the refuge, embracing the largest mountains of the Brooks Range and their foothills sloping north to the coastal plain and southward toward the Yukon River as a book of life the way God wrote it: page after page vibrant with grizzly bears, wolves, caribou, moose, Dall sheep, polar bears, eagles, peregrine falcons, seabirds and songbirds, and with the native people we call Eskimos, who have dwelled in this north country since their ancestors crossed the land bridge from Asia countless centuries ago. In the history of conservation, certain events, principles and individuals stand out as preeminent—for example, the establishment of Yellowstone in 1872 as the first national park, or the designation of the Gila in 1924 as the first wilderness. The Murie expedition and the people associated with it belong in that class.

The leader of the group, Olaus J. Murie, was no stranger to the Alaska wilderness. As a field biologist for the Bureau of Biological Survey (later the Fish and Wildlife Service), Murie had made a series of trips to the Brooks Range as early as the 1920s. Often his partner on the trail was his wife Margaret, or Mardy, whom he had married two months after she became the first woman graduate of the University of Alaska. In the mid-1930s, Olaus and Victor Scheffer conducted a pioneering ecological inventory of the Aleutian Islands, while Mardy stayed on St. Lawrence Island, in the Bering Sea 40 miles from Siberia, in company with the native people and studying the archaeology of their ancestors.

In the 1950s Olaus had left government service to play an active role as citizen-scientist. In his capacity as director of the Wilderness Society, he equated this goal with the work of Robert Marshall, the principal founder of the Wilderness Society who had made an extended stay in the Arctic in the early thirties and had written, in his classic book *Arctic Village*, about freedom, tolerance, beauty and contentment in the north.

The issue was not whether the area should be designated a national park. Murie envisioned the emphasis on wilderness and wildlife rather than on people. In the expedition of 1956 the principals in the party included Olaus and Margaret Murie; Dr. Brina Kessel, a young biologist of the University of Alaska; and two promising graduate students, Robert Krear and George Schaller. They made their way by bush plane to the northeast corner of Alaska bordering the Yukon basin in Canada. Once they were finished, the campaign to protect the area began in earnest. Under auspices of the Conservation Foundation, Olaus showed slides of the Sheenjek in Alaska and felt heartened by public "willingness to help in any movement to preserve some of the choice parts of the wilderness." Or as Mardy wrote, "Thoughtful people in and out of Alaska were concerned, for the Age of the Bulldozer had arrived."

The Interior Department responded by inviting Olaus to make a formal presentation in Washington, after which Secretary Fred Seaton in November 1957 identified nine million acres for the future establishment of the Alaska National Wildlife Range. Mining and other commercial interests complained about "sacrificing development for the benefit of a handful of elite hunters, scientists and tourists." They wanted state control, multiple use, flexibility. But on December 6, 1960, over the objections of Alaska's congressional delegation, governor, state legislature, and fish and game commission, Secretary Seaton signed an order creating ANWR and closed it to entry under the mining laws. The two Alaska senators, Ernest Gruening and Bob Bartlett, though progressives on most issues, struck back by blocking appropriations for years.

The oil development at Prudhoe Bay brought new attention to this great preserve. In circles where commerce comes first, a nature sanctuary is scarcely considered inviolate. Despite its doubling in size and redesignation as a refuge by the historic Alaska Lands Conservation Law of 1980, the pressures for oil exploration have only intensified.

Last November the Senate rejected a move to allow oil rigs to invade the refuge. That was heartening. Moreover, many senators and House members are sponsoring bills to make the disputed coastal plain protected wilderness.

Senator William V. Roth (R-Delaware) has gone farther. Impressed with the opportunity to protect a magnificent ecosystem shared by two nations, he is sponsoring a bill to establish a Northern Yukon-Arctic International Wildlife Refuge. The Northern Yukon National Park is already there as a Canadian nucleus, and Canada is hoping soon to establish a second border park just to its south. There is a potential, working with the Native peoples of the region, for something still grander. Now the responsibility lies with the United States to protect fully its own wilderness resource in this corner of our Arctic. Leadership, true leadership, in safeguarding endowments of nature makes for better international relations than force of arms.

As for the Murie party, one day last summer George Schaller, now a renowned natural scientist in his own right, arrived at Mrs. Murie's log home in the Tetons. He thought he was there to make film footage for a documentary on the life of Mardy Murie. He was in for a surprise. It was a Sheenjek reunion, with Bob Krear, now retired after a career of university teaching, and Brina Kessel, still going strong at the University of Alaska and compiling a study on the birds of Alaska. Olaus's memory was with them as they relived their adventure.

"We celebrated with a little cake, white on top," Mardy Murie told me about this reunion. "We looked back at the '50s and '60s and felt we had achieved a little victory in gaining the refuge." There was nothing small about it, Mrs. Murie. That was a blessing for Alaska and us all, one we are only beginning to appreciate.

CHAPTER VI

ON MEDIA AND EDUCATION

I remember almost thirty years ago when Tom Bell began his own paper, the fortnightly *High Country News,* because the media in his native Wyoming and Rocky Mountain West generally failed to cover critical environmental issues. He labored endless hours and invested all his savings. It was definitely not a venture for profit.

Tom has long been out of it, but *High Country News* perseveres, even prospers, run by a nonprofit foundation and read by 15,000 subscribers. Betsy Marston, the editor, calls it "a presumptuous little paper that attempts to cover ten western states, believing it *is* possible to cover a green beat fairly, yet care passionately about the issues that involve wildlife, public lands, and rural communities." Perhaps the most presumptuous part of it is that advertising is discouraged—subscribers pay for the stories they read, not for refrigerator ads.

Having watched the media and its treatment of the environment through the years, the point that stands out to me now is not what the mass media, "the mainstream," does, or fails to do, but the advent of a whole new alternative genre pioneered by *High Country News.* I look across the West and see a wide variety of publications like *Environment Hawaii, Wild Forest Review,* and *Cascadia Times,* all professionally designed and written, plus the desktop-published magazines and newsletters of grassroots environmental groups like *Raven Call* (Southeast Alaska Conservation Council), *Networker* (Alliance for the Wild Rockies), and *Northwest Conservationist* (Northwest Ecosystem Alliance). They fill a niche the mainstream media has chosen to bypass.

At a conference on Northwest Media and the Environment, conducted at Bellingham, Washington, in October 1993, Bill Dietrich, science reporter of the *Seattle Times,* was incredibly frank:

> *Environmental coverage is generally in full retreat. In my tenure at the Times, we've gone from two or three reporters routinely covering the environment to one, while doubling the size of the business page staff. Most reporters at the Times are consumption reporters: We advise what foods to eat, gadgets to get, businesses to buy stocks in, fads to conform to. Two-thirds of the newspaper is devoted to advertising urging people to consume. To this a periodic lonely environmental story is regarded by some as a dire threat to American civilization.*

But there's always a better way. Looking to the future, thirty years hence, I envision the print alternatives as only the beginning. Developments in telecommunications and cyberspace await those smart enough to use them. I look for new networks providing environmental news and inspiration in forms to which people can respond and enjoy.

I wish I could say the same for education, waiting somehow for its alternative. That day will come, when professors become risk-takers and lead their classes outside the classrooms to learn from life through activism. I believe it fitting here to cite the career of Richard Neuberger. Born in Portland in 1912, he became a student editor at the University of Oregon, campaigning for abolition of mandatory military training and compulsory student fees. His grades were low and he left without graduating—then wrote for the Portland *Oregonian, New York Times,* and many of the best magazines. In time he grew from an observer of politics into a participant, first as a member of the Oregon House of Representatives, then the State Senate, and in 1954 as a member of the United States Senate, breaking a Republican monopoly on Oregon politics. Until his untimely death in 1960, he was associated with every positive piece of environmental legislation, and was known in the Senate as "Mr. Conservation." Yet he still thought of himself as a writer and in a *Harper's* article (February 1947) wondered aloud about the propriety of his political activism. But,

> *When I see Oregon's teachers paid the lowest salaries on the Coast, when I see a private utility company selling the power from the dam at Bonneville which the people built and paid for, when I see a Japanese-American soldier with forty-one blood transfusions denied a hotel room on a rainy night, when I see a million-dollar race track rising while veterans cannot construct homes—then my blood pressure rises too, and I wonder if any case is strong enough to impel abdication in favor of those who tolerate these things.*

I didn't find this quotation in a textbook; I wish that I had.

Where Are the Muckrakers?

Defenders of Wildlife
March 1992

Steve Stuebner's editors at the *Boise Statesman* discovered last year that he was undermining the sacred objectivity of their news columns by injecting what they considered his own personal pro-environment bias. They caught him doing this subtly and slyly, for example by referring to a contested Idaho roadless area as a "wildlife sanctuary."

So the editors of the *Statesman,* a unit of the Gannett chain, called Stuebner in, cited the evidence and announced they were shifting him from the environment beat, after five years with a string of awards, to cover city-county news. Stuebner conceded ruffling feathers now and then but felt victimized by the management's demand for blandness. "Milquetoast reporting," he calls it—and he quit.

Stuebner isn't the first to go down, then out the door for reporting and writing about the environment as though it really matters. Richard Manning, who worked for the *Missoulian,* the daily newspaper in Missoula, Montana, attracted wide attention in 1988 with a hard-hitting series on the exploitation of Montana forests. It was no small venture, involving weeks of interviews, backcountry legwork and painstaking examination of documents. He won awards for investigative reporting, but his bosses at the paper felt squeamish. They squelched him by transferring him to another beat, and he quit.

Manning might still be hacking out tame features in Missoula predicated on the passive "he said, she said" newspaper formula. I'm glad he didn't. Instead, he wrote a fine book, *Last Stand,* which tells a lot about him, the newspaper business and the forces controlling the forests.

Journalists attempting to cover the environment are subject to this kind of treatment more often than you would think. I know, having been there myself, remembering how *Field & Stream* in 1974 dismissed me as conservation editor. "Virtually every veteran environmental writer I know has been threatened with the loss of his or her job at one time or another," says Jim Detjen of the *Philadelphia Inquirer.*

It happens to the best of people in the best of places. Philip Shabecoff for

32 years worked as a reporter for the *New York Times,* including stints as foreign correspondent in hot spots of the world. For 14 years he covered the environmental beat in Washington, a pacesetter in his profession, turning up one major story after another. I never realized until recently that while Shabecoff was respected and admired on the outside, he was rowing upstream on the inside.

A profile he wrote during the early Reagan days of James G. Watt, then Secretary of the Interior, was rejected by the *New York Times Magazine* because he, Shabecoff, was "ahead of the curve." Other articles were not published. *Times* editors told him he was stale, biased, "too close to environmentalists"— exactly the same message, in almost the same words, that Manning and Stuebner heard from their bosses. When he was taken off his beat and switched to cover the Internal Revenue Service, Shabecoff quit and established *Greenwire,* a valuable daily computer briefing service on environmental news all over the world.

Institutions and professions of our time tend to be conformist and conservative, breeding young talent into good old boys and good old girls who play it safe, careful not to rock the boat. The media ought to be different, the one institution of society that watchdogs all the others and keeps them honest. . . .

The truth is that big environmental stories seldom are broken by the mainstream media. Most of those stories appear first in alternative publications that lately have emerged because the mainstream has failed. Thus I should not have been surprised at speeches I heard at the first annual meeting of the Society of Environmental Journalists last October. Yes, there is such a group, but don't think it's about to incite a green revolution—it isn't that kind.

I would like to have heard a keynote speaker boldly define the most critical environmental problems—ozone depletion, overpopulation, accumulation of toxic wastes, threats to biotic diversity or whatever they may be—and challenge the media to raise public awareness in support of global strategies to avoid disaster. Instead, the keynote was delivered by William Ruckelshaus, the old EPA administrator, now a mogul of waste-management entrepreneurs. He was dreary and discouraging, preaching a gospel that environmentalism has gone too far, sounding as if he were talking to the chamber of commerce.

Perhaps the mainstreamers in charge wanted someone of prominence or prestige to grace their first convention and thus legitimize it. I would like to have heard from Hugh Kaufman, the courageous EPA whistleblower, or Dave Foreman, the Earth First founder, about his bitter encounter with the FBI, or Peter Raven or Paul Ehrlich on the global struggles for biodiversity. Instead,

I heard speakers talk about the goodies in pesticides, the bad side of the 1990 Clean Air Act and how there really are no health benefits to improving visibility at the Grand Canyon and the eagles won't notice the difference anyway.

Such presentations assure a generous serving of requisite "balance," but the best talk I heard was given by Betsy Marston, editor of the feisty *High Country News*. She said simply: "We do have a beat, the environment, and we do care about the land, the animals and plants that live on and with the land, and the communities that have a stake in the West. We think of ourselves as the grassroots, on-the-ground newspaper. Our job goes beyond reporting to interpretation and understanding."

That makes sense to me as journalism playing its rightful role, and while the big papers complain about loss of circulation, advertising and influence, the biweekly *High Country News* keeps growing. It is published by a non-profit educational foundation that doesn't depend on advertising, so it doesn't waste paper. I find hope in *High Country News* and other regionals coming along, such as *Environment Hawaii* edited and published by Patricia Tummons. Society needs them—more of them in every part of the country—to tell it straight, going beyond reporting to interpretation and understanding.

Plenty of good journalists are ready, like those I mentioned above who would rather quit than cave in. They follow the best tradition of their profession, my profession, as practiced by Lincoln Steffens, Upton Sinclair and the other muckrakers early in this century. "A newspaper is indeed like a woman or a politician," wrote Steffens in his celebrated autobiography. "When it is young, honest, and full of ideas, it is attractive, trusted, and full of the possibilities of power. Powerful men see this, see its uses, and so seek to possess it. And some of them do get and keep it, and they use, abuse, and finally ruin it." No wonder he and others did most of their writing for magazines and alternative papers.

Steve Stuebner calls his old bosses "Gannettoids" and their products "McPaper." Maybe so, but the media have a powerful role to play beyond their current meager efforts. It's more difficult for editors to ask, "What's really going on? What does it mean? Where's the rest of the story?" And even more so to come up with hard answers, as a handful do at the risk of their careers. But as a reader once wrote to me, "History books are records of events and the doings of individuals who didn't go with the flow." Let truth hang out and consequences follow. It's the way to keep the system honest and working.

Outdoor Educators Must Stop Playing It Safe

High Country News
April 24, 1989

My theories of education begin with the principle that learning derives from life, all of life, as an unending process from birth to death. John Muir, who left the University of Wisconsin to matriculate in what he called the "University of Wilderness," provides a classic example to prove the point.

That much is simple. It may also be simple to say that modern American education emphasizes the cognitive—that is, a focus on facts, with abilities to analyze, calculate and memorize, and to use language. Yes, it provides a practical means of acquiring information, but the intuitive, ethical and spiritual are largely omitted. Imagination is often repressed or undervalued, so that only a limited portion of one's capacity is trained. And the task remains of becoming a whole person.

"Our imaginations have been industrially deformed to conceive only what can be molded into an engineered system of social habits that fit the logic of large-scale production," writes Ivan Illich in his marvelous little book, *Tools of Conviviality:*

> *People feel joy, as opposed to mere pleasure, to the extent that their activities are creative; while the growth of tools beyond a certain point increases regimentation, dependence, exploitation and impotence. . . . Convivial tools are those which give each person who uses them the greatest opportunity to enrich the environment with the fruits of his or her vision.*

In this vein, I will cite the work of Michael H. Brown, a psychologist and educator, who conducts wilderness vision quests to help "explore and develop valuable human resources which lie dormant in us all." He concentrates on spiritual dimensions of contact with the natural world. As he puts it, "It is time to deliberately focus on and consciously work toward the constructive discovery, exploration, healing, enrichment and growth of the human spirit."

That idea to me marks another key principle in education, as it relates to the large wild outdoors of the national forests and national parks, but also to small fragments of wilderness close to home. In a technological, super-civilized world, they provide "tools for conviviality."

A growing number of colleges and universities recognize the benefits of conducting programs in river running, backpacking, rock climbing, and snow climbing. They encourage individual independence, group cooperation, ecological awareness and an environmentally simpler life. Some include literature, history, anthropology, and ecology with the wilderness experience. That's all to the good.

I recall during a recent summer arriving at the Yellowstone Institute, located in an old national park facility, the historic Buffalo Ranch, near the east entrance to Yellowstone National Park. There I met Wayne Phillips, normally a range ecologist for the U.S. Forest Service, preparing to teach a two-day course in wildflowers and their environment. During this brief period he would lead pleasant walks and an evening seminar, providing practical guidelines to wildflower identification and plant ecology. Most students stayed in simple cabins and did their own cooking in a community kitchen, all of which enriched the experience and kept the cost low. Such institutes continue to emerge in national parks—and that's to the good, too.

People learn in different ways, at different ages and stages; I would hardly claim one approach to be most correct, but plainly it doesn't take a lot of lecturing when lessons are manifest in sky, earth, water, weather.

For example, another friend, Sam West, worked as a guide and field manager for OARS, a large outfitting firm, on Colorado River trips through the Grand Canyon. OARS detailed Sam for a time to Nepal to establish a guide program in the Himalayas. He climbed mountains with Tibetans and Nepalese and studied Eastern philosophy. Then he returned to the Grand Canyon to work several years as a river ranger for the National Park Service.

"I've seen people who have spent a week or two on the Colorado River and changed their lives," Sam once said to me. "They would go home and quit their jobs. That place has the power to do it. It has a precious kind of energy that can be tapped—just by going there and relating to it in a respectful way."

The experience and his Buddhism changed Sam's life, too. He left the security of federal employment to work on a program introducing city people to the outdoors, and then with prisoners and others of society's dispossessed. Nobody told him or taught him to do so; it was a progression in his own growth derived largely from learning in the wild outdoors.

We all come in somewhere, not knowing where the trail will lead. Mark Dubois, as a kid in Sacramento, prowled the caves and limestone canyon bluffs above the Stanislaus River in the Mother Lode country. In time he became a river guide, working on raft trips on the undammed nine-mile section of river through the Stanislaus Canyon. After two years of commercial river running, Mark and friends started doing free river trips with kids, mostly inner-city kids, delinquents. As Mark told me:

> We didn't get paid, it just felt good doing it and we needed just enough for gas and minimal expenses. We taught stars, edible plants and how to identify the critters. We would lead the blind into caves, switch off the light, and let them lead the way out. It's amazing how much you can learn being blind.
>
> We recognized that on the rivers there isn't such a thing as a delinquent. The only reason there's delinquency is when you don't have anything to do and you break a window. Out in the wild places, all of a sudden "delinquents" and "normal" kids, you can't tell the difference anymore, because there are so many things to occupy their attention that they're all the same.

When he began, Mark knew nothing about dams, but he knew more about the Stanislaus than anybody, and likely loved it more, too—certainly enough to lead the heroic fight against the New Melones Dam. In 1979 he demonstrated his commitment by chaining himself to a boulder at a remote spot along the river and threatening to stay until the waters covered him or until he received assurance that the Stanislaus would not be buried under 200 feet of reservoir water. Mark's willingness to sacrifice himself worked, but only for a time. Ultimately the project was completed. Some time after, I canoed with Mark and Sharon, his wife, on flat water that once flowed free. While camping on a rocky bluff, we talked long and late. Mark said:

> The word "need" to me is really a funny word. Everybody uses it, but I more and more question what you really need. Ghandi has a quote that says, "There's enough in this world for every man's need, but not for every man's greed." I somehow feel that greed is too harsh a word. It's not just greed: There's an ignorance of thinking these things are going to give us happiness. Wild places teach people that you don't need all those things.

Such dialogue reminds me of where I came in, of the experience that changed my own life. It was more than 30 years ago on a trip sponsored by the American Forestry Association, "Trail Riders of the Wilderness," to the Bridger Wilderness in Wyoming.

Looking back, I recall serious deficiencies that I would not now approve: too many riders, too many horses, too much booze, and power saws to cut firewood. But I also remember the trail leading through a natural kingdom of tall timbers and a thousand clear lakes, weaving among massive rock formations to compare with those in Yosemite Valley. We camped upon the very scenes painted by Alfred Jacob Miller in 1837, the Wind River places that he had found "as fresh and beautiful as if just from the hands of the Creator."

A psychologist might explain the appeal of that sweeping scene in the sheer absence of critical or harmful human actions, or perhaps by saying that through solitude in the primeval one feels liberated of strain and stress. In any case, the individual acquires a sense of scale, feeling that he or she belongs at the bosom of a much greater and peaceful whole, larger and longer lasting than anything known before.

Here at last the individual has at hand an environmental model from which to measure the restorative impetus needed to cope with alienation from nature. Or as Shakespeare summed it up in Act II of *As You Like It*, "And this our life, exempt from public haunt, finds tongues in trees, books in the running brooks, sermons in stones and good in everything."

From the beginning, I learned other lessons by studying wilderness: its history, values, administrations and uses—including use as a learning resource. The University of the Wilderness, of which Muir wrote, could hardly be more real or vital to our times. However, I determined that with opportunity goes responsibility: I must be more than a user but a guardian as well.

It isn't enough to view national parks, or wilderness, as Enos Mills did, as "the school of nature." It isn't enough to accept Freeman Tilden's uplifting idea as expressed in *Interpreting Our Heritage*:

> *Thousands of naturalists, historians, archaeologists and other specialists are engaged in the work of revealing, to such visitors as desire the service, something of the beauty and wonder, the inspiration and spiritual meaning that lie behind what the visitor can with his sense perceive.*

That to my mind is the introductory part of it. The challenge is to contribute consciously and conscientiously to making the out-of-doors into genuine demonstration models of ecological harmony, while imparting an understanding of actions necessary to protect the natural system from the abundant threats against it. I can't say that I see many outdoor educators doing this.

Moreover, nature reserves cannot be uncoupled from the world around them. They cannot endure as valid ecological sources of inspiration and spiritual meaning in surroundings of worsening environmental decay. What we need today is a revolution of thought to challenge and revamp old institutions:

medicine, religion, economics, education, science, politics, communications, and natural resource administration. Today's conditions demand a critical examination of old national goals and traditional personal goals measured in terms of comfort and security, alongside new social standards based on sharing, caring, and risk-taking.

Nuclear weapons will never force nations to join in recognizing the limitations of a fragile earth. But environmental educators could lead in pledging allegiance to a green and peaceful planet, based on the concept of husbanding and sharing resources, instead of allowing them to be cornered and squandered.

The trouble is that most outdoor educators are careful to avoid critical issues. This is especially the case in national parks, where employees want to get ahead or be sure of re-hire the following summer. As evidence I cite an exception to prove the rule, my friend Alfred Runte, historian and educator (author of a well-respected history, *National Parks: The American Experience*). While working as a seasonal interpreter in Yosemite National Park during the summer of 1980, Runte talked to visitors about national park ethics and ideology. He would begin by asking his audience to recognize that national parks are in jeopardy, then adding: "What would you be willing to do to see that national parks remain part of the fabric of American society for generations to come? Would you be willing to give up some power so that geothermal development would not destroy Old Faithful? Would you be willing to give up some lighting so that strip mines and coal-fired power plants would not be needed in the Southwest?"

For his troubles Runte was directed to a week of "rehabilitation training," during which the chief park interpreter and assistant superintendent listened to the tape of a talk he had given to park visitors, reviewed the transcript and made corrections. Then, dressed like tourists, they accompanied him while he led groups of visitors and made further changes. Runte was undismayed; following "rehabilitation," he delivered his message as he chose. Later, he told me: "I think that a program, any program, any lecture, whether in a university or a public setting, without a theme, a message, is pointless. Dispensing information for information's sake is not what the Park Service ought to be doing."

The same holds true for any educational institution. I appreciate the role of the many nature centers functioning across the country, yet I lament the studied avoidance of critical issues across the fence. Or, as the director of the Palm Springs Desert Museum—a classy oasis filled with natural science exhibits, yet surrounded by a deteriorating environment—told me in 1978: "Our board doesn't want us to be involved."

But what is the rightful role of education, educators, and the educated? I think again of the social criticism of Ivan Illich:

> *The present world is divided into those who do not have enough and those who have more than enough, those who are pushed off the road by cars and the rich anxious to get more. . . .*

Paul Sears, the pioneer ecologist, once defined conservation as a point of view involved with the concept of freedom, human dignity, and the American spirit. Gifford Pinchot expressed much the same idea, declaring that the rightful use and purpose of natural resources in a free society is to make all the people strong and well, able and wise, well-taught, well-fed, full of knowledge and initiative, with equal opportunity for all and special privilege for none.

We need to get on with this mission. "A nation that continues year after year to spend more money on military defense than on programs of social uplift is approaching spiritual death," wrote Martin Luther King, Jr., who embodied the challenge to spiritual life. I yearn for the time when green and growing things will become part of what we now call "the ghetto," and when education in the wild outdoors will serve the impoverished and dispossessed. We know already that getting drug victims away from environments where they have failed into settings where they find their own ways in solitude helps give them a new outlook on life. Mental patients who haven't been out of hospital walls in years have shaken off habits of defeat, dependence, helplessness, and passive compliance by achieving some personal success through wilderness learning and adventure.

Thus I feel that outdoor environmental education is only at the beginning. Those wild places will prove invaluable in the learning that derives from life, all of life, if only society is smart enough to save them.

In Defense of Wildlife and Open Expression

Wild Earth

December 1992

Wild Earth *editor's note: We present here, as words of caution, the letter as well as the column of Michael Frome concerning his recent dismissal from* Defenders. *This dismissal is both sad and predictable. Michael Frome whom Dave Foreman once described as America's best environmental journalist has a history of honorable discharges: Several periodicals have terminated Frome's tenure with them after he dared write truths that rocked the establishment. Defenders of Wildlife members should paddle hard to free that organization from the mainstream.*

In late October James Deane, editor of *Defenders*, telephoned to dismiss me as columnist of the magazine to which I had contributed without interruption for more than seventeen years.

Deane said my dismissal was ordered by Rodger Schlickheisen, the new president and executive director of Defenders of Wildlife, who had decided to restructure the publication, with himself in complete charge of editorial content. Deane explained that Schlickheisen does not want expression of independent ideas in the magazine, and that he saw my column as comprising two pages which he personally could not control.

I do not dispute Schlickheisen's right to run his organization, including its periodical, as he wishes. However, various colleagues in journalism, members of Defenders of Wildlife, and friends have asked me questions that merit an open response.

I believe it appropriate, therefore, to provide here my last column for *Defenders*, submitted but not published. Note the second paragraph, in which I expressed my opinion that when the issue arises of clearing a public area of campers or of bears, I say: Close the place to camping; safeguarding bears, or any native species, comes first. In the subsequent paragraph I wrote that wildlife doesn't get much help in the very settings where help and compassion are most expected.

That is the point. I endeavor to focus on specifics, accountability and action, where an organization like Defenders evidently prefers the benign, environmentally politically correct approaches associated with biodiversity, Amazon rain forest, whales and wolves and, as in the current issue, "The Leopold Legacy"—catchy issues that appeal to public sentiment without offending potential contributors.

In 1990 Deane told me of a communication from an influential member of the Defenders board of directors decrying the use of the word "environmentalist" because it might turn some people away. Several years ago he rejected a column of mine because, he said, it was critical of Republicans in Congress and might discourage Republican contributors to Defenders. The column was about politics, not Republicans, but the admonition I received was part of a continuing message: It's okay to be bold, but not too bold; be reasonable.

In December 1990 Deane called me about a column I had just submitted. He explained that a Defenders lobbyist was upset about a section of my column citing an action by Neal Sigmon, a congressional committee staff member, who personally deleted the appropriation for a National Park Service house organ, the *Courier*, because of something written by a ranger-reporter that he, Sigmon, didn't like. The lobbyist feared my reference to Sigmon would endanger her influence with the congressional subcommittee and I was asked to eliminate the reference in my column. I found the idea of political pandering very disturbing, but offered to compromise by omitting Sigmon's name. Deane lectured me sternly, reminding me that *Defenders* is not a general circulation publication, but represents the special interests of Defenders of Wildlife—which to me is all the more reason to be wholly truthful. Writers and editors, particularly of environmental periodicals, need to shuck cosmetic coverage of tough issues and place responsibility wherever it may belong.

In 1991 I wrote a column that was rejected. It began with reference to the conformist and conservative character of institutions and professions, and to the penalties imposed on individuals who break ranks on issues of principle. I cited the harsh experiences of John Mumma, a regional forester of the U.S. Forest Service, when he tried to halt overcutting of public forests in Montana and northern Idaho, and of Philip Shabecoff, the environmental reporter of the *New York Times*, a pacesetter in his profession, who was taken off his beat and switched to cover the Internal Revenue Service because his editors considered him biased, "too close to environmentalists." Shabecoff quit and environmental coverage became appropriately—as they say of the *New York Times*—"gray."

I was admonished. Deane told me on the phone that two influential members of the board disapproved of my work, that I was not free to choose my own subjects, that *Defenders* was the board members' magazine, that I had elicited criticism from Governor Walter Hickel over the column I had written about wildlife in Alaska. I wrote that of course there would be criticism—for anyone claiming to be an environmental journalist who fails to expose an issue of controversy and to stir debate is not doing his or her job.

I have never met Rodger Schlickheisen and confess that I never heard of him until his selection as president of Defenders. I have read that he is experienced in direct mail promotion and is a former administrative assistant to Senator Max Baucus of Montana. At Defenders, he succeeds as president Dr. Rupert Cutler, who served for three years, and Joyce Kelly, who served for two years before Cutler. I received only encouragement and support from them.

The Last Column

I was pleased at first when the ranger, C., phoned in June from Mesa Verde National Park in Colorado, on behalf of several colleagues who wanted to trust me with important information. I like to be trusted by caring personnel struggling to serve public principle in a bureaucracy driven by politics. But presently I felt saddened by the news, then downright angry as it settled in. I'm still upset at the very idea that in this day and age two innocent black bears should be shot to death for living in their space as God taught them.

That is what C. reported happened at Mesa Verde on June 18, 1992. That the bears wandered into a campground hardly makes them criminals. If the bears poached for food, it was because campers weren't sufficiently cautious or properly advised by the Park Service to keep supplies out of temptation's way. Besides, if it's a question of clearing an area of campers or bears, I say: Close the place to camping; safeguarding bears, or any native species, comes first.

Wildlife needs all the help it can get, and it doesn't get much in the very settings where help and compassion are most expected. After hearing from ranger C., I decided to ask questions. In due course I received a response from Robert Baker, regional director of the National Park Service. Once the two bears were observed in the campground, Baker wrote, it was decided to immobilize them with tranquilizing chemical injections. The rangers obviously botched the injections; the bears remained mobile, and so were shot dead. A subsequent investigation, according to Baker, concluded this horrible act was justified to prevent "an unacceptable risk to human safety and property."

I can't agree. Anyone going to a national park or wilderness or sanctuary for wild animals ought to prepare for risk and be properly advised to do so. Many of these places, unfortunately, are run like zoos, or entertainment centers, popcorn playgrounds where visitors are invited to observe wild animals in padded comfort. Thus visitors become snared in a loop serving the business interests of concessionaires and chambers of commerce.

In August I visited the renowned Boundary Waters Canoe Area Wilderness, showpiece of the Superior National Forest in northern Minnesota. I spent a week paddling, portaging, and camping—and it was a shocking eye-opener. The Forest Service leadership crows about the BWCA as one of its "crown jewels," but I found it badly overused and abused, being loved to death in a recreational orgy. The Forest Service likes to point to a permit system, visitor quotas, and endless research, but I saw badly eroded campsites, traffic congestion at the portages, and scant opportunity for promised solitude.

A new report by the Friends of the Boundary Waters shows that too many fishing people overharvest lake trout and walleye, that walleyes and smallmouth bass stocked in lakes where they never before existed degrade native lake trout. Black bears are forced into abnormal feeding habits and locations. Many loons leave their nests and produce fewer offspring. This may be true as well for bald eagles and ospreys. On behalf of wildlife, visitor quotas to the BWCA need to be sharply reduced and rigorously enforced, but that calls for more courage to resist local business pressure than Forest Service officials thus far have shown.

The trouble is that what's good for business comes first. In fact, "What's Good for Business Has Been Good for the Park" was the title of an article by Russell Berry, superintendent of Voyageurs National Park, an area adjacent to the Boundary Waters, published in the *Courier*, the National Park Service house organ, in August 1987. That's a terrible notion: When business comes first, trouble for wildlife always follows close behind. Berry's focus was on tourism, complete with snowmobiling, the most alien activity yet sanctioned in a national park. Berry was promoted to superintendent of Denali National Park in the wild heart of Alaska, where the tourism boom of the past thirty years has been accompanied by sharp wildlife declines.

Politics is a powerful influence. For instance, when Mike Hayden, the Bush administration Assistant Secretary of the Interior in charge of parks and wildlife programs, recently went to see Voyageurs, he said he wanted to do something to help the resort owners with all their power boats and snowmobiles. So he came up with "a good compromise plan, a middle ground" for management; never mind protecting wolves and other wildlife in the snowmobilers' path. "People's recreational needs are changing," says Hayden. "That's why the multiple-use concept is so important." National parks were never meant for multiple use; their mandate is specific for preservation and protection. But political cronies in key posts in government don't know that, and don't want to know.

A few years ago, I visited Tanzania, in East Africa. While I saw extensive herds of wild animals, I was most deeply impressed by the simple yet lofty text of a manifesto President Julius Nyerere had issued in 1961, the year his country gained independence: "In accepting the trusteeship of our wildlife, we solemnly declare that we will do everything in our power to make sure that our children's grandchildren will be able to enjoy this rich and precious heritage." Tanzania is still learning, but that struggling young country spends a greater portion of its income on wildlife protection than does the United States.

We need such a manifesto, a solemn declaration of trusteeship that ethical right transcends all business and politics. I believe that people who care, who aren't on anybody's payroll, can make it happen. They are making it happen. Thanks to Elizabeth Hartwell of Virginia, the Mason Neck National Wildlife Refuge was established twenty miles south of the national capital, for the protection of bald eagles. Thanks to Beulah Edmiston of California, the tule elk, smallest of the wapitis, was rescued from the brink of extinction and assured adequate habitat.

Thanks to Elizabeth Sizemore and Marcia Sullivan, leaders of the Mexican Wolf Coalition, their state of Texas is being pressed to support restoration of the Mexican wolf in Big Bend National Park and adjacent Big Bend Ranch State Park, the area where the last wild wolves of Texas were recorded killed in 1970. As Elizabeth notes, if attitudes then were not of indiscriminate killing and total disregard of our natural heritage, the Texas Threatened and Endangered Species List of 1992 would not contain so many animal species (more than 200 in 1992).

Attitudes are different now. We are changing direction, learning the rights of other species and the responsibilities—and opportunities—of humankind. To have our children's grandchildren enjoy a rich and precious heritage should be the dream of the rangers in Mesa Verde National Park, and of the strangers who come to them to learn that the life of a bear is sacred life.

Censored but Never Sued

The Autumn 1971 issue of *Living Wilderness* (later renamed simply *Wilderness*), published by the Wilderness Society, recounted "The Strange Case of Michael Frome, Lover of Trees and Bête Noire of the Lumber Industry." The article focused on my difficulties with the American Forestry Association (AFA) and was preceded by an editorial note telling something about me:

> *In his American Forests column Mike used to probe into anything and everything related to our nation's forests and range lands. His approach was direct, his style incisive. He gave quarter to no one he thought deserving of criticism. Oftentimes he was critical of the U.S. Forest Service and/or the timber industry.*

Thirteen pages of letters and reprints of two newspaper articles began with a copy of a memorandum dated March 4, 1971, from the executive vice president of AFA, William E. Towell, to James B. Craig, the editor of *American Forests*. The purpose of the memo was to clarify in writing decisions already made. My column was to be "censored" by the editor. I was not to write critically about the U.S. Forest Service, the forest industry, or about controversial forestry issues. A disclaimer was to precede my column. My response to Towell and Craig followed:

> *I cannot agree not to write critically about the U.S. Forest Service, the forest industry or about controversial forestry issues. I cannot, do not and will not accept censorship as a requisite to continue publication in American Forests.*

Thus I became a bit of a cause célèbre. Senator Lee Metcalf of Montana introduced the entire material from *Living Wilderness* into the Congressional Record on January 21, 1972. He said:

> *It is certainly the prerogative of the American Forestry Association to publish what they wish, but it is a sad day when they can no longer look at all sides of forestry. When they openly advocate censorship of their columnists, whose propaganda line are we reading?*

The role of the journalist, as I saw it then and see it now, is to illuminate issues of importance and thus enable citizens to participate intelligently in the democratic process of decision-making. That was what I learned from the work of Lincoln Steffens and Bernard DeVoto. That is what reporting is about, real reporting, tracking the issue wherever it may lead, reaching a conclusion and expressing it, without fear or favor. There isn't much of this kind of journalism, not in television, radio, nor the mainstream magazines and newspapers. But it's the kind I've tried to practice and to teach. In 1975, Dan Saults, the chief of public information for the U.S. Fish and Wildlife Service, wrote as follows:

> He [Frome] has built a good reputation as lecturer, magazine writer, author and bluetail fly who keeps biting the horses on which our masters ride. For a half-score years he used to phone me from his lair in Alexandria, Virginia, across the Potomac from my den in Interior in Washington, and ask questions to which I sometimes thought there were easy, honest answers. The discussion generally turned out better when I didn't think that.
>
> This did not make the Frome columns beloved around that set of government offices, although we could take some solace on occasions when Agriculture got a worse blistering. We didn't have great affection for Mike in federal information centers, but we respected the hell out of him in part because he didn't believe our news handouts, in part because we learned he had done his homework before he called up. Mike and I had been friends before I went to Washington; we were still friends at cocktail parties there; but when we were working, Frome and Saults weren't buddies. And he wasn't always fair. Neither of course, was I. True objectivity is as hard to define as beauty, anyway.

It's tragic that continued degradation of the environment gets such short shrift from the mass media. It takes a catastrophe, like Chernobyl, Bhopal, or the Exxon oil spill in Alaska, to make the nightly news, and then it is reported as a "story," with scant attention to fundamental cause or broad effect. Conglomerate control of the media stifles initiative. Newspapers in cities without competition profit more by covering less of the news and avoiding in particular anything offensive to advertisers. Newspapers, broadcasting, motion pictures are all, like advertising, components of a seductive system whose products work as merchandise but fail as enlightenment.

I learned that education is like that too. Textbooks in school generally must be free of value judgments; teachers show both sides of controversy without sharing their opinions—they're apt to get in trouble if they do. For a professor to be involved as a citizen activist is not "professional" and induces loss of "credibility." I recall the admonition of my department head at the University of Idaho: "Michael, you're not training students to think—you're teaching them to be like you. You're opinionated. You should provide the data and allow students to reach their own conclusions."

I questioned this academic approach, whereby the instructor is presumed to have no opinion and thus issue no challenge. I observed undergraduates conditioned to multiple-choice or true-false exams, and to memorization, where there must be a "right" answer, not his or her own answer. I saw graduate students writing bland theses in archaic language, proving competency in statistics and established research methods, and fluency in jargon, and professors writing articles to be judged by their peers for publication in scholarly journals read mostly by the authors.

Considering that we teach more by what we do than what we say, students tend to imitate their instructors, finding in their example a convenient way to stay out of trouble. Education and the media, where they should furnish the solution, instead are part of the problem.

Nevertheless, I've been blessed with good fortune in both teaching and journalism. Serious students have shown me their determination to make a difference and taught me to keep the faith.

The connection with *Field & Stream* began in the mid-1960s when I met the editor, Clare Conley, at a dinner in Washington. (I had seen that magazine on newsstands, but doubt I had ever read it seriously.) A few months later Conley wrote to me: He had read an article of mine on the politics of conservation and asked something to the effect of, "When are you going to write this for us?" I recognized the opportunity to reach a large audience of outdoors people. *Field & Stream* was nothing to be ashamed of, considering that fine writers and conservationists like Aldo Leopold, Zane Grey, Corey Ford, and Robert Ruark had been there before me. I contributed two features, and when, soon after, the conservation editor died, I was appointed to succeed him.

It was a wonderful position. The magazine at that time was owned by CBS, the Columbia Broadcasting System, which evidently let the magazine management run its own affairs. Conley encouraged me to tackle one tough issue after another. When one article exposing the Corps of Engineers wasn't enough, he allowed me space for a second, and a third. Readers wrote warm letters. I received mail from all kinds of people, college professors and rednecks who wrote in a penciled scrawl. It was news to many of them that there is more to conserving than killing. I learned a lot too, about wildlife, biology, politics in game commissions, the pros and cons of hunting.

Conley and I initiated the *Field & Stream* Action Group, awarding citations and pins to readers who did something to protect the environment in their own localities. We hit the politics at the core of America's environmental decay. In September 1968 we launched "Rate Your Candidate," a feature that included a series of questions which readers could send to their elected representatives and candidates for election. It included a rating of selected congressmen, some of the best and some of the worst. In 1970 we expanded the questionnaire in such a way that readers could clip and mail it to candidates. In 1972 we rated every member of the Senate and House, based on a questionnaire to which we had received replies from 220 members of the House and 58 members of the Senate. Following publication, the magazine was attacked by a score of congressmen in letters to their constituents, letters to CBS, and speeches on the floor. But it was clear they no longer could placate sportsmen with gun control alone but must address fundamental environmental issues.

But changes were taking place at the magazine. *Field & Stream* had been independently owned for years before it was acquired by Holt, Rinehart & Winston, the book publisher. Then Holt was taken over by CBS. It didn't show at the time, but it's never healthy when book publishing, magazines, and radio and TV networks and stations are commonly controlled under the same roof.

First, Conley was fired. Jack Samson, the new editor, assured me that all was well, but soon directed that I lay off the politicians. He wanted me to write in generalities without naming names. There would be no "Rate Your Candidate" in 1974, and before that year was over I was fired.

Many individuals and organizations protested my dismissal. TIME wrote about me as "A Voice in the Wilderness." I received letters of support, faith, and confidence that gave me new strength and commitment. Fifty people picketed CBS in Washington, carrying signs reading CBS—Censored Broadcasting System; Mike Frome—America's Most Courageous Conservationist—Sacked!; CBS Censors Field & Stream; Free Mike to Monitor; Friends of the Earth Love Mike Frome. "We tout our system as being one of freedom for the individual, and we particularly tout our freedom of speech and expression," editorialized Tom Bell in *High Country News*. "His [Frome's] experiences give the lie to just how much freedom we really do have." Brock Evans in the *Sierra Club Bulletin* of February 1975 wrote:

> *Threats to jobs are nothing new, of course, for those who dare to take on the timber industry and its powerful friends. People in Alaska have lost their jobs, people in Montana have been threatened into silence, and people in*

*Oregon have been beat up—all for daring to speak out against the timber
industry's voracious designs on the national forests. But it is hard to believe
that a nationally respected outdoors magazine would do likewise. Frome's
fate gives us a taste of the sort of pressures we may have to face, of the sort of
tactics we can expect, in our fights to save the wilderness.*

Samson tracked those who supported me and struck at them. He com-
plained to the executive director of the Sierra Club about Brock Evans, and to
TIME. Because *Montana Outdoors* and *Massachusetts Wildlife*, both official state
agency publications, came to my defense, he dispatched letters of protest to
the fish and game commissions and the governors of the two states. After
Outdoor Life published an interview with me, he wrote the editor, Chet Fish,
"If you think that much of Frome, why don't you hire him?" And to Don
Aldrich, of the Montana Wildlife Federation: "You remind me of the preservationists who, in screaming that we had defiled their hero, Mr. Frome, and
stilled a voice crying in the wilderness—demanded that we cancel their sub-
scriptions. It was a pleasure for us to find out that 99% had never subscribed
to this outdoor magazine and had probably never even read it!"

Samson's view was that ecology, per se, is anti-hunting and anti-gun, and
that it has no place in the lexicon of the outdoors. Still, I had strong support
from the outdoors groups. Ray Scott in *Bassmaster Magazine* (February 1975)
wrote that he was "shocked and sickened" when he learned of my dismissal.
"Mike Frome in my opinion is one of America's greatest living conservationists. No spokesman for conservation ever spoke more clearly or more directly
about the problems and problem causers than Mike Frome. He was clearly
concise and attacked the rapist of our outdoors in a no-holds barred manner."
And Jack Lorenz in *Outdoor America*, published by the Izaak Walton League,
stated, "'It's every man for himself,' said the elephant as he danced among the
chickens. The big spenders didn't get big by being stupid. I've felt that the
growing economic crunch would land right on our backs. It's not surprising
that the first tangible footprints should appear on one Mike Frome. . . . CBS
couldn't stand the heat so they kicked the stove out of the kitchen."

Half a dozen members of Congress, Republicans and Democrats, in both
houses, expressed concern over my dismissal and the dangers of media monopoly. Conley, my old editor, felt much the same. On a radio interview we did
together in New York, he said my dismissal was an example of monopoly capital
tightening the stranglehold on the mass media. I myself felt victimized by conglomerate control stifling open discussion of critical issues in a free society. The

chairman of CBS, William S. Paley, wrote to protesting congressmen and conservation leaders that he had investigated my dismissal. I doubt he checked very closely, but that's not the point. CBS, or any institutional entity, must bear corporate responsibility for the decisions and actions of its subsidiaries. CBS installed Jack Samson as editor, certainly not to conduct a conservation crusade, but to end one that had been underway. Brent Blackwelder, of the Environmental Policy Center, in a memo of November 20, 1974, wrote: "As owner of *Field & Stream,* the Columbia Broadcasting System must bear the full responsibility for the censorship and firing which have occurred, although the exact extent of CBS's involvement is hard to ascertain."

I was hopeful somehow of bringing legal action and looked to writers' groups, environmental lawyers, and the American Civil Liberties Union for guidance. That was no easy doing. I learned that while the First Amendment guarantees freedom of speech and press, that freedom goes to the owner of the press. Anti-trust laws might apply, but only if I could prove a conspiracy to deprive me of my ability to earn a living. "The firing of a writer is vaguely assumed to be justified by peers who otherwise are loud defenders of citizens' rights," concluded Victor Navasky in the *Authors Guild Bulletin* after investigating my dismissal. But he may have been recording his own assumption, for his report lacked any serious sense of wrongdoing or outrage.

The Society of Magazine Writers (later renamed American Society of Journalists and Authors, ASJA) responded more positively, though only after painful soul-searching. Here was a professional society whose members were concerned with making a living and the issues related to that effort. The society scrupulously avoided taking stands—the one exception was a 1969 resolution demanding immediate, complete, and unconditional withdrawal of American troops from Vietnam. When my case was discussed at the membership meeting in New York on March 13, 1975, some said the editor, right or wrong, must be entitled to run his magazine as he wishes. But others insisted that unless writers speak in behalf of free expression the media would be sterile; that the organization to maintain its integrity must face issues of professional concern. Finally the members authorized the Professional Rights Committee to prepare and issue a white paper about my dismissal.

The chairman of the committee, Patrick M. McGrady, Jr., knew about censorship, having worked in Moscow for *Newsweek.* He knew, also, how to dig after data. Thus he interviewed Samson, who told him the following:

He [Frome] was going so heavy on the exposés. Above all, the thing I

really objected to when he was doing those exposés—I mean filling the whole
article with names of people. He didn't have to do that! I don't mind an exposé
every now and then, but when you start putting the names in, embarrassing
people, you're going too far.

Maybe so, but the naming of names, holding individuals and institutions
accountable for their words and deeds—that is what journalism and open
expression are about. McGrady, at a meeting of the society on May 8, 1975,
declared:

> *It is important to us as writers not to be treated as dogs, not to be treated*
> *as chattel, and to be treated as human beings entitled to an explanation.*
> *Now he [Samson] could have said, "I fired Mike Frome because I didn't*
> *like him." I would have found this perfectly acceptable. But he has given*
> *many different reasons, in private and in public, for that firing, and these*
> *reasons don't make sense at all. It is clear, since Mike has decided to make*
> *an issue of this, that there is a good possibility he was fired for being a very*
> *hard-hitting and effective exposé writer. I think we, on a citizen level, can*
> *be very proud that we have people like Mike and when he is stomped on and*
> *eliminated, without any proper explanation, I think we have a right to insist*
> *on a full explanation.*

All that is history. The white paper McGrady and committee produced is
in the files. It may not have gotten me reinstated, but it proved that writers
care about more than the paycheck. Samson claimed the real reason he fired
me was that I am anti-hunting, although he had no evidence except that I've
never hunted, and we joked about that. My theory is simple: Hunting ought
to involve environmental satisfactions, an authentic immersion in nature, with
hard efforts in tracking, scenting, and in pinpointing the game for hours or
even days if necessary. The quality of the hunt should be measured by the
experience of woodsmanship, thinking like the animals, perceiving surroundings from their viewpoint. "Honest sweat should be part of any hunt," as my
old *Field & Stream* colleague, Ted Trueblood, wrote.

I would miss my readers, but I was only dismissed, I didn't die. Jeff Cox,
a friend at Rodale Press, gave me a lift with a note, "There is nothing like the
winds of change blowing through your life to clean out the stale air." Then
Wayne Barrett, the editor of *Defenders of Wildlife*, called. He had talked with
the directors and was authorized to offer me a column, in which I could say
anything I wanted as long as it didn't get the outfit sued for libel. That went
on for years and *Defenders* never was sued.

CHAPTER VII

THE WEST BEYOND TOMORROW

The American West at the close of the twentieth century is far from being the place it was at the opening of the century, except for physical location on the globe and perpetuated frontier legend and myth. This is a different age, light years beyond the time when states here were still territories. The West is not an isolated, remote province but part of a tight little world wired together, with all things and all people connected.

A century ago the United States achieved its high standard of living through ingenuity in harnessing natural resources. Then Gifford Pinchot, the innovator and apostle of conservation through wise use, warned that civilizations live or die, rise or fall, on the extent to which they pursue sound management, proper development, and protection of their reserves. Pinchot's principle has been proven to work in this country. Nevertheless, we now live on a planet deeply wounded, troubled by global warming, acid rain, destruction of tropical forests, loss of wildlife habitat, toxic waste. Nations are interdependent, destined to rise or fall in a common future. Plainly the time is at hand to apply the principle of stewardship, real stewardship, to our entire planet, with the United States as the exemplar. That should be the public interest in charting the future of the Western environment.

Nor can the discussion of the environment be separated from critical social issues. New York, as they say, is ready to explode; likely Philadelphia and Miami are too. Violence and killing are common fare in urban America. But when I read about a teenage gunman taking over a classroom in Rapid City, South Dakota, and holding children hostages or about the latest drug raid in beautiful Bellingham, Washington, I realize how dysfunctional things have gotten to be everywhere. The rape of three-year-old children, serial killings, drug abuse, child abuse, gender abuse, ethnic animosities, human degradation and despair seem to be close at hand, wherever one goes, wherever one lives.

Society needs transformation. It needs a wholesome natural environment as the basis of a wholesome, prosperous human environment, for one doesn't work without the other. Luckily for the West, the environment is still its greatest asset, the foundation of a new consciousness of harmony with the essence of life, replacing the aggression and violence shown by television and the media. Society needs a new way of teaching and learning. In schools children acquire the desire for power. The history they are taught shows only the power of domination and conquest, instead of the power of service, of caring, for the earth and for each other.

John Collier on the first page of his classic primer, *Indians of the Americas*, defined the power of life as "the ancient, lost reverence and passion for human personality, joined with the ancient, lost reverence and passion for the earth and its web of life." He decried the loss of this power in our modern world. I see a loss of power for real learning through feeling and independent thinking—and loss of power in institutions for restoring harmony to human society. The analytical type of thinking that gives power over nature has smothered the powerful in ignorance about being part of nature.

Now it is time to come of age, to learn from history and build an ethical future. To consciously advance respect for living nature through private and public institutions and the professions and through individual concern is to advance the cause of human dignity. This isn't easily done, however, in a land of illusion and myth. As Thomas Merton warned in *Conjectures of a Guilty Bystander*, a myth is apt to become a daydream and a daydream an evasion. Myths rationalize bigotry, exploitation, homelessness, war, and degradation of the environment, as if they aren't there or don't count.

For four hundred years the dominant European/American policy toward the indigenous people of this country has been one of continuous genocide. Theodore Roosevelt's *Winning of the West* (which earned him presidency of the American Historical Association) extolled what he considered the manifest destiny of frontiersmen "upright, resolute, and fearless, loyal to their friends, and devoted to their country" who cleared the wilderness of red savages. Indigenous animals were accorded the same fate as the Indians. Even now the grizzly is widely regarded as a "savage killer." Snakes are "slimy," though their skin is very dry; the coyote is "cowardly," the mountain lion "ravenous and craven." Merton wrote that the word "frontier" began as the symbol of adventure and clear-eyed innocence but acquired pathetic innocence in Kennedy's New Frontier, trying to keep the myth alive, rather than recognizing that America had become prisoner of frontier mythology.

It's hard for society to face and to free itself of its myths. In what we like to regard as an open society, students are rarely taught, challenged, or inspired to be thinkers. It is too easy for teachers to rely on a structured program involving little more than presenting information and testing recall of "facts," which may not be factual after all. Higher education generally does little to encourage innovative, nontraditional teaching methods, and the grind of class work keeps students isolated from society and nature—the world for which they are preparing.

A society less than open, and living with myth, is likely to pay a bitter price. For example, before the collapse of the Soviet Union, I wondered why a socialist nation presumably serving the common good with integrated planning and comprehensive control of production and distribution, should be plagued with horrendous environmental problems. Factories and cities along the Volga were dumping 280 million cubic feet of raw sewage into the river every twenty-four hours. Industrial plants throughout the Soviet Union were focused on production, ignoring even the barest minimum standards to protect air and water. The same system applied in all the countries of Central and Eastern Europe under Soviet hegemony. Conditions worsened with time: The Chernobyl disaster symbolized environmental collapse throughout the Soviet bloc.

My initial thought was that the Soviet government had been forced (a) to industrialize in a short period of time a backward agrarian land and (b) to concentrate on defending itself in a world of unfriendly nations. But the Russians themselves in time told it otherwise. They defined the cause of failure as "bureaucratic parochialism" or "the unreasoned, unjustified decision making of administrative dogmatism," as practiced by the head of one industrial ministry or another trying to forward what he considered his "own" industry, or fulfill his "own" plan and quota, while committing violence to nature in the process. Russians have told me that the collapse of the Soviet Union, the massive upwelling to throw off the yoke of repression, resulted in large degree from pent-up public fury over the degraded and degrading natural environment.

That system failed because it had no checks or balances, no tolerance for differing views, let alone dissent; it suffered institutional inbreeding, denying the means to renew itself. Any system based on deceit and ruled by force only erodes trust, effectiveness, and leadership. It destroys initiative, programming people to conform, to adapt their personalities and goals to established standards of society, rather than cultivate their own potential or challenge society and thus contribute to its enrichment.

I find a powerful message in the European experience, a signal of warning that we must examine critically our own institutions—political, industrial, economic, educational, cultural, all of them—to reassess their validity as we near the turn of another century. Hierarchical, top-down, closed systems don't work, wherever they may be. Public involvement, alertness, and open dialogue are essential to good government. That is why, to my own surprise, I find it fitting to listen closely to the wise-use/property-rights groups that scored heavily with the election of conservative Republicans in 1994.

I could readily rationalize that Big Money influenced the outcome; that many voters were fed up and stayed home, allowing winners to be elected by a minority, and that, anyway, the Democrats will do better next time. But the truth is that money doesn't vote, only people do, and those who cared enough turned out to express their strong feelings, principally that they don't trust government.

I'm not a property-rights person and I confess that I don't trust government either. Something about it has gone sour and stale. I don't have to be a political conservative to make that observation. "The first thing is, every government is run by liars and nothing they say should be believed," I. F. Stone, the ultra-liberal iconoclast, wrote twenty-five years ago. And he continued, "A government finds it very hard to absorb intelligence that runs counter to its own preconceptions." Stone was not speaking at a time when Reagan was president, or Nixon, but rather in the era of a Democrat, Lyndon Johnson.

To be sure, considerable damage has been done consequent to the 1994 election. The *New York Times* on June 18, 1995, editorializing on "The Endangered West," noted anti-environmental actions by state legislatures and governments, including the following: Montana, rewriting water pollution laws as a favor to the mining industry; Idaho, awarding potential polluters a major voice in setting clean water standards; Utah, rebuffing citizen proposals to protect 5.7 million acres of public land as wilderness; Washington, adopting the nation's most far-reaching "taking law," weakening essential land-use controls; and Wyoming, authorizing a bounty on wolves—defying wolf reintroduction into Yellowstone National Park and protection accorded the wolf by the Endangered Species Act.

Congress moved along the same lines, with legislation enacted or pending to ban new listing of endangered species, expand logging in the Tongass National Forest in Alaska, open the Arctic National Wildlife Refuge to oil exploration, close national parks, drain wetlands, transfer millions of acres administered by the Bureau of Land Management to states so livestock grazers would be free of federal environmental regulations.

Thus the *Times* was led to observe:

> *The war in the West and the war in Congress on basic environmental protection have much in common. First, both are being driven and in some cases underwritten by big business. Second, both are being waged to save the "little guy" from Federal tyranny. Third, this little guy is nowhere to be found when the time comes to draft crippling legislation. Indeed, his wishes have been largely ignored. Poll after poll suggests that what ordinary citizens want is more environmental protection, if it means a cleaner environment and a healthier society.*

One lesson may be that it's time to reexamine government at all levels and the citizen role in making it work. That little guy needs to be better heard, informed, and involved in decision making. Yes, government is needed. Yes, there are competent, committed public servants, but many I know are frustrated by their inability to perform fully in the public behalf. Able personnel are apt to be punished for doing their jobs. Dan Kemmis, mayor of Missoula, Montana, has advanced a thoughtful proposal on how to make things work. In his book, *A Tale of Two Cities: Community and the Politics of*

Place, he urges that communities establish a system of public hearings, at which citizens hear each other; that communities become more self-sufficient and keep locally earned dollars at home, arguing that cities and their regions are more effective economic units than states; that residents of the West be given more control over policies affecting nearby federal lands; and that people learn to inhabit a given place on the place's own terms.

That differs from the old model of "job-based economy" that has left ghost towns, pollution, and erosion across the West, but, then, nature should be a guiding force for society, with decentralized responsibility essential to making a region valid and vital. History is already running ahead of decision makers: Mining, logging, and ranching, the old extractive industries, still exercise political power, even while declining and being supplanted by new industries—financial, engineering, software, and recreation. Statistics show the West growing as fast as any region in the United States, if not in the world. And the most important reason is that people want the amenities and quality of life derived from a landscape of natural beauty.

The West beyond tomorrow needs a new way of examining itself. So do environmentalists need new ways. Until now we have focused on public lands (as I certainly have done), but we need to think whole, about cities, towns, suburbs, about private lands in the valleys, floodplains, and streamsides, about community growth boundaries as a first step to preserving the amenities, and about more effective communication between government, business, and citizens.

Maybe environmental organizations need to renew themselves too. Some rely heavily for their funding on direct mail, exploiting products of the very forests we claim to be determined to protect. Or they rely on grants from foundations, leading to a private poker game with those in political power that almost always results in a disappointing losing hand. I would rather see the organizations speak boldly and honestly, hewing to principle, without hate, anger, or intolerance.

Society needs a revolution in ideas and ideals, but it's hard to break through old western barriers of polarization between "them" and "us." Yet I think that most people deep down share common goals and common fears and that the challenge is to work through them to build a common answer that works for the long run. Every individual has the need and desire to do good and be identified as one who cares. Several years ago I was on a program of the Society of American Foresters in Spokane, Washington. During the discussion a representative of the Western Pine Association asked, "But aren't there more elk now?" His emphasis was on the positive side of wildlife. A retired woods manager of the Potlatch Company said, "I was concerned with the total ecology. . . . " He didn't want to be told that for forty years he might have been placing timber profits first.

In November 1986 on a trip to Washington, D.C., I interviewed Donald Hodel, the Secretary of the Interior (who followed James G. Watt). "Call me Don," he said. He didn't want to come across as a stuffed shirt with a closed mind. He wore western boots, had a fire in the fireplace, and showed me a picture of himself climbing in Yosemite; moreover, he told me of how his father had helped to save a free-flowing river in Oregon from a proposed dam. Hodel outlined his pet program, Take Pride in America. It didn't go anywhere, but it was a good slogan. We need to take pride in America, we need to take pride in the West.

When I think of what I may have learned over the years, I hope that it's been to stick to principle, setting aside fear and apprehension; to seek friendship and understanding, accepting the light and truth in people whose ideas differ from mine; and to believe that ultimately right will prevail so that the West beyond tomorrow will benefit from the best we do for it now.

RECOMMENDED READING LIST

Abbey, Edward. *Desert Solitaire: A Season in the Wilderness.* New York: Ballantine, 1968. In his first important book, Abbey records everything he found and felt significant as a park ranger in Utah.

Austin, Mary. *The Land of Little Rain.* 1903. Albuquerque: University of New Mexico Press, 1974. A pioneering writer pictures the desert, its landscape and people, at the turn of the century.

Bass, Rick. *The Nine-Mile Wolves.* New York: Ballantine, 1992. With focus on a Montana wolf pack, Bass debunks old myths and fears.

Craighead, John J., Jay S. Sumner, and John A. Mitchell. *The Grizzly Bears of Yellowstone: Their Ecology in the Yellowstone Ecosystem, 1959–1992.* Washington, D.C.: Island Press, 1995. Craighead and associates crystallize years of long-term ecological research.

Douglas, William O. *Go East, Young Man.* New York: Random House, 1974. Though en route East, Justice Douglas records experiences and philosophy nurtured in the West.

Foreman, Dave. *Confessions of an Eco-Warrior.* New York: Harmony, 1991. The radical activist tells of emerging from conservatism to crusade for wilderness.

Jacobs, Lynn. *Waste of the West: Public Lands Ranching.* Tucson: Lynn Jacobs, 1991. Everything about grazing—history, politics, alternatives, future—and he published it himself.

Kemmis, Dan. *Community and the Politics of Place.* Norman: University of Oklahoma Press, 1990. The mayor of Missoula, Montana, connects people and place with sustainable community.

Limerick, Patricia. *The Legacy of Conquest: The Unbroken Past of the American West.* New York: Norton, 1987. A progressive historian depicts economic realities behind the early West.

Mills, Stephanie. *In Service of the Wild.* Boston: Beacon, 1995. Restoration—the road ahead.

Murie, Adolph. *A Naturalist in Alaska.* 1961. Tucson: University of Arizona Press, 1990. The life-cycles of Alaska wild animals are recorded in first-rate writing by a pioneer field biologist.

Murie, Margaret. *Two in the Far North.* 2d ed. Edmonds, Wash.: Alaska Northwest, 1978. Step-by-step the author walked with her husband, Olaus, in the campaign to save the Arctic National Wildlife Refuge.

Parkman, Francis. *The Oregon Trail*. 1849. With a foreword by A.B. Guthrie 1962. New York: New American Library. Parkman saw the wildlands of Pawnee, Sioux, and buffalo as they were, and witnessed their conquest.

Peacock, Douglas. *Grizzly Years*. New York: Holt, 1990. Thoughtful reflections from a man who has shared the wilds with the great bear.

Power, Thomas M. *Extraction and the Environment: The Economic Battle to Control Our Natural Landscapes*. Washington, D.C.: Island Press, 1996. A professor of economics explains the value of protected landscapes to local economies using case studies.

Shanks, Bernard. *This is Your Land: The Struggle to Save America's Public Lands*. San Francisco: Sierra Club, 1984. A chronicle of the history of public lands, with a critical look at the federal government's management and at the Sagebrush Rebellion.

Stegner, Wallace. *Beyond the Hundredth Meridian*. New York: Viking (Penguin paperback), 1992. Stegner recounts the life of John Wesley Powell, and the challenge of balancing land and water in the growth of the West.

Stegner, Wallace. *The Uneasy Chair*. Lynton, Utah: Peregrine Smith Books, 1988. Stegner admired Bernard DeVoto, but this biography shows his friend with warts and all.

Turner, Frederick. *Beyond Geography: The Western Spirit Against the Wilderness*. New Brunswick: Rutgers University Press, 1983. A scholar reviews spiritual history leading to European domination of native cultures in the New World.

Wilkinson, Charles. *Crossing the New Meridian: Land, Water and the Future of the West*. Washington, D.C.: Island Press, 1992. Wilkinson, a professor of western environmental law, defines broad problems and proposes solutions.

Williams, Terry Tempest. *Refuge*. New York: Random House, 1991. A touching work combining a personal family saga with ecological issues at the Great Salt Lake.

Wolke, Howie. *Wilderness on the Rocks*. Tucson: Ned Ludd, 1991. Marshalling a body of facts and events, Wolke offers a comprehensive ecological argument for preservation of wilderness.

Wyant, William K. *Westward in Eden*. Berkeley: University of California, 1982. Leading up to and concentrating on the 1970s, Wyant traces the history of American land settlement from the American Revolution.

INDEX

ABOUT THE AUTHOR

Author, educator, and tireless environmental advocate, Michael Frome began his illustrious career as a newspaper reporter and travel writer. He went on to serve as conservation editor of *Field & Stream* and as a columnist for the *Los Angeles Times* and the magazines *American Forests, Western Outdoors,* and *Defenders of Wildlife.* His books include *Conscience of a Conservationist; Whose Woods These Are: The Story of the National Forests; Strangers in High Places: The Story of the Great Smoky Mountain;* and *Regreening the National Parks.* He has won numerous awards, including the Marjory Stoneman Douglas Award (for his work on behalf of national parks), an Award of Merit from the Desert Protective Council (1993), and the highest conservation award , the Jade of Chiefs, from the Outdoor Writers Association of America (1994). He spent four years teaching at the University of Idaho, which established the Michael Frome Scholarship of Excellence in Conservation Writing in his honor. Prior to his retirement in 1995, he directed the pioneering program in environmental journalism and writing at Western Washington University. A longtime resident of the western United States, he lives with his wife June in Bellingham, Washington.

Founded in 1906, The Mountaineers is a Seattle-based non-profit outdoor activity and conservation club with 15,000 members, whose mission is "to explore, study, preserve, and enjoy the natural beauty of the outdoors . . . " The club sponsors many classes and year-round outdoor activities in the Pacific Northwest, and supports environmental causes by sponsoring legislation and presenting educational programs. The Mountaineers Books supports the club's mission by publishing travel and natural history guides, instructional texts, and works on conservation and history. For information, call or write The Mountaineers, Club Headquarters, 300 Third Avenue West, Seattle, Washington, 98119; (206) 284-6310.